THE BOOKS AND THE PARCHMENTS

ΗϹΕΝϹΗΜΕΙΟΝᵡ
ΓΟΝ·ΟΥΤΟϹΕϹΤΙΝ
ΑΛΗΘωϹΟΠΡΟΦΗ
ΤΗϹΟΕΙϹΤΟΝΚ°ℰᴹ°
ΕΡΧΟΜΕΝΟϹ·
Ι͞ϹΟΥΝΓΝΟΥϹΟΤΙ
ΜΕΛΛΟΥϹΙΝΕΡΧ Ε
ϹΘΑΙΚΑΙΑΡΠΑΖΕΙΝ
ΑΥΤΟΝΚΑΙΑΝΑ ᴥΙΝΑΠΟΙΗ
Ν͞Α ΑΝΕΧωΡΗϹΕΝ Κ͞ΝΥΝΑΙ ΒΑϹΙΛΕΑ ϹωϹΙΝ
Δ ΦΕΥΓΕΙΠΑΛΙΝΕΙ Τ°
ΟΡΟϹΜΟΝΟϹΑΥΤ ᵒᶜ·

A Portion of the Codex Sinaiticus showing John 6. 14, 15

ΡΞΔ ϹΛΕΓΕΝΑϹΚΑΙΤΟΙϹΟΧΛΟΙϹ·ΟΙᴧ
ℰ ΙΔΗΤΕΝΕΦΕΛΗΝΑΝΑΤΕΛΛΟΥϲᴧ
ΑΠΟΔΥϹΜωΝΕΥΘΕωϹΛΕΓΙϲ
ΤΑΙΟΤΙΟΜΚΡΟϹΕΡΧΕΤΑΙΚΑΙΓϲ
ΝΕΤΑΙΟΥΤωϹΚΑΙΟΤΑΝΝΟΤΟ
ΤΠΝΕΟΝΤΑΛϹΓΕΤΕΟΤΙΚΑΥϹωΝ
ΕϹΤΑΙΚΑΙ ΓΙΝΕΤΑΙ ΥΠΟΚΡΙΤᴧ
ΤΟΠΠΡΟϹωΠΟΝΤΗϹΓΗϹ ΚΑΙΤΟ Υ
ΟΥΝΟΥΟΙΔΑΤΕΔΟΚΙΜΑΖΕΙΝ
ΤΟΝΔΕΚΑΙΡΟΝΤΟΥΤΟΝΠωϹ
ΟΥΔΟΚΙΜΑΖΕΤΕ ΤΙΔΕΚΑΙΑΦ Ε
ΛΥΤωΝΟΥΚΡΙΝΕΤΕΤΟΔΙΚΑΙΟ
ΡΞℰ ωϹΓΑΡΥΠΑΓΕΙϹΜΕΤΑΤΟΥΑΝΤΙ
ℰ ΔΙΚΟΥϹΟΥΕΠΑΡΧΟΝΤΑΕΝΤΗ
ΟΔωΔΟϹΕΡΓΑϹΙΑΝΑΠΙΑΛΛΑΧΘΑΙ
ΑΠΑΥΤΟΥ·ΜΗΠΟΤΕΚΑΤΑϹΥΡ·

A Portion of the Codex Alexandrinus showing Luke 12. 54-58

THE BOOKS
and the
PARCHMENTS

SOME CHAPTERS ON THE TRANSMISSION
OF THE BIBLE

REVISED EDITION

F. F. BRUCE

FLEMING H. REVELL COMPANY

First Published 1950
Second Edition 1953
Third and Revised Edition 1963

FROM THE PREFACE TO THE FIRST EDITION

THIS volume gathers together a number of articles written and papers read at various times on the transmission of the Bible. It is intended for non-specialists like those who have read them or heard them in their earlier forms, and who have frequently expressed a desire to have them in this form.

It is gratifying to mark the eagerness with which people of widely divergent interests listen to a simple account of how the Bible has come down to us. In revising these chapters I have tried to bear in mind the questions which are most frequently asked about these matters, and to answer them to the best of my ability. I hope that the volume may thus prove interesting and useful to the many who, without aiming at any specialist knowledge of Biblical learning, would welcome a handbook dealing with these questions.

The mixed origin of the contents no doubt betrays itself in a certain haphazardness in the topics selected, though I have tried to smooth out the worst roughnesses and cut down too much over-lapping.

The three chapters on the Biblical languages are not intended to teach readers the elements of these languages but simply to say some interesting things about them.

There are many aspects of Biblical study which are not touched upon here. Questions of higher criticism, introduction, exegesis, and even of Biblical archaeology, interesting as they are, lie outside the scope of the volume. So also does the theological approach to the Bible (although theology has done its best to creep into Chapters VI, VII, and VIII).

There is little that is original in these pages, and my debts to others are acknowledged throughout the work. Mr. G. C. D. Howley has given valued help in the reading of the proofs. Nor should I omit a word of gratitude to all those whose keen interest in the subjects here dealt with has encouraged me to present them in this form. A teacher of any subject, and especially of Biblical studies, can have no greater reward than to see others fired with enthusiasm for his subject.

F. F. BRUCE

March, 1950.

PREFACE TO SECOND EDITION

IN this second edition I have brought the contents up to date in several respects and corrected a number of inaccuracies. I am indebted for help in these matters to various readers and reviewers. In many subjects which are under debate, I may seem to have expressed myself with more assurance than the present state of knowledge warrants; this is perhaps inevitable in a work of this kind.

F.F.B.

January 1, 1953.

PREFACE TO THIRD EDITION

IN going through these pages and revising their contents afresh after eight years, I have tried to resist the temptation to make so many changes that the work would no longer be recognizably the same. One thing that has impressed itself upon me time and again has been the wealth of fresh discovery that has had to be recorded during these last years. Much more is now known about the Dead Sea Scrolls, although even yet much remains to be known. Publication has begun of the manuscripts from the Gnostic library from Chenoboskion. The ancient Greek 'Linear B' script has been deciphered, and perhaps also 'Linear A'. A complete text of the Palestinian Targum on the Pentateuch has been found; and the Abisha' manuscript of the Samaritan Bible, if not exactly 'found', has at any rate been 'found out'. Other discoveries include the Bodmer papyri of the Gospel of John and other New Testament books, and the Syriac text of Ephrem's commentary on the Diatessaron. Some attention has been paid to all these in this revision. And in the year following Bible Year it is surely appropriate that a new chapter should be added, taking some preliminary account of the New English Bible.

April, 1962.   F.F.B.

CONTENTS

ILLUSTRATIONS

THE BOOKS AND THE PARCHMENTS

THE BOOKS AND THE PARCHMENTS

A BOUT the middle of last century there came to light a letter in William Tyndale's hand, written in Latin to someone in authority (possibly the Marquis of Bergen), which had lain unread in the archives of the Council of Brabant for three hundred years. The letter has a special human interest because it was written during the last winter of Tyndale's life (1535-36) while he lay in prison 'for the word of God and the testimony of Jesus', and it shows us how the great Bible translator's enthusiasm for his work remained unimpaired to the last, in spite of the most discouraging circumstances. This is what he wrote:

> I believe, right worshipful, that you are not unaware of what may have been determined concerning me. Wherefore I beg your lordship, and that by the Lord Jesus, that if I am to remain here through the winter, you will request the commissary to have the kindness to send me, from the goods of mine which he has, a warmer cap, for I suffer greatly from cold in the head, and am afflicted by a perpetual catarrh, which is much increased in this cell; a warmer coat also, for this which I have is very thin; a piece of cloth, too, to patch my leggings. My overcoat is worn out; my shirts also are worn out. He has a woollen shirt, if he will be good enough to send it. I have also with him leggings of thicker cloth to put on above; he has also warmer night-caps. And I ask to be allowed to have a lamp in the evening; it is indeed wearisome sitting alone in the dark. But most of all I beg and beseech your clemency to be urgent with the commissary, that he will kindly permit me to have the Hebrew Bible, Hebrew grammar and Hebrew dictionary, that I may pass the time in that study. In return may you obtain what you most desire, so only that it be for the salvation of your soul. But if any other decision has been taken concerning me, to be carried out before winter, I will be patient, abiding the will of God, to the glory of the grace of my Lord Jesus Christ; whose Spirit (I pray) may ever direct your heart. Amen.
>
> W. TINDALUS

It requires little imagination to sympathize with his desire for warmer clothes; a damp, draughty, unheated cell is no place to pass the winter in, and it is difficult to concentrate the mind on study if the body is shivering. But we get the impression that Tyndale's desire for warmer clothes was but a means to an end; he wished to reduce his bodily discomfort sufficiently to let his mind get on with its chosen work. Most of all he wants his Hebrew books. And why? Because a good part of the Old Testament remained to be translated. Some years previously he had translated the New Testament into English (the first time that it had ever been englished from the Greek original), and he was at work on the first translation of the Old Testament from Hebrew into English when he was arrested. The Pentateuch had been published in 1530; the historical books had also been translated but not yet published. So he was anxious to press on with the task. But the completion of it must be left to others; on the 6th October, Tyndale himself, in the words of John Foxe, 'was brought forth to the place of execution, was there tied to the stake, and then strangled first by the hangman, and afterwards with fire consumed, in the morning at the town of Vilvorde, A.D. 1536; crying thus at the stake with a fervent zeal and a loud voice: "Lord, open the King of England's eyes"'.

We cannot read the letter which Tyndale wrote from prison without remembering the remarkably similar request made by the Apostle Paul in remarkably similar circumstances. It was just before the last winter of his life, while he lay in prison in Rome awaiting the death-sentence and the executioner's sword (according to the traditional account), that he sent a message to his friend, Timothy, in Asia Minor: 'Do your best to come to me soon. . . . When you come, bring the cloak that I left at Troas with Carpus, and the books, especially the parchments. . . . Do your best to come before winter'.[1]

The comfort of the body is not to be neglected, but something to occupy the mind is the main thing. 'Most of all . . . the Hebrew Bible' was Tyndale's plea; 'especially the parchments' was Paul's.

It has been suggested that the word translated 'cloak' in Paul's message was not really a cloak. The Greek word is *phailonēs*, borrowed from the Latin *paenula*; and sometimes it means a piece of cloth to wrap round books to protect them against the weather. And it is suggested that Paul was more concerned about protecting his books than about protecting his body. Perhaps we can have it both ways. Paul may have left his cloak at Troas wrapped round the books, but in view of his reference to the approach of winter it

[1] There is an interesting reference to this passage of Scripture in F. W. Newman's *Phases of Faith* (1850), pp. 29 f. In recording his intercourse with one whom he calls 'the Irish clergyman' (actually J. N. Darby), Newman says: 'I once said: But do you really think that *no* part of the New Testament may have been temporary in its object? For instance, what should we have lost if St. Paul had never written the verse, "The cloak which I have left at Troas, bring with thee, and the books, but especially the parchments." He answered with the greatest promptitude: "*I* should certainly have lost something; for that is exactly the verse which alone saved me from selling my little library. No! every word, depend upon it, is from the Spirit, and is for eternal service."'

is not difficult to surmise that he asked Timothy to bring it so that he could wrap it round himself. And then, with a little less discomfort, he could get down to the books and the parchments.

But what were these books, and what were the parchments which Paul was so specially anxious to have? The Greek words that he uses to indicate them are interesting; they denote primarily the material of which the two classes of documents were made. The word for 'book' is *biblion*, and that for 'parchment' is *membrana*.

A *biblion* was more particularly a roll of papyrus or byblus. This was a reed-plant, growing beside rivers and marshes and such places, the inner bark of which was extracted and dried in flat strips. When these strips were dried, a row of them was laid side by side, and above this another row was laid in criss-cross fashion, and the two rows were gummed together. The result was a piece of writing material. Several of these pieces could be joined together end to end so as to form a long strip which was then rolled up into a scroll of convenient size, called in Greek a *biblos* or *biblion*. This name was derived from one of the names of the plant itself, *byblos*, which is related in turn to the name of a town in Phoenicia which the Greeks knew as Byblos.[1] (The form *biblion* is really a diminutive of *biblos*, but lost its diminutive sense. In the New Testament *biblion* simply means a 'roll' or 'book'; when a diminutive word is required, as for the little book which John was told to eat in Rev. 10. 9, the form *biblaridion* is used.) It is from *biblion*, in fact, that our word 'Bible' is derived. The plural of *biblion* is *biblia*, and the whole collection of Old and New Testament books came to be known by Greek-speaking Christians as *ta biblia*, 'the books'. Latin-speaking Christians then borrowed the word *biblia* but treated it as a singular noun, and from its Latin use the English word 'Bible' and similar forms in many other languages have been derived.

The other documents which Paul asked Timothy to bring were parchments. The Greek word here is *membrana*, a word borrowed from Latin, from which, of course, comes our English word 'membrane'. This is an animal and not a vegetable product, the skin of sheep, goats, antelopes, and similar animals, which was shaved and scraped to provide a more durable writing material than papyrus. The word 'parchment' comes from the name of the city of Pergamum, in Asia Minor, for the production of this

[1] Its Phoenician name was Gebal: in this form it is named in the Old Testament (Psa. 83. 7; Ezek. 27. 9; its inhabitants are called Gebalites in Josh. 13. 5; 1 Kings 5. 18). See further on pp. 21 f., 30.

writing material was at one time specially associated with that place. Parchment made from calf-skin is called vellum.

In New Testament times parchment, being more durable and more costly than papyrus, was used chiefly for documents of greater value, or for such as were constantly in use and were, therefore, exposed to greater wear and tear. What the parchments were which Paul so particularly desired Timothy to bring we cannot be sure, but it is a reasonable guess that they contained portions of Holy Scripture.

A book with pages in the form familiar to us was not used in New Testament times, though this kind of book (known technically as a *codex*) made its appearance not long after the end of the apostolic age and quickly became popular in Christian circles. The books mentioned in the Bible were rolls of papyrus. The use of papyrus for writing purposes in Egypt goes back to *c.* 3000 B.C., and we have evidence that by the end of the twelfth century B.C. it was exported in large quantities from Egypt to Phoenicia for the same purpose. Such a papyrus roll is that which John saw in his vision of heaven (Rev. 5. 1), which contained so much writing that the outside (*verso*) was covered with it as well as the inside (*recto*), and which when rolled up was secured with seven seals. Usually rolls bore writing on one side only, the side on which the fibres ran horizontally and which was therefore easier to write on. The Roman poet Juvenal satirizes one of his contemporaries who wrote a tragedy called *Orestes*, which was inordinately long—so long that it covered the outside of a roll as well as the inside, and was not finished even then:

scriptus et in tergo necdum finitus Orestes![1]

The longest books of the New Testament (which, in descending order of length, are Luke, Acts, Matthew, John) represent the amount of written matter which a roll of normal size contained. A roll could not exceed a certain length without becoming inconvenient for use. One of the reasons why Christian communities so quickly adopted the codex form in preference to the roll form, from the beginning of the second century onwards, was probably that the new form allowed them to have several documents together in one book, such as the four Gospels, or the collection of Pauline epistles, and later, of course, the New Testament or even the whole Bible. The writing on a roll was arranged in columns of convenient breadth. In the account of the roll of

[1] '*Orestes*, written on the back as well and even so not yet finished' (Juvenal *Satire, i.6*).

Jeremiah's prophecies that was read in the presence of King Jehoiakim (Jer. 36. 21-25), it was not three or four *leaves* that Jehudi read, as the text of the A.V. and R.V. says, but three or four *columns*, as the R.V. margin and R.S.V. rightly have it; Jehudi had no time to read more, for the king seized the roll, cut it up and threw it into the brazier. As the roll was read it was unwound with one hand and wound up with the other, rollers being provided round which it could more easily be wound.

When the roll was wound up, a slip containing the title of the work and the name of the author was usually pasted on the outside. This could easily fall off, leaving the work without a name. It may be that something like this happened to the Epistle to the Hebrews. This Epistle bears no writer's name, although it was not intended to be an anonymous letter; its recipients no doubt knew quite well who had sent it to them. A number of rolls would be kept together in a cylindrical box, which the Romans called a *capsa*. If an anonymous roll was kept in a box along with a number of other rolls by a known author, the nameless roll was apt to be credited to that author too. Thus, if the Epistle to the Hebrews was kept along with letters of Paul, it was not unnatural that Paul's name should come to be attached to it.

For writing on papyrus or parchment a pen and ink were used, as is indicated in 3 John 13, where the Elder has much to say to Gaius which he is unwilling to communicate by means of 'ink and pen'. (In a similar passage in 2 John 12 the phrase 'paper and ink' is used, where the Greek word for 'paper' is *chartēs*, another word for papyrus.) The pen was a reed (Greek *kalamos*), pointed at the end. The ink was compounded of charcoal, gum and water; the Greek word used by John is simply *melan*, i.e. 'black'.

Temporary notes were often made with a metal stylus or stiletto on a wax tablet—a flat piece of wood covered with a film of wax. The writing could be effaced by being rubbed over with the blunt end of the stylus. A very widespread writing material favoured by the common people was a piece of unglazed pottery, which readily took ink. Great numbers of these inscribed pot-sherds—*ostraca*, to give them their technical name—have been found in Egypt and Palestine. They served for writing letters, for keeping accounts, and a hundred and one other purposes.

The most durable form of writing is that referred to in Job 19. 24, the engraving of rock-inscriptions with an 'iron pen'. Another very durable form of writing, widely used in the Middle East in Old Testament times, was with a sharp instrument on tablets of soft clay, which were then baked hard. Vast quantities of these clay tablets have come to light, principally in the Euphrates-Tigris valley, where the kingdoms of Babylonia and Assyria flourished, but also in Persia, Syria, Asia Minor and Egypt. A line incised in a clay tablet with the three-sided stylus with bevelled head favoured for this purpose was naturally thicker at the beginning of the stroke than at the end, and this produces the characteristic appearance of the wedge-shaped or 'cuneiform' script in which so many languages of Western Asia were written.

These brick tablets were very durable, but their bulk and weight made them terribly inconvenient. Our paper books are heavy enough in all conscience, as we know to our cost when even a modest library has to be moved by road or rail; but imagination staggers at the problems that would arise if we had to keep their equivalent in inscribed bricks! Papyrus, on the other hand, was very convenient, but not at all durable. Only in such conditions as are provided by the dry sands of Egypt and the volcanic ash of Herculaneum have papyrus documents been preserved; in humid climates they soon rotted away. So, while we can read the original inscriptions of the Assyrian and Babylonian kings and the notes which common people wrote on pieces of pottery in eighth-century Samaria and sixth-century Lachish, the autographs of the Hebrew prophets who were their contemporaries have disappeared long ago, as also have the autographs of all the other Biblical writers, most—probably all—of whom wrote on papyrus. But these autographs were copied before they perished, and throughout the intervening centuries they have been copied and re-copied continually. Until the invention of printing five centuries ago all this copying had to be done laboriously by hand, one copy at a time; since then, the printing presses have sent out whole editions where previously single manuscripts were produced by individual scribes.

CHAPTER II

THE BIBLE AND THE ALPHABET

WHEN we speak of the *Bible*, we use a word which originally referred to a particular kind of writing material. When we speak of the *Scriptures*, we use a word which etymologically denotes the writing and not the material. We have discussed the early forms of writing material; now we are to think of early forms of writing.

The invention of printing in Europe in the fifteenth century A.D. was an event of great importance in the history of the transmission of the Biblical text, as well as in the general history of culture. But we sometimes forget that it is far outweighed in importance by the invention of writing. Without the invention of writing we should have had no Bible at all, for the Bible is God's Word *written*. God's Word came to the fathers through the prophets and became incarnate in Jesus Christ; but we should be very much poorer if we had no written record of what God said but had to rely on oral tradition. That, of course, might have mattered less if phonographic methods of recording the spoken word had been in use in Biblical times. But these methods are, in fact, of recent invention, whereas writing was in use in those days and so was naturally the means employed for perpetuating the revelation of God.

The first person who is represented in the Bible as writing anything is Moses. There are six things which Moses in the Pentateuch is explicitly said to have written: (1) the memorial concerning Amalek;[1] (2) the Book of the Covenant;[2] (3) the Ten Commandments;[3] (4) the itinerary of the Israelites in the wilderness;[4] (5) the Deuteronomic law-code;[5] (6) the Song reproduced in Deut. 32.[6] At one time it was widely supposed that Moses was the first man who ever committed anything to writing, and that he learned the art directly from God[7] (possibly when he received the two Tables of the Law at Sinai inscribed by 'the

---

[1] Exod. 17. 14.　　[2] Exod. 24. 4.　　[3] Exod. 34. 27, 28.　　[4] Num. 33. 2.
[5] Deut. 31. 9, 24.　　[6] Deut. 31. 22.

[7] This idea is at least as early as the second century B.C., when it was put forward by the Hellenistic Jewish writer, Eupolemus. It is interesting, however, to note that Josephus ascribes the art of writing to the generations immediately following Adam, perhaps thinking particularly of Enoch, who is regarded by some forms of Jewish and Samaritan tradition as having committed divine revelations to writing.

finger of God').[1] This was a perfectly reasonable supposition in days when no writing was known earlier than the time of Moses; now, however, we can look at actual records written many hundreds of years before Moses, written more than 5,000 years ago.

Writing is not the only method of keeping memoranda and communicating information otherwise than by word of mouth; other devices are known, such as those practised by the American Indians and by the Peruvians in the Inca Age. But none of these other devices has proved capable of being developed to anything like the same degree as writing. Writing developed out of drawing; and something of the development of the art of writing can be grasped if we compare a modern treatise on some abstract subject with the earliest known forms of picture-writing.

The form of writing with which we are specially concerned in this chapter, however, is alphabetic writing, not simply because it is the form of writing which we practise ourselves (by contrast, for example, with the Chinese), but especially because the Bible, as far as we can tell, was from the beginning written in alphabetic writing. Alphabetic writing is the form of writing which has a distinct character for every significant sound in a language—in principle, at least, for in practice (as we know in English) the same sound may be indicated by more letters than one and the same letter may be pronounced in more ways than one.[2]

In tracing the development of writing in general and of alphabetic writing in particular it is a good scheme to begin with our own alphabet and work backward, for then we are proceeding from the well known to the less well known, and that is always a sound method. Our English alphabet has twenty-six letters: A B C D E F G H I J K L M N O P Q R S T U V W X Y Z. We need concern ourselves only with the capitals; the 'lower case' letters are simply modifications of these. We have inherited our alphabet in the first instance from the Romans, along with several other useful things. The Roman alphabet, however, had only twenty-three letters; A B C D E F G H I K L M N O P Q R S T V X Y Z. Our I and J are by origin variant forms of one and the same Roman letter; the same is true of U and V; while W is just what we call it, a double U (or, as the French call it, a double V).

---

[1] Exod. 31. 18.

[2] Thus the same sound is denoted by *c*, as in *car*; by *k*, as in *kite*; by *kh*, as in *khaki*; by *ck*, as in *sack*; by *ch*, as in *chasm*; by *gh*, as in *hough*. The letter *g* is pronounced differently in *get* and *gem*; and think of the variety of ways in which *gh* is pronounced! English, of course, is a notorious example of defective correspondence between sound and symbol; but the same defect is present in some degree in all written languages.

As for the Latin alphabet of twenty-three letters, its last two letters, Y and Z, were imported from the Greek alphabet in the first century B.C., not to represent true Latin sounds, but to help the Romans to represent certain Greek words more accurately in their alphabet—those Greek words containing the letters Υ (*upsilon*), which was pronounced like the modified *u* in French or the German *ü*, and Z (*zeta*), which was pronounced like *dz* or *zd*. Neither of these sounds was found in any native Latin word. Before these two letters were appended, then, the Roman alphabet had only twenty-one letters.

The Romans in their turn received the alphabet from the Etruscans, and the Etruscans received it from the Greeks—more particularly from those Greeks who had settled in Southern Italy from the eighth to the sixth centuries B.C. There were variations between the various forms of alphabets used by the Greeks, but in all of them the third letter, Γ (*gamma*), had the voiced sound of *g* as in English *gather*. How comes it, then, that the third letter in the Roman alphabet, C, has the unvoiced sound of *c* as in English *can*? It is not that the Romans had no use for the voiced sound of *g*; they had, and if they had derived their alphabet direct from the Greeks, they would have pronounced C like Greek *gamma*, the more so as there were already two letters in the alphabet which had the sound of *c* in *can*—namely K and Q. But the Etruscans had no voiced *g* sound in their language, so when they took over the Greek alphabet they gave *gamma* the corresponding unvoiced sound (as though the name of the letter were pronounced *kamma*). Thus, in the alphabet which the Romans took over from the Etruscans, there were three letters which had practically the same unvoiced sound—C, K, and Q. Later, when the Romans felt the need of a separate letter for the *g* sound, they used G, which was really a variant form of C, and put it in the seventh place in the alphabet. This was the place occupied by the Greek letter *zeta*, but, as we have seen, the Romans had no such sound, and so they jettisoned it from the alphabet, little thinking that their descendants would one day bring it back and put it at the end of the alphabet. They also jettisoned five other letters from the Greek alphabet since they had no sounds corresponding to them.

There were numerous varieties of the Greek alphabet in use all over the Greek world, from Asia Minor to Marseilles. One of these was the 'West Greek' alphabet, from which the Roman alphabet was derived through Etruscan intermediation. Another was the 'East Greek' or 'Ionic' alphabet, which was officially introduced at Athens in 403 B.C., and in time replaced the local varieties of alphabet in other parts of Greece. This is the alphabet of twenty-four letters which we commonly call the 'Greek alphabet'. The following table will help to show the relation which these two forms of Greek alphabet bore to each other and to the Roman alphabet. Note that, so far as the table goes, it indicates the relationship of the letters and not of the sounds which they represented.[1]

One of the chief differences between the West Greek and the Ionic alphabet is that in the former H represents an aspirate sound, while in the latter (since most of the Ionic Greeks dropped their aitches) there was no need of a letter to indicate the aspirate sound, and so H (*eta*) was used to represent a long open *e* sound, similar to the sound of *ea* in English *bear*. In this as in some other respects, such as its retention of the letters *digamma* (whence F) and *koppa* (whence Q), and its giving to X the value of *ks* and not *kh*, the West Greek alphabet, along with the Roman alphabet, was nearer to the original Greek alphabet than the Ionic alphabet was. The earliest inscriptions in the Greek alphabet occur in Athens and the islands of Thera, Melos and Crete; they belong to the ninth or eighth century B.C.

Greek tradition derives the alphabet from the Phoenicians. It is significant that Cadmus, whom the Greeks regarded as having introduced the alphabet among them, was not only a Phoenician according to legend, but bears a Phoenician name. The Cadmus legend is well worth studying for its own sake, but all we need to say here is that the traditional Greek ascription of their alphabet to the Phoenicians is confirmed by the actual facts of the case. The earliest form of the Greek alphabet *is* the Phoenician alphabet, with a few adaptations to the necessities of the Greek language, which was a totally different language from the Semitic tongue of the Phoenicians. The most important of these adaptations was the use of five Phoenician letters (which in the Semitic alphabet repre-

[1] This table is simplified; the earlier inscriptions in each of these alphabets show a greater variety of forms than it is necessary to indicate here. The three letters omitted from the Ionic Greek alphabet were retained in use to denote certain numerals, *digamma* to denote 6, *san* or *sampi* to denote 900 (for which purpose it was placed after *omega*, the sign for 800), and *koppa* to denote 90. Twenty-seven letters instead of the normal twenty-four of the Ionic alphabet were required to denote the numerals, the units from 1 to 9, the tens from 10 to 90, and the hundreds from 100 to 900; hence these three letters, otherwise jettisoned, were still used in this way. Similarly, three Greek letters which were not used in the Latin alphabet were employed as Latin numerals: θ (*theta*) as 100 (later simplified to C, the more naturally as C is the initial of Lat. *centum*, 'hundred'); φ (*phi*) as 1,000 (later simplified to M, the more naturally as M is the initial of Lat. *mille*, 'thousand'); the sign φ when halved (D) denoted the half of 1,000 (500); ψ (West Greek *khi*, Ionic *psi*) denoted 50 (it was simplified to ⊥ and then to L).

West Greek alphabet		Pronunciation	Ionic alphabet — Name	Ionic alphabet	Minuscule	Pronunciation	Etruscan alphabet — Earlier	Etruscan alphabet — Later	Early Roman alphabet
A	A	a	alpha	A	α	a	A	A	A
B	B	b	bēta	B	β	b	𐌁	B	B
Λ	C	g	gamma	Γ	γ	g	𐌂	C	C
Δ	D	d	delta	Δ	δ	d	D	D	D
E	E	e	epsilon	E	Є	ě	Ǝ	Ǝ	E
	F	w	(digamma)				ꟼ	ꟻ	F
	Ɪ	zd, dz'	zēta	Z	(zeta)	zd, dz	I	I	(G inserted here later)
⊟	H	h	ēta	H	η	ē	⊟	⊟	H
⊗	Θ	th	thēta	Θ	θ	th	⊗	⊕	
	I	i	iōta	I	ι	i	I	I	I
	K	k	kappa	K	κ	k	K	K	K
	L	l	lambda	Λ	λ	l	𐌋	L	L
M	M	m	mu	M	μ	m	M	M	M
N	N	n	nu	N	ν	n	N	N	N
			xi	Ξ	ξ	x	⊞	⊞	
	O	o	omicron	O	O	ŏ	O	O	O
Γ	Π	p	pi	Π	π	p	ꓶ	Γ	P
	M	s	(san)				M	M	
	Q	k, q	(koppa)				Q	Q	Q
R	P	r	rhō	P	ρ	r	q	P	R
S	ξ	s	sigma	Σ	σ, s	s	ξ	ξ	S
	T	t	tau	T	T	t	T	T	T
V	Y	u	upsilon	Υ	υ	ü	Y	V	V
Φ	Φ	ph	phi	Φ	φ	ph	Φ	Φ	
+	X	x	khi	X	χ	kh	X	X	X
Ψ	Ψ	kh	psi	Ψ	ψ	ps	Y	V	(Y.Z. added
			ōmega	Ω	ω	ō			in 1st Cent.B.C.)

sented three gutturals and two semi-vowels) to indicate Greek vowels.[1] All twenty-two letters of the Phoenician alphabet represented consonants. Of the five Phoenician letters which the Greeks adapted as vowel-signs, four represented Semitic sounds which were not required in Greek speech. These were the gutturals corresponding to Hebrew א ('aleph), ה (he), and ע ('ayin), and the semi-vowel indicated in Hebrew by י (yod). But one of the letters used by the Greeks to denote a vowel-sound—Semitic waw, used as Greek Υ (v, upsilon), was also required by the Greeks in its original function as the letter indicating the semi-vowel w. So the Greeks used it twice over in their alphabet, in two variant forms—once in its Semitic position, No. 6, to denote the w sound, and again as an extra letter at the end of the alphabet, No. 23, in its new character as the vowel-letter upsilon. As No. 6 among the Greek letters, with the value of w and the name digamma, it appeared in the West Greek alphabet and most of the other local Greek alphabets, but was lacking in the Ionic alphabet, because the Greeks who originally used the Ionic alphabet stopped using the w sound. It is therefore absent from the classical Greek alphabet, which is based on the Ionic form. The letters which follow v (upsilon) in the Greek alphabet were added a considerable time after the Greeks originally acquired the alphabet from the Phoenicians and do not concern us at this stage in our inquiry.

Not only the forms of the Greek letters, but the names of most of them, betray their Semitic origin. For most of the names were taken over into Greek along with the letters. Alpha, beta, gamma, delta, and so on, are meaningless in Greek except as names of the letters which they denote; but the Phoenician names which lie behind them, which are practically identical with the Hebrew forms 'aleph, beth, gimel, daleth, and so on, are not only the names of letters but have a meaning of their own besides—they appear for the most part to denote the objects originally represented by the shapes of the respective letters in the earliest form of the Semitic alphabet, namely, ox, house, throw-stick,[2] door, etc.

[1] Why five? There were seven distinct simple vowel-sounds in classical Greek (quite apart from the differences of quantity)—those represented in the Ionic alphabet by α, ε, η, ι, ο, υ, ω. But there were five vowels in the Cypriote syllabary, and possibly the pre-Greek system of writing which originated in Crete and spread from there to Cyprus and elsewhere had some influence on the adaptation of the Phoenician alphabet to Greek usage. See Sir George Hill, History of Cyprus, Vol. I (1940), p. 53, where further reference is made to Rhys Carpenter in the American Journal of Archæology, 42 (1938), p. 67.

[2] So G. R. Driver, Semitic Writing (1948), pp. 155, 163 f. Another and older suggestion is that gimel means 'camel.'

The Semitic alphabet from which the Greeks derived theirs was written from right to left, as four forms of the Semitic alphabet —Hebrew, Samaritan, Arabic, Syriac—are written to the present day. The earliest Greek writing also ran from right to left. After a time the Greeks introduced the practice of writing alternate lines from right to left and from left to right; this practice was called writing *boustrophēdon* (ox-turning-wise), as it resembled the alternate directions followed in ploughing, up one furrow and down the next. This was followed by the third stage, in which the left-to-right direction was standardized, and this has remained the direction in which the Greek alphabet (with its derivative, the Roman alphabet) is written to this day.

This matter of the direction of writing has no such metaphysical significance as some people are inclined to read into it; it is a matter of convention and convenience. For right-handed writers the left-to-right direction has the advantage that one is less likely to smear or deface the words already written. The cuneiform writing of Babylonia and surrounding lands was originally in columns read downwards, arranged from right to left; but after 2500 B.C. or thereabout it regularly ran from left to right. The Egyptian hieroglyphs were usually written from right to left (as the derived hieratic and demotic scripts always were), but sometimes from left to right, and sometimes in vertical columns. The Sinaitic alphabetic script was written indifferently in any of these three directions. The Indian *nāgarī* script, whose ultimate prototype is the Aramaic form of the Semitic alphabet, is written from left to right. The oldest extant piece of Latin writing runs from right to left (as the early Etruscan alphabet did): this is the inscription of *c*. 600 B.C. found on a fibula at Præneste (Palestrina) which reads: *Manios med fhefhaked Numasioi* ('Manios made me for Numasios').[1] The earliest extant Latin inscription in stone, which is not later than 400 B.C., is written in vertical columns reading from bottom to top and from top to bottom alternately, the letters lying, as it were, on their sides.

How old is the Phoenician alphabet from which the Greek alphabet is derived? It is found in inscriptions of various kings of Gebal who reigned between the fourteenth and ninth centuries B.C. Gebal, known to the Greeks as Byblos, is (interestingly enough) the city from whose name the Greeks derived one of their names for papyrus[2] (and from which in due course our word 'Bible'

---

[1] In classical Latin this would be *Manius me fecit Numerio* ('Manius made me for Numerius'),   [2] See p. 11.

came): we have the record of a large quantity of papyrus which was sent there from Egypt shortly before 1100 B.C.—for what purpose if not for writing? The oldest of these royal inscriptions at Gebal is that of King Shaphatbaal,[1] and is dated about 1250 B.C. Then we have two inscriptions from the tomb of King Ahiram of the same city, two or three centuries later. There are also shorter inscriptions, such as a piece of pottery bearing the potter's name, 'Abda, son of Kelubay the potter', from about the same time as Shaphatbaal's inscription, and a bronze spatula bearing an inscription which contains the owner's name, Azarbaal,[2] roughly contemporary with the Ahiram inscriptions. A vessel found in the same city of Gebal, belonging to the time of King Amenemhet IV of Egypt (shortly after 1800 B.C.), has marked on it two signs which are pretty certainly the Phoenician letters 'ayin and kaph.[3]

So we can trace the Phoenician alphabet back at least to the eighteenth century B.C. We call it rightly the Phoenician alphabet, because in the present state of our knowledge the Phoenicians appear to have been the first people to use it, but it is the alphabet which before long came into use throughout Syria and Palestine among other Semitic-speaking peoples beside the Phoenicians, and it is therefore known also by the more general name of the North Semitic alphabet. In this alphabet, for example, we have such documents as the 'Gezer Calendar', the oldest piece of Hebrew writing known to be extant, which dates from the time of David or thereabout (c. 1000 B.C.) and contains a list of farming operations month by month; and King Mesha's Moabite Stone, which gives the Moabite version of the revolt mentioned in 2 Kings 1. 1 (c. 850 B.C.).

So far we have traced our alphabet back to the Phoenician alphabet of the eighteenth century B.C. without having to postulate missing links. When we come to consider how the alphabet arose, however, we have to exercise a certain degree of imagination.

The origin of writing long antedates the origin of the alphabet. Simple and convenient as alphabetic writing appears to us, it was at a comparatively late stage in the development of writing that the alphabetic principle made its appearance. In view of the

---

[1] The name means 'Baal has judged'; cf. the recurring Old Testament name, Shephatiah (2 Sam. 3. 4, and elsewhere), meaning 'Jehovah has judged'.

[2] The name means 'Baal has helped'; in its Carthaginian form Hasdrubal, it appears as the name of a brother and brother-in-law of Hannibal. Cf. the Old Testament name, Azariah, meaning 'Jehovah has helped'.

[3] See C. F. A. Schaeffer, The Cuneiform Texts of Ras Shamra-Ugarit (1939), p. 36; G. R. Driver, Semitic Writing, p. 190.

apparent development of writing from drawing, this was inevitable. A picture of an old man, the sun, a bear or a bee, so long as it represents one or other of those objects and nothing else, remains a picture only. We might group the pictures together in such a way as to tell a story of a bear stealing an old man's honey as he lay asleep in the sun, while the bees buzzed angrily but ineffectively around, but so long as the pictures denoted only these concrete objects they would be nothing more than pictograms. Such picture-writing is not unknown even in modern civilization; it is employed, for example, in advertisements such as those which by a picture-sequence show the wonderful change in a lady's nervous system on washing-day after she has learned how to make a certain cleansing substance do the hard work for her;[1] it is employed, too, and very effectively, in such road-signs as those which indicate the proximity of cross-roads and other types of road-junction.[2]

But if the picture of an old man is used to express old age, if the picture of the sun is used to express heat, if the picture of the bear is used to suggest a person or perhaps a nation characterized by some quality of bearishness, if the picture of a bee is used to suggest busy-ness (or honey), then we have moved a step—and a long step—in the direction of writing; the picture is no longer a pictogram but an ideogram, because it expresses some idea associated with the things shown in the picture. Thus, until a few years ago in our system of traffic signs, a torch did not denote a literal torch, but the torch of learning, which by a further extension of meaning was (in this particular context) intended to indicate the presence of a school. (This ideogram has now been replaced by a pictogram in which two schoolchildren are seen coming out of school.)

Or we may extend the use of our pictograms in another direction. We may use the picture of the sun to denote not 'sun' but 'son'; the picture of a bear to express not the animal but the verb 'to bear'; the picture of a bee to express the verb 'to be'. If we do that, we are concentrating on the sound instead of the sense; we use the signs now not as pictograms but as phonograms.

But mark: pictograms and ideograms convey the same sense to readers whose languages may be widely different from each other, whereas phonograms are restricted to one particular language: for example, the use of the picture of the sun to denote the word 'son' is possible only with reference to a language in which the

[1] See also D. Diringer, *The Alphabet*, p. 32.
[2] Cf. F. Bodmer and L. Hogben, *The Loom of Language* (1943), p. 49.

two words meaning respectively the chief heavenly luminary and one's male offspring happen to have the same sound, as they have in English.

We have a few well-known ideograms which are common to most nations to-day, the most obvious being the signs for numbers. If I write 'four', only a reader who understands English will know what I mean; but if I write 4, my meaning is understood at once by any Frenchman, German, Russian, Israeli or any other reader who may see it. They will pronounce it differently—*quatre, vier, tchetyre, arba,* and so on—but they will all understand the same idea by it, because it expresses an idea and not any particular sound.

I can go farther and build up words syllable by syllable, charade fashion, by the use of ideograms and phonograms. If I want to express 'before' in writing, I can use the picture of a bee followed by the ideogram 4. If I wish to write 'sonship' I can combine the pictures of the sun and a ship. This may seem a fantastic procedure to us, but it is exactly the way in which writing developed. The representation of every syllable by a distinct sign is a real advance on the earlier stage in which ideograms and logograms (signs denoting whole words) were the only available symbols. The number of possible syllables in any language, though large, is limited; with a syllabary, therefore (a set of signs denoting syllables), we are on the way to a more convenient system of writing. The number of signs in a syllabary can be further reduced if, instead of having a separate sign for every possible syllable, we have signs for only the simpler syllables, say of the vowel-plus-consonant or consonant-plus-vowel type, or even of the consonant-plus-vowel type only. Thus, instead of writing a word like 'Manchester' with three syllabic signs, Man-ches-ter, one could use simpler signs and write it Ma-an-che-es-te-er, or even Ma-na-che-se-te-re. The last effort looks queer, but it is the way in which Greek was written for long in the island of Cyprus, where a syllabary of fifty-four signs was in use, indicating open syllables (syllables ending in a vowel) only. Thus in this Cypriote script a king called Stasikypros has his name written Sa-ta-si-ku-po-ro-se.

In point of fact, it was seldom that one of these improvements was adopted in the ancient East to the complete exclusion of the earlier stages. Thus, in the cuneiform writing of the Euphrates-Tigris valley and adjacent lands we find intermingled the simpler syllabic writing, the more complicated syllabic writing, and ideograms.

This script is called cuneiform or wedge-shaped from the shape of the signs which was the natural result of the instrument and material used for writing it—a metal stylus with bevelled head which traced marks in soft clay, which was then baked hard. The cuneiform script was used by the Sumerians, an early population of Mesopotamia, for writing their language. It goes back to c. 3000 B.C. Around that time we find two distinct forms of writing in Mesopotamia and Elam, which lay to the east—the semi-pictographic script of Elam and Jemdet Nasr (near Kish), and the proto-cuneiform of Ur and Lagash. Both were probably derived from a common pictographic origin, but the Sumerians made a more rapid advance from it than the Elamites did. From the Sumerians the cuneiform script was taken over by other peoples for other languages—Elamite, Akkadian, Hurrian, Hittite, and others.

There were other ideographic and syllabic scripts in use in the Middle East in the third and second millennia B.C.—the hieroglyphic script of Egypt, with the simpler systems derived from it; the hieroglyphic script used in the later Hittite kingdoms; the script printed[1] on the Phaestus disc (which, though found in Crete, is thought to be of Anatolian origin); the varieties of linear script of Minoan Crete, which was carried thence to the Greek mainland and to Cyprus. (It was from a form of the Cretan linear script that the Cypriote syllabary mentioned above was derived—originally for a pre-Greek language.)

The Cretan linear scripts, which also go back to a pictographic stage, remained undeciphered for long. The inscriptions were published in Scripta Minoa, by Sir Arthur Evans (Vol. I, 1909; Vol. II, edited by Sir John Myres, 1952). The clue to their decipherment came within reach in 1939, when Professor C. W. Blegen found about 600 tablets, written in one of the Cretan linear scripts ('Linear B'), at Navarino in south-west Greece, near the site of Nestor's city of Pylos. Many more tablets in the same script have been found in recent years, not only there but also in Mycenae. The credit for deciphering 'Linear B' belongs to the late Michael Ventris, who showed in 1952 that the language written in this script, both in Crete and on the mainland, was an early form of

---

[1] Yes, printed with movable stamps! Sir Arthur Evans thought that the inscription was a religious chant in honour of the Anatolian Goddess-Mother. It shows forty-five different signs. See Evans, Scripta Minoa, i (1909), pp. 22 ff., 273 ff.; D. Diringer, The Alphabet (1947), pp. 78 f.

Greek (c. 1200 B.C.).[1] It should not be long now before an earlier form of the Cretan script ('Linear A') is deciphered; the language written in it is not Greek, but is probably related to one of the language-groups of Western Asia.[2]

While these syllabaries were in official use in the great Middle East Empires of the second millennium B.C., the first experiments were being made in alphabetic writing. The Egyptian scribes, as early as 3000 B.C., began to develop out of their hieroglyphic writing a sort of alphabet of twenty-four signs, representing all the consonants current in their language. These signs were in their origin the signs for roots which consisted of one strong consonant and one or two weak consonants which tended to be disregarded or dropped. The signs thus came in each case to designate the surviving strong consonant. They were only a potential alphabet, however; apart from serving to spell foreign words and to fulfil some grammatical functions, they were not generally used. This potential alphabet never became a real alphabet; it never became independent of the cumbersome hieroglyphic system but merely supplemented it where some such supplementary aid was required.

Yet it is commonly thought that the Egyptian potential alphabet gave the idea of a real alphabet to some of the Semitic peoples inhabiting the parts of Asia nearest to Egypt. This is not proved, but Egyptian derivation is less unlikely than derivation from any other source. We must remember, however, that it is not necessary to suppose that the alphabet must have evolved step by step from an earlier system of writing. The alphabetic idea, so simple once it has been suggested and worked out in practice, is the sort of idea that very possibly originated as a brain-wave in the creative mind of some inventive genius. 'For this achievement,' says Dr. Diringer, 'simple as it *now* seems to us, the inventor, or the inventors are to be ranked among the greatest benefactors of mankind. ... The more or less civilized peoples of Egypt, Mesopotamia, Crete, Asia Minor, Indus Valley, China, Central America, reached an advanced stage in the history of writing, but could not get beyond the transitional stage. A few peoples (the ancient Cypriotes, the Japanese, and others) developed a syllabary. But

---

[1] Cf. M. Ventris and J. Chadwick, *Documents in Mycenaean Greek* (Cambridge, 1956); J. Chadwick, *The Decipherment of Linear B* (Cambridge, 1958); L. R. Palmer, *The Interpretation of Mycenaean Greek Texts* (London, 1962).

[2] On April 3, 1962, Professor C. H. Gordon of Brandeis University, Waltham, Massachusetts, announced that he had discovered conclusive evidence for his view that the language of the Linear A inscriptions was Phoenician; and indicated that his decipherment would be published in the *Journal of Near Eastern Studies* in July, 1962.

only the Syro-Palestinian Semites produced a genius who created the alphabetic writing, from which have descended all past and present alphabets'.[1]

One point in favour of the Egyptian derivation of the North Semitic alphabet is that it lacks vowel signs. True, the Semitic languages are of such a nature that their written forms can dispense with vowel signs less inconveniently than many other languages; yet it is probably not a coincidence that the Egyptian potential alphabet was also vowelless. Other points of contact between Egyptian writing and the North Semitic alphabet are affinity in writing materials (though this is by itself quite inconclusive), and similarity in the form and direction of the characters.

If we wish to trace a closer connection between the Egyptian potential alphabet and the North Semitic alphabet, however, we must look for a missing link; the gap between the two is too wide for us to believe that the latter was an immediate development from the former. It has been argued in a very persuasive manner that the missing link is to be found in the script found in the Sinai Peninsula, at Serabit el-Khadem, where turquoise mines were worked on behalf of the Egyptians in the earlier part of the second millennium B.C. These Sinai inscriptions were discovered by Flinders Petrie in 1905, and are now in the Cairo Museum. Sir Alan Gardiner, who was a pioneer in the decipherment of these inscriptions, assigned them to the period of the Twelfth Egyptian Dynasty (c. 1989-1776 B.C.), and concluded that this script was the origin of the North Semitic alphabet, largely on the ground that the *names* of the North Semitic letters designate the *objects* depicted by the Sinaitic symbols. A corollary of this is the view that each symbol indicates the initial sound of the name of the object which it depicts; for example, the North Semitic letter *beth*, which originally was the picture of a house and whose name means 'house', is the symbol for the sound *b*. This is what is called the acrophonic principle. It is difficult to account for all the letters of the original alphabet on this principle, but it does seem to have played a prominent part in the formation of the alphabet.

But the view that the Phoenician alphabet is descended from the Sinaitic script is likely to be modified or even given up as a result of Professor W. F. Albright's study of the Sinai inscriptions in the winter of 1947-8. Professor Albright now holds that the date of the inscriptions must be reduced by three or four centuries

[1] *The Alphabet*, pp. 216 f.

from the date assigned them by Sir Alan Gardiner, and considers the script 'as normal alphabetic Canaanite from the early fifteenth century B.C.'[1] In that case it is later than our earliest evidence for the North Semitic alphabet, and it looks as if the Sinai script and the North Semitic alphabet had a common ancestor. If we look for this common ancestor, we are confronted with the fact that in the period with which we are dealing Syria and Palestine formed the arena of a considerable number of competing experiments in alphabetic writing. The exact circumstances in which the alphabet originated, and the nature and extent of its dependence on an Egyptian prototype cannot be determined in our present state of knowledge.

The excavations at Tell ed-Duweir (identified with the Biblical Lachish), begun in 1933, provided further examples of early alphabetic writing, including an inscription on a dagger of the sixteenth century B.C., and four pieces of pottery of the thirteenth century B.C. bearing marks 'which are unmistakably the letters of an alphabet'.[2] Comparable inscriptions have been found on various objects at Gezer, Shechem, Megiddo, Beth-shemesh and elsewhere. These early Canaanite inscriptions fall into three groups, concerning which Dr. Diringer remarks: 'For those readers who have a fondness for curious facts, I should like to point out that, probably by a sheer coincidence, the three groups of the early Canaanite inscriptions correspond roughly, the first to the Age of the Patriarchs; the second, to the Age of Joshua; the third, to the Age of the Judges; and that the *lacuna* of two or three centuries between the first and the second groups corresponds roughly to the period of oppression of the Israelites in Egypt'.[3]

There was one early form of alphabet used in the North Semitic area which did to a limited degree express vowel distinctions. This was the cuneiform alphabet of Ras Shamra (the ancient Ugarit), used for the texts discovered there from 1929 onwards and dating from *c.* 1400 B.C. This cuneiform alphabet is not a development from the cuneiform script of Mesopotamia; its wedge-shaped character is the result of writing with a metal stylus on clay tablets. It was, probably enough, invented by a native of Ugarit or the neighbourhood who knew the North Semitic

---

[1] Professor Albright's account is given in the *Bulletin of the American Schools of Oriental Research*, April, 1948, pp. 6-22. His dating marks a return to that suggested by Flinders Petrie, *Researches in Sinai* (1906), pp. 129-131.

[2] G. R. Driver, *Semitic Writing*, p. 101.

[3] *The Alphabet*, p. 211. See also F. M. Cross, 'The Evolution of the Proto-Canaanite Alphabet', *Bulletin of the American Schools of Oriental Research*, April, 1954, pp. 15-24.

alphabet, and on the basis of that made up an alphabet suitable for the writing materials with which he and his fellows were familiar. Some, but only some, of the Ras Shamra characters appear to be copies of the corresponding characters of the North Semitic alphabet, adapted to the different writing material; others may have simply been invented on principles of general convenience. The form of the letters is a very unimportant matter compared with the basic alphabetic principle. The Ras Shamra alphabet is so well advanced at the date of the inscriptions in which we know it that it can hardly have originated later than the sixteenth century B.C.,[1] and the alphabet on which it was based must be still older. This agrees with the evidence we have already noted for tracing the North Semitic alphabet back to the eighteenth century. Instead of having but one letter corresponding to 'aleph, the first letter of the North Semitic alphabet, the Ras Shamra alphabet has three, according as the guttural sound 'aleph (something like what we know as the 'glottal stop') was followed by an a, i, or u vowel-sound. It has been suggested that this departure from general Semitic practice where the alphabet is concerned may have been due to requirements of non-Semitic languages for which the Ras Shamra alphabet was also used.[2] The Ras Shamra alphabet has some thirty letters; this excess over the number in the North Semitic alphabet is accounted for in part by the three letters corresponding to 'aleph and in part by its making provision for a greater complement of guttural and sibilant sounds than the North Semitic alphabet—some of these sounds having been amalgamated with others in later North Semitic speech but kept distinct to this day in Arabic. It is to be expected that if we found earlier monuments of the North Semitic alphabet we should find these sounds represented. Professor Albright has identified letters representing some of them in the Sinai script,[3] which seems to be derived from an earlier form of the North Semitic alphabet than we know yet.

So we have not come quite to the end of our quest; more light must yet be thrown on the origin of the alphabet. When that light is sufficient to show exactly where the alphabet came into being,

---

[1] C. F. A. Schaeffer, *The Cuneiform Texts of Ras Shamra-Ugarit*, p. 36. More recently, in November, 1949, Professor Schaeffer found at Ras Shamra a tablet of the fourteenth century B.C., on which are inscribed thirty letters of the Ras Shamra alphabet in what was presumably their alphabetic order. The Ras Shamra letters listed on p. 32 are set out in the order in which they appear on this tablet. The close approximation of this order to the known order of the Phoenician or North Semitic alphabet further supports the view expressed above that the Ras Shamra alphabet is based on that alphabet.

[2] See C. H. Gordon, *Ugaritic Handbook* (1947), pp. 10 ff.

[3] *Bulletin of the American Schools of Oriental Research*, April, 1948.

it will not be surprising if it turns out that Gebal was the place. Gebal was in close touch with Egypt; at Gebal, too, there was in use a system of writing 'lying midway between the Egyptian hieroglyphic script and the Phoenician alphabet'[1] which may prove to be the missing link.[2] More than this we cannot say.

What has all this to do with Biblical studies? Much every way. These researches incidentally increase our knowledge of the milieu in which the ancestors of Israel lived. What Professor Albright says of the Sinai inscriptions may be extended to most of the subject-matter which we have been discussing: 'The discovery of more inscriptions in Serābît will thus have considerable importance for Israelite origins as well as for the history of the alphabet'.[3] Again, in view of the classic Protestant belief that the Scriptures should be made available to the common people in their own language, it is worth noticing that it was the alphabet that made it possible for all classes to be literate; its invention is therefore a landmark of great importance in the history of civilization. The older systems of writing, being much more complicated, required long study and practice and were the preserve of priestly and clerkly castes.

But once the alphabet was invented, it was a simple matter for anyone to learn to read and write. In Judges 8. 14 we read how Gideon laid hands on a young man of Succoth in Transjordan, who, according to the text of the A.V. and R.V., 'described' to him the chief men of his city. The margins of both versions, however, point out that the ordinary sense of the word is 'wrote'. But that a chance youth should have been able to write at this time may have seemed too unlikely. When the R.V. was produced, the oldest alphabetic autograph known was Mesha's Moabite Stone, three centuries later than Gideon's time. Now, however, it seems most reasonable to take the narrative literally and conclude that the youth 'wrote down' for Gideon a list of the elders of Succoth, as the R.S.V. rightly says.

As we have seen, Moses is the first person in the Bible who is said to have written anything, and what he wrote has formed part ever since of 'God's word written'. It is clear that Moses could perfectly well have written in an alphabetic script, and it is most likely that he did so. In days when alphabetic writing at so early a period was not known, it was reasonable to suggest that Moses

---

[1] G. R. Driver, *Semitic Writing*, p. 93.

[2] It is a syllabary containing at least 80 signs.

[3] *Bulletin of the American Schools of Oriental Research*, April, 1948, p. 22.

wrote in the cuneiform script on clay tablets like those discovered at Tell el-Amarna in Egypt.[1] But now there is no ground for thinking that the Bible was not written from the very beginning in an alphabetic script. The history of the Bible is thus closely bound up from the start with the history of alphabetic writing. Believers in the providence of God may well conclude that it was by that providence that, when the Bible first began to be written, there lay ready to hand for the purpose a form of writing, recently invented, the understanding of which was not restricted to specially trained readers but lay within the capacity of Everyman.

[1] A. E. Cowley, in *Aramaic Papyri of the Fifth Century B.C.* (1923), p. xxv, suggested that the original documents which eventually formed part of the Hebrew Torah 'were written in cuneiform and probably in the Babylonian language.' But this is much less probable now than it seemed forty years ago.

Ras Shamra		Sinaitic	Early North Semitic	Early Greek	Moabite Stone	Samaritan	Aramaic and Square Hebrew	Hebrew name and meaning	Value of Hebrew letter
	('a)		K	K	⋠ ⋈ (a)				'aleph (ox)	'
	(b)		9	9	∂ B (b)	9	9		beth (house)	b
	(g)		∧	1	7 (g)	⊐	Y		gimel (throw-stick)	g
	(ḥ)									
	(d)		△	△	△ △ (d)	△			daleth (door)	d
	(h)		⊟	⊟	⊟ (e)	⊟			he (lo!)	h
	(w)		Y	Y	⊣ (w)	Y			waw (peg)	w
	(z)		I	I	I (z)	I			zayin (weapon)	z
	(ḥ)		⊟	⊟	⊟ (h)	⊟			heth (hedge)	ḥ
	(ṭ)		⊕	⊗	⊕ (th)	⊕			teth (shake)	ṭ
	(y)		ι	ι	ιι (i)				yodh (hand)	y
	(k)		v	v	v (k)	Y			kaph (palm)	k
	(š)									
	(l)		v	∠	v7 (l)	∠			lamedh (goad)	l
	(m)		₹	y	y (m)	y			mem (water)	m
	(dh)									
	(n)		₹	y	y (n)	y	y		nun (fish)	n
	(ẓ)									
	(s)		₮	₮	(x) ₮	₮			samekh (fish)	s
	(')		O	O	(o) O	O	V		'ayin (eye)	'
	(p)		⊃	7	11 (p)	7			pe (mouth)	p
	(ṣ)		T	M	(ṣ)				sadhe (cricket)	ṣ
	(q)		φ φ φ	φφ	(q) φ	φ			qoph (monkey)	q
	(r)		9	9	4 (r)	4	9		resh (head)	r
	(th)		w	₹₹ζ	(s) w				shin (tooth)	š, ś
	(gh)									
	(t)		+	X	T (t)	+			tau (mark)	t
	('i)									
	('u)									
	(ś)									
	(u)				vy					

CHAPTER III

THE HEBREW LANGUAGE

OUR discussion of the script which was used in writing the Scriptures leads us on inevitably to some consideration of the languages which were written in those scripts.

The languages of the Bible are not, as is sometimes imagined, dead languages. All three of them are alive and in use to-day. Hebrew is the official language of the young State of Israel, and during the period of the British Mandate it was one of the three official languages of Palestine, Arabic and English being the other two. Aramaic is spoken by the small remnant of Assyrian Christians in Syria, Iraq and Persia. Greek is the language of between seven and eight million Greeks. There are naturally differences between the modern forms of these languages and the forms spoken in Biblical times. Change is necessary to life on earth. Only when a language becomes dead does it cease to change. In that sense classical Latin is a dead language.[1] But there is much less difference between modern Hebrew and Biblical Hebrew, between modern Greek and Biblical Greek, than there is between modern English and English as spoken in 1066.

By far the greater part of the Old Testament is written in Hebrew. The language is not called 'Hebrew' in the Old Testament itself, however. There it is variously called 'the Jews' tongue' (Isa. 36. 11; Neh. 13. 24) and 'the lip of Canaan' (Isa. 19. 18). In the New Testament it is called 'Hebrew' in Rev. 9. 11; 16. 16.[2]

Hebrew belongs to what is called the Semitic family of languages. This name 'Semitic' is now so firmly established in this sense that it is not worth changing it, although it is not an ideal term for the purpose. (But while it is convenient and fairly unobjectionable to use it in a linguistic sense, it is misleading and invidious to use it in a racial sense.) It is an adjective derived from the name of Shem, one of the three sons of Noah, from whom

---

[1] Ordinary spoken Latin, on the other hand, did not die; it continued to be spoken and gradually changed into the modern Romance languages: French, Spanish, Catalan, Portuguese, Provençal, Italian, Romansch, Romanian, etc.

[2] Where the 'Hebrew' language is mentioned elsewhere in the New Testament, the Aramaic language is meant.

several Semitic-speaking groups are derived in Gen. 10 and 11.[1]

When we speak of languages as belonging to one family of languages (in this instance the Semitic family), we mean that these languages have developed from what were dialects of one original language. As the people who spoke that language spread out from a common centre, they and their descendants deviated increasingly from each other in their speech, owing to a variety of factors, until what at an earlier stage were mutually intelligible dialects became distinct languages. The geographical factor was one of the most potent in producing this diversity of speech, and so it is natural to group the languages of the family in a geographical arrangement. Hebrew belongs to the North-west Semitic group, more particularly to the Western division of the group, which included Canaanite, Moabite and Phoenician, the Semitic languages with which Hebrew was most closely akin. To the Northern division belonged Amorite and Aramaic. Ugaritic, the language of the Ras Shamra texts, discovered in North Syria in 1929 and following years, has generally been classified as a Canaanite language, but it has some affinities with other branches of the Semitic family as well, and perhaps should simply be called North-west Semitic. The East Semitic group comprises the Semitic languages of Babylonia and Assyria, generally referred to comprehensively as Akkadian. The South Semitic languages are those of Arabia and Ethiopia. Since the seventh century A.D. the Arabic language has spread west and east from its Arabian home; it is by far the most widely spoken Semitic language nowadays.

This geographical classification is only a matter of expediency, however; it must not be thought of as rigid or scientific. For example, although Hebrew is classified among West Semitic languages, it has various features which are rather distinctive of Akkadian, Arabic, and even Egyptian. These features have led some scholars to make such exaggerated statements as Professor Margoliouth made in the beginning of the present century when he wrote that 'it is now possible to treat the Old Testament as a part of Arabic literature, just as it has long been possible to treat Hebrew as a dialect of Arabic'.[2] Another learned Orientalist is quoted as having said that 'a good Arabic dictionary is of greater

---

[1] E.g., the Hebrews, Assyrians, Aramæans, and Arabs. But Elam and Lud, other sons of Shem (Gen. 10. 22), were not Semitic-speaking. On the other hand, some of the children of Ham were Semitic-speaking, e.g., Canaan (Gen. 10. 6) and those sons of Cush who are listed in Gen. 10. 7. The genealogical tables of Gen. 10 and 11 do not denote linguistic divisions but geographical and political relationships.

[2] D. S. Margoliouth, *Lines of Defence of the Biblical Revelation* (1903), p. v.

use for the understanding of the Old Testament than all possible commentaries'.[1] More recently, Dr. A. S. Yahuda has overstated the case for Egyptian linguistic influence on Biblical Hebrew in a manner which has secured the general assent neither of Semitists nor of Egyptologists.[2] And other scholars have looked in other directions for the main affinities of the Hebrew language. Such conclusions are really the result of concentrating on the connections which Hebrew has with one language-group or another; they have all a greater or lesser degree of truth, and are valuable in so far as they remind us that the classification of the Semitic languages—or of any other family of languages— is no simple matter.

Hebrew was no isolated language in Old Testament times. It was exactly what Isaiah calls it—the 'language (literally, 'lip') of Canaan'. It had only dialect-variations from Phoenician, the language of Tyre, Sidon, and Gebal and of their colonies farther afield, like Carthage; or from the language spoken by the Moabites, who lived east of the Dead Sea. In the days of the Roman wars with Carthage (third century B.C.) the chief magistrates of Carthage were called by practically the same title as the judges of Old Testament times. The judges were called *shōphĕtīm* in Hebrew; the Romans replaced the Semitic plural ending by a Latin ending (*-es*) and called the Carthaginian magistrates *suffetes*. The names of many Carthaginians are easily intelligible to anyone with a knowledge of Hebrew. Thus Hannibal, the great Carthaginian general, has a name which means 'grace of Baal'; compare the Old Testament name Hanniel (Num. 34. 23; 1 Chron. 7. 39), which means 'grace of God (*'El*)' or 'God is gracious'. His father, Hamilcar, was given the surname Barca ('lightning') which is identical with the name of the Hebrew judge, Barak. The name Hamilcar itself is not so obviously interpreted; it is actually a rather broken-down form of *'Abd-Melqart*, 'servant of Melqart', a leading deity of Phoenicia. It was Melqart who was worshipped in Israel as Baal (lord) in the time of Ahab and Jezebel, for Jezebel was a Phoenician princess. Melqart is actually *Melk-qart*, 'king of the city'; *melk* being the equivalent of Hebrew *melekh*, 'king', and *qart* being a Phoenician word meaning 'town', the same word as

---

[1] The Orientalist is quoted but not named by B. Manassewitsch in *Die Arabische Sprache* (1891), p. v. Much of the importance of Arabic in this respect lies in its wealth of vocabulary and its preservation of many grammatical forms which Biblical Hebrew had lost.

[2] Principally in his book, *The Language of the Pentateuch in its Relation to Egyptian* (1933). Egyptian is not a Semitic but a Hamitic language, but the Semitic and Hamitic families are so closely related that many scholars envisage a primitive Hamito-Semitic speech-unity.

Hebrew *qiryath* which occurs as an element in some Hebrew place-names.[1] Phoenician *qart* appears in the very name of Carthage, which is Phoenician *Qart-chadast* (New Town); the second element in the name is the feminine form of the adjective meaning 'new' (Heb. *chādāsh*, feminine *chădāshāh*).

Older documents in the Phoenician language are those inscriptions mentioned on pages 21 f. The inscription on the sarcophagus of King Ahiram[2] of Gebal, for example, is written in a language almost identical with Hebrew. Its translation runs: 'Ittobaal (Ethbaal), son of Ahiram, king of Gebal, made this coffin for Ahiram his father as an abode for ever. And if any king among kings or governor among governors pitches a camp against Gebal and uncovers this coffin, let the sceptre of his authority be broken and the throne of his kingdom be overthrown, but let peace rule over Gebal. Whoso effaces this writing, let his seed perish'.

The Tell el-Amarna tablets, which contain the diplomatic correspondence of the Egyptian court during the reign of the Pharaoh Akhnaton (1377-1360 B.C.), are written mostly in the Akkadian tongue, but contain here and there Canaanite glosses in cuneiform script.

The first really long inscription in any Canaanite language, however, which has survived, is the Moabite Stone of King Mesha,[3] bearing an inscription of date about 850 B.C. Here again we find a language substantially the same as Hebrew; the inscription presents no difficulty to any reader with an adequate knowledge of Hebrew.

Among the Israelites themselves there were no doubt dialect variations in their use of Hebrew, but unfortunately we have no inscriptions from the northern kingdom comparable to those from the southern kingdom, which might enable us to know what these variations were. From the northern kingdom we have the Gezer calendar (see page 22) and a number of short inscriptions on pieces of pottery (ostraca), the most important of these being seventy-five ostraca from the royal palace in Samaria, belonging to the reign of Jeroboam II (785-745 B.C.), and containing notes on supplies of oil and wine. But from the southern kingdom we have more continuous inscriptions—we have the six lines of the inscription from near the exit of the Siloam tunnel,[4] describing how the

---

[1] As in Kiriath-sepher ('city of books').

[2] *'Achi-ram*, meaning 'brother of the High One,' or 'the High One is brother.' The name of Hiram, king of Tyre, is a shortened form of Achiram.

[3] See p. 22.

[4] This tunnel carries water from the Virgin's Fountain to the Pool of Siloam. The construction of the tunnel is usually connected with Hezekiah's operation mentioned in 2 Kings 20. 20; 2 Chron. 32. 3 f., 30. The inscription is now in Istanbul.

workmen, tunnelling from either end, struck pick against pick (c. 700 B.C.); and about one hundred lines of readable Hebrew in the Lachish Letters,[1] discovered in 1935 and 1938, and written in the summer of 588 B.C. These have proved very important for many aspects of Hebrew and Old Testament study. Of the first discussion to be published of the Lachish Letters (that contributed by Professor H. Torczyner to the Bialik memorial volume in 1935), Professor D. Winton Thomas remarks: 'It is of some interest that this first discussion of them was written, two thousand five hundred years later than the period to which the ostraca belong, in the language of the ostraca themselves, in Hebrew'.[2]

After the Jews' return from the Babylonian captivity, the use of Hebrew as a spoken language declined; for vernacular purposes it was increasingly superseded by Aramaic. Hebrew, however, remained the sacred language; it was used for long by the Rabbis in their discussions, and as a literary medium it never fell into complete disuse. Some scholars have contended that even as late as the time of Christ Hebrew was the vernacular of Judaea, as does Professor M. H. Segal, although he concedes that 'with regard to the language of Jesus, it is admitted that in the Roman period, and perhaps earlier, Aramaic was the vernacular of the native Galilean Jews'.[3] Professor T. W. Manson has suggested that, in His more formal disputations with the Pharisees, Jesus may have used Hebrew, as they did.[4] This Rabbinical Hebrew (which represents a later development of Biblical Hebrew) was the language of the Mishnah, a codification of the traditional oral law which was committed to writing about A.D. 200.[5] For this reason it is commonly known as Mishnaic Hebrew.

The use of Hebrew as a literary language continued into the Middle Ages. The history of modern Hebrew literature goes back to the period of the Enlightenment in the eighteenth century,

---

[1] These letters were written on ostraca during Nebuchadnezzar's siege of Lachish (Jer. 34. 7).

[2] 'The Prophet' in the Lachish Ostraca (1946), pp. 5 f.

[3] Mishnaic Hebrew Grammar (1927), p. 17. There was a patriotic revival of Hebrew during the rising led by Judas Maccabaeus and his family (167 B.C. and the following years); and letters written by participants in the Bar-kokhba rising of A.D. 132-135 are written, apparently indiscriminately, in Hebrew, Aramaic and Greek.

[4] The Teaching of Jesus (1931), pp. 46 ff.

[5] Further commentaries grew up around the Mishnah in Babylonia and Palestine. These commentaries are known as Gemaras. The Mishnah with Palestinian Gemara is called the Palestinian or Jerusalem Talmud; the Mishnah with Babylonian Gemara is called the Babylonian Talmud. The Palestinian Talmud was committed to writing c. A.D. 400; the Babylonian Talmud c. A.D. 500. The latter is fuller and generally regarded as the more authoritative. Another collection of tradition parallel to the Mishnah but independent of it is the Tosephta. Mishnah and Tosephta are in Hebrew; the Gemaras mainly in Aramaic.

and more recently the ancient language has renewed its youth like the eagle and become the vigorous vernacular of Israel.

The ancestors of the Israelites apparently spoke Aramaic; that at any rate, is the language which was spoken in Paddan-Aram by the relatives whom the patriarchs left behind them there.[1] By the time of Jacob, however, the branch of the family that had settled in Canaan spoke in the 'lip of Canaan'. This may be deduced from the statement that when Jacob and Laban piled a cairn in Transjordan to demarcate their respective spheres, Jacob called it by a Hebrew name, while Laban gave it the corresponding Aramaic name.[2]

From the foregoing chapter it will be seen that the Hebrews wrote their language in the standard North Semitic alphabet of twenty-two letters, running from right to left. This direction has been maintained in Hebrew writing ever since, and while beginners in Hebrew study may find it strange at first, it is something to which they soon become used. Until about 200 B.C. they used the form of the letters which we find in the Phoenician inscriptions —a form in which the letters have an angular shape.[3] This is the form in which the earlier Hebrew documents are written—the Siloam inscription, the Lachish Letters, and so forth, not to mention the Moabite Stone and other inscriptions in other varieties of Canaanite. The script in which the Samaritan manuscripts and their printed copies are written is an ornamental development of this angular script. Among the Aramaic speakers, however, another variety of the Semitic alphabet was developed, in which the letters acquired a square shape rather than an angular one, and this square character was taken over by the Jews for the writing of Hebrew as well as Aramaic about 200 B.C. It is in this square character that most manuscripts of the Hebrew Bible are written; it is this, too, which is used for Hebrew printing. Jewish tradition ascribes the change-over in the script to Ezra, but it is probably later than his day.

The names of the twenty-two Hebrew letters are familiar to the reader of the English Bible from Psalm 119, in which each section of eight verses is named after a Hebrew letter. This is because the Psalm, consisting of twenty-two sections of eight verses each, is an acrostic Psalm in Hebrew. Each of the first eight verses begins with the letter א ('aleph), the first letter of the Hebrew alphabet; each of the second eight verses begins with ב (beth),

---

[1] See p. 48.   [2] Gen. 31. 47.
[3] For various forms of the Semitic alphabet see table on p. 32.

the second letter, and so on. There are other acrostic compositions in the Psalms and elsewhere in the Old Testament, though Psalm 119 is the most elaborate. The first four chapters of Lamentations are acrostic chapters; chapters 1, 2, and 4 have twenty-two verses each, each verse beginning with a different letter of the Hebrew alphabet, in the proper order; chapter 3, with sixty-six verses, has the first three verses beginning with א (*aleph*), the second three beginning with ב (*beth*), and so on. (Chapter 5 has also twenty-two verses, but it is not an acrostic.)

All twenty-two letters of the Hebrew alphabet represent consonants, though some of these are unknown in our language. Hebrew, like other Semitic languages, was rich in gutturals, though not so rich as Arabic. The Hebrew gutturals were א (*'aleph*). ה (*he*), ח (*cheth*), ע (*'ayin*), and ר (*resh*). *'Aleph* denoted what phoneticians call the glottal stop, a momentary closing of the air-passage before a vowel or between two vowels. It is not represented by any sign in ordinary written English, but its presence can be detected if we pronounce the phrase 'at all' with a momentary break between 'at' and 'all', instead of saying 'a-tall'. The glottal stop is also heard in some of our English dialects as a substitute for the 't' sound. When Hebrew is transcribed into our alphabet, *'aleph* is commonly indicated by the sign '. *'Ayin* was a similar sound, but the closure of the air passage takes place farther back in the throat and is accompanied by vibration of the vocal chords. There is no need to attempt this sound, however, as modern Hebrew speakers ignore it in pronunciation. It is still pronounced in Arabic. In transcription it is denoted by the sign '. *He* is an ordinary 'h' sound; *cheth* is more vigorously aspirated, rather like the panting of a dog after exertion. The latter sound is indicated in transcription by *ch* (as in this book) or by *h* with a dot below it. *Resh*, the 'r' sound, was also treated as a guttural by the Hebrews, so we conclude that it was produced at the back of the mouth, somewhat like a Northumbrian 'r'.

The letters ב (*beth*), ג (*gimel*), ד (*daleth*), כ (*kaph*), פ (*pe*), ת (*tau*) form a special group of six. They ordinarily represent the sounds *b, g, d, k, p, t*; but when preceded by a vowel they were pronounced as 'spirants' instead of 'stops', and in that case are sometimes transcribed by *bh, gh, dh, kh, ph, th*. These transcriptions represent respectively the sounds of English *v*; *g* in German *sagen*; *th* as in English 'then'; *ch* as in Scottish 'loch'; *ph* like *f*; and *th* as in English 'thin'.

In point of fact, however, the guttural distinctions and the double pronunciation of the letters *b*, *g*, *d*, *k*, *p*, *t*, were not in antiquity and are not to-day so closely observed as the grammarians might lead one to suppose. In the standard pronunciation of modern Palestinian Hebrew only three of these last six letters have their double pronunciation preserved: *b*, *k*, and *p*.

There are two 't' sounds—ת (*tau*), transliterated *t*, and ט (*teth*), normally transliterated *t* with a dot below it.[1] There are two 'k' sounds—כ (*kaph*), transliterated *k*, and ק (*qoph*), transliterated *q* (as in this book) or *k* with a dot below it. No distinction in pronunciation is maintained between *tau* and *teth* or between *kaph* and *qoph*, although these distinctions are still made in Arabic. ו (*waw*) is pronounced *w*, י (*yod*) is pronounced *y*,[2] ל (*lamed*) is pronounced *l*; מ (*mem*) is pronounced *m*; נ (*nun*) is pronounced *n*. That leaves only the sibilants or hissing sounds, of which there are five. ז (*zayin*) is *z*; ס (*samekh*) is *s*. שׁ (*shin*) was usually pronounced *sh*, but sometimes had a sound almost identical with that of *samekh*. In that case the letter was called *sin* instead of *shin*. To distinguish the two pronunciations of שׁ, the Palestinian Masoretes[3] placed a dot over the right prong for the sound *sh* (שׁ) and one over the left prong for the sound *s* (שׂ). Another sibilant was denoted by the letter צ (*çade*); this was, perhaps, more sharply hissed, with the tongue in a different position from that required for the pronunciation of *samekh*. It is transcribed ç (as in this book) and also by *ts* or by *s* with a dot below it; the *ts* pronunciation is that adopted in Israel to-day and, although it is not an ancient pronunciation, it is convenient to use it in practice to distinguish this sound from other sibilants.

Even in ancient times there were dialect variations in the use of sibilants, as the Shibboleth-Sibboleth incident of Judges 12. 6 makes clear.[4]

At a later date the Galileans had the reputation of confusing or dropping their gutturals, and it may have been some provincialism of this sort that made Peter's speech 'bewray' him in the courtyard of the high priest's palace.

The letters כ (*kaph*), מ (*mem*), נ (*nun*), פ (*pe*) and צ (*çade*)

---

[1] In this work no distinction is made in transliteration between *tau* and *teth*, for typographical convenience.

[2] In the English Bible, Hebrew proper names with *yod* are represented with *j*, which in modern English has quite a different sound from *y*. Thus 'Jehovah-jireh' would have been pronounced in Hebrew something like *Yahweh yeereh*. In the square Hebrew alphabet י (*yod*) was the smallest letter; hence the Gospel expression 'jot and tittle' to denote 'minutiæ.' The tittle was a small ornament added to a letter.

[3] See pp. 117 ff.   [4] Heb. *shibbōleth* means an ear of corn or a stream.

THE MOABITE STONE
(Page 36)

had special forms for use when they came at the end of words: these were respectively ך, ם, ן, ף and ץ.

The similarity between certain letters of the Hebrew alphabet is frequently responsible for scribal errors. The letters ד (*daleth*) and ר (*resh*) are particularly liable to be confused. For example, the son of Javan (Greece) who is called Dodanim in Gen. 10. 4 is called Rodanim in 1 Chron. 1. 7 (R.V.). The true form is Rodanim, which denotes the inhabitants of the island of Rhodes, but the initial ר became corrupted to ד in the textual transmission of Genesis. For the same reason there is frequent confusion between the two nations Aram (Syria) and Edom in the Old Testament. Thus, when we read in 2 Sam. 8. 13 of David 'smiting the Syrians (Heb. *'Aram*) in the valley of salt', a comparison of 1 Chron. 18. 12 and the title of Psalm 60 shows that the true reading is *'Edōm* (the difference was that between ארם and אדם).

As the Hebrew letters denoted consonants only, vowels were unrepresented in writing. People who knew the language could read it easily without any signs denoting vowels. Even to-day people who are really familiar with Hebrew can read it easily in the consonantal text alone; some say they can read it more easily this way, as the vowel-signs hold them up in the course of reading. A glance at a modern Hebrew newspaper will show that it is printed without vowel-signs, but those readers for whom it is intended have no difficulty in reading it. The vowel-signs, however, provide a very welcome crutch to less competent readers.

We can trace various stages in the representation of vowels in Hebrew writing. The first stage began to be introduced as early as the ninth century B.C. It was designed to represent the more important long vowels, and for this purpose four of the consonant letters were used with a secondary function. To represent long *a*, ה (*he*) or א (*'aleph*) was used; to represent long *o* or *u*, ו (*waw*); to represent long *e* or *i*, י (*yod*).

This was very inadequate as a method of vowel-representation, however, and in the early centuries A.D. further methods were devised. Some accurate system was necessary to guide the public readers of the Scriptures in the synagogues, for in an age when Hebrew was not much used as a language of ordinary intercourse the exact pronunciation might be forgotten. The vowel-signs (or vowel-points, as they are usually called) which were finally established as standard about A.D. 900 superseded earlier schemes, of which some evidence survives in old manuscripts. The victorious scheme was the work of the Masoretes of Tiberias in

Palestine, and represents the pronunciation of Hebrew vowels current in Palestine from the end of the eighth century A.D. onwards.[1]

These vowel-points were added to the consonantal text in much the same way as the vowel-signs are indicated in Pitman's shorthand. If we look at a page of the Hebrew Bible we see above and below the line of consonants (and sometimes half-way up) a series of dots and dashes. Most of these are the Masoretic vowel-points, while others are further aids to the pronunciation and punctuation.

We can best illustrate the vowel-points by placing each between two consonants to show their positions; for this purpose we may choose the consonants ה (h) and ס (s), without considering whether the resultant syllables have any sense or not.

has would be written	-	-	הַס
hās[2]	„	„	- - הָס
hes	„	„	- - הֶס
hēs	„	„	- - הֵס
his	„	„	- - הִס
hos[2]	„	„	- - הָס
hōs	„	„	- - הֹס
hus	„	„	- - הֻס

But what happened when certain vowels had already been denoted by consonants? By the Masoretic period these consonants had become fixed as part of the inviolable consonantal text. They were therefore left in undisturbed possession, and the newer and more comprehensive system was superimposed upon them.

Hebrew grammar is simple and logical, but it seems difficult at first because it is so different from the grammar of those languages with which we are familiar in Western Europe.

Most Hebrew words are derived from roots containing three letters. Take, for example, the root קׁ דׁ שׁ q-d-sh, which denotes

[1] See pp. 117 ff. The antiquity and authority of the Hebrew vowel-points was a subject of much debate for some two centuries after the Reformation.

[2] Note that *ā* is represented by the same sign as *o*. This shows that at the time when this system of vowel-points was fixed there was no distinction in quality between these two vowels. There was such a distinction in Palestine before about A.D. 750, and that distinction was maintained in Babylonia, from which the pronunciation used by Sephardic Jews (those of Spain and Portugal) was derived. The pronunciation of the Palestinian Masoretes, which did not distinguish *ā* from *o*, influenced the pronunciation of Ashkenazic Jews (those of North Europe). Thus the Ashkenazim, for example, pronounce שָׁם ('there') as *shom*; the Sephardim pronounce it as *shām*. The standard pronunciation of modern Israeli Hebrew approximates to the Sephardic rather than to the Ashkenazic.

the idea of holiness. From this root a number of different forms can be composed, by means of various vowels, prefixes and suffixes, or such devices as the doubling of the middle letter. Thus we have *qōdesh*, 'holiness'; *qādōsh*, 'holy'; *qodshō*, 'his holiness'; *qādēsh*, 'a sanctuary' (as in place-names like Kadesh-Barnea, Kadesh-Naphtali); *qĕdēshīm* and *qĕdēshōth*, the male and female attendants at Canaanite sanctuaries whose functions involved sexual vice. From the same root we have verb forms; *qādash*, 'he was holy'; *qaddēsh* or *haqdēsh*, 'to make holy', 'to sanctify'; *mĕqaddēsh* or *maqdīsh*, 'sanctifying'; *mithqaddēsh*, 'sanctifying oneself'; *'eqdash*, 'I will be holy,' and so forth.

From the adjective *qādōsh*,[1] which is masculine singular, we can form the feminine singular *qĕdōshāh*, the masculine plural *qĕdōshīm*, and the feminine plural *qĕdōshōth*. From this it will be seen that *-āh*[2] is the characteristic feminine singular ending, and that the plural endings *-īm* and *-ōth* are characteristic of the masculine and feminine respectively. There are exceptions to every rule, however, as will be appreciated when it is considered that the distinctively masculine word 'father' has its plural in *-ōth* (*'ābhōth*), while the essentially feminine word 'woman' has its plural in *-īm* (*nāshīm*)![3]

In addition to the singular and plural numbers, Hebrew has also the dual number, which is used chiefly of persons or things which habitually go in pairs. The dual ends in *-ayim*. Thus from *'ōzen*, 'ear', we have the dual *'oznayim*, 'ears'; from *'ayin*, 'eye', we have *'ēnayim*, 'eyes'; from *sāphāh*, 'lip', we have *sĕphāthayim*, 'lips'.

When one noun follows another so that the second bears a 'genitive' relationship to the preceding one, as in the phrase 'man of God' (Heb. *'īsh 'Elōhīm*), Hebrew has no word corresponding to English 'of', and no change takes place in the second of the two nouns. The first noun, however, commonly assumes a shorter form. Thus *'Elōhīm* is 'God', but 'God of Israel' is *'Elōhē Yisrā'ēl* (see Gen. 33. 20, where 'El-elohe-Israel' is 'God, the God of Israel'). When two nouns occur in such a relationship as this, the former is said to be in the 'construct state'; a noun in the construct state is not preceded by the definite article.

[1] The adjectival sense may also be expressed by using the abstract noun *qōdesh*, 'holiness'; thus *har qōdesh*, 'hill of holiness,' means 'holy hill'; *har qodshī*, literally 'hill of my holiness,' means 'my holy hill'; *rūach qodshō*, literally 'spirit of his holiness,' means 'his holy spirit,' and so on.

[2] This *-āh* was previously *-āth*, which is preserved in the construct state. So we have feminine *tōrāh*, 'law,' but *tōrath 'Elōhīm*, 'law of God.'

[3] *Nāshīm* is the irregular plural of *'ishshāh*, 'woman.' *'Ish*, 'man,' has its plural *'ănāshīm*. The other common word for 'man', *'ādām*, has no formal plural; one either uses the singular *'ādām* in a collective sense (which is its normal usage), or says *bĕnē 'ādām*, 'sons of man.'

The definite article in Hebrew is *ha*, which is attached to a following noun in accordance with certain rules which need not be detailed here. When a noun preceded by the article is accompanied by an attributive adjective, that adjective must also be preceded by the article. Thus 'the great man' would be *hā-'īsh ha-gādōl*—literally, 'the man the great (one)'.

Instead of using possessive pronouns, Hebrew attaches suffixes to the noun. Thus from *'īsh*, 'man', we find *'īshī*, 'my man'; *'īshō*, 'his man'; *'īshēnu*, 'our man', and so on.

The verb in Biblical Hebrew does not have what can properly be called tenses, distinguishing past, present, and future time. It has instead what are technically called 'aspects', which distinguish the character of the action as being completed or incomplete. The two aspects are known as 'perfective' or 'imperfective'.[1]

Then, in place of what we call 'voices', the Hebrew verb has a number of forms called 'conjugations' which express various forms of the verbal action. The normal conjugations are seven in number, though not every verb has all seven. The first is the Qal or 'light' conjugation, which expresses the ordinary form of the verbal action. The second conjugation is the Niph'al, which expresses firstly a 'tolerative' sense, secondly a reflexive or reciprocal sense, and thirdly a passive sense. The tolerative sense is well illustrated by the well-known words of Isa. 55. 6, which really mean: 'Seek ye the Lord while *He lets Himself be found*' (the form used being the Niph'al of *māçā*, 'find'). The third or Pi'el conjugation has normally intensive force, and its distinctive feature is the doubling of the middle letter of the root. Thus the root *sh-b-r*, which in the Qal means simply 'break', appears in the Pi'el as *shibbēr*, 'break in pieces'. A further sense which the Pi'el may bear is the causative one; from the root *l-m-d*, which in the Qal means 'learn', we have the Pi'el form *limmad*, 'cause to learn', i.e. 'teach'. The more usual form by which causative meaning is expressed, however, is the Hiph'il conjugation. Thus *pāqad* (Qal) means 'oversee'; *hiphqīd* (Hiph'il) means 'cause to oversee', i.e.

---

[1] If we call them perfect and imperfect, we are liable to confuse them with the perfect and imperfect tenses of other languages; such confusion is even more likely if we follow older text-books and call them past and future. T. Newberry, in *The Englishman's Bible*, calls them the short and long tenses, and marks them in the text by a dot and an upright stroke respectively. The perfective and imperfective aspects of the verb will be familiar to students of the Slav languages, where they play an important part alongside the ordinary tenses. Even Biblical Hebrew preserves some vestiges of older Semitic tense-forms over and above the regular aspect-forms, notably in the '*waw* consecutive' construction, which is too technical a matter to deal with here. In Modern Hebrew the perfective and imperfective aspects have become the past and future tenses respectively, while the participle discharges the function of a present tense.

'entrust to'. The Pu'al and Hoph'al conjugations are the passives of Pi'el and Hiph'il respectively. And the Hithpa'el conjugation is primarily the reflexive of the Pi'el; thus from the root *q-d-sh* noticed above the Qal means 'be holy', the Pi'el 'make holy', and the Hithpa'el 'make oneself holy'. The Hithpa'el has also frequently the sense of giving oneself out as doing something; thus from the root which gives us *nābī*', 'a prophet', we have a Hithpa'el conjugation *hithnabbē*', meaning 'to act the prophet'.

The names of the conjugations Niph'al, Pi'el, Pu'al, Hiph'il, Hoph'al, Hithpa'el, are actually the forms taken by these conjugations in the case of the verb *pā'al*, 'make' or 'do'.

Much of the vivid, concrete and forthright character of our English Old Testament is really a carrying over into English of something of the genius of the Hebrew tongue. Biblical Hebrew does not deal with abstractions but with the facts of experience. It is the right sort of language for the record of the self-revelation of a God who does not make Himself known by philosophical propositions but by controlling and intervening in the course of human history. Hebrew is not afraid to use daring anthropomorphisms when speaking of God. If God imparts to men the knowledge of Himself, He chooses to do so most effectively in terms of human life and human language. So, where *we* should say that Moses, in his solitary communion with God on Mount Sinai, 'suddenly became aware of the afterglow of the divine glory, so to speak', the book of Exodus (33. 20-23) is much more vigorous and tells how God told Moses that he could not see His face, but would have an opportunity of seeing His back.

Indirect speech is unknown to Biblical Hebrew; all speech is reported in the direct form, whether the words recorded were the actual words spoken or represent the general purport of what was said.

Nations or groups of people are frequently given a personality and called after the name of their ancestor in such a way that one might almost think that an individual was being spoken of. When we open the book of Judges and read of Judah and Simeon his brother agreeing to help each other to take possession of their allotted territories, it is not the actual sons of Jacob that are meant, but the tribes descended from them. Another example of this sort of thing is the way in which the northern kingdom is personalized as Ephraim in the prophecy of Hosea. This expresses a Hebrew attitude to which the name 'corporate personality' has been given. So, too, when we read in Malachi 1. 2-3: 'Was not

Esau Jacob's brother? saith the LORD: yet I loved Jacob; but Esau
I hated'; it is not so much the two sons of Isaac that are meant but
the two nations of Israel and Edom. (So also in the birth-oracle
to Rebekah in Gen. 25. 23, the words 'the elder shall serve the
younger' refer, not to the individuals Jacob and Esau, for Esau
never served Jacob in that sense, but to the nations descended from
the two brothers, for during long stretches of their history Edom
was subject to Israel or Judah.)

But the words of Malachi, 'I loved Jacob; but Esau I hated',
illustrate another feature of Hebrew thought and speech. Here a
contrast is stated in extreme terms for the sake of emphasis. Of
course, in this instance what is being emphasized is that Israel,
by contrast with Edom, was the object of God's electing love.
But the same two words are used in contexts where it is as clear
as daylight that 'hate' is not to be taken literally. We think of our
Lord's solemn affirmation: 'If any man cometh unto Me, and
hateth not his own father and mother and wife and children and
brethren and sisters, yea, and his own life also, he cannot be My
disciple' (Luke 14. 26). The Teacher of the law of universal love
does not intend His followers to indulge in unnatural hatreds!
What He means, of course, is that His disciples must give all other
objects of love a second place in relation to their devotion to Him;
the parallel passage in Matt. 10. 37 gives the sense in less paradoxical
language: 'He that loveth father or mother more than Me is not
worthy of Me; and he that loveth son or daughter more than Me
is not worthy of Me'. But the paradoxical idiom preserved in
Luke's version is in the true Hebraic style.

If some expositors had been mindful of this type of idiom,
they might not have been so quick to conclude that the Hebrew
prophets denounced the whole idea of ritual sacrifice root and
branch when they record God as saying, for example: 'I desire
mercy, and not sacrifice' (Hos. 6. 6). Large areas of the Pentateuch
certainly represent God as ordaining sacrifices. Are the prophets
concerned to say that this is a misrepresentation? It has very
frequently been thought so. We get a similar sentiment to Hosea's
in Jeremiah 7. 22-23: 'For I spake not unto your fathers, nor
commanded them in the day that I brought them out of the land
of Egypt, concerning burnt offerings or sacrifices: but this thing
I commanded them, saying, Hearken unto My voice, and I will be
your God, and ye shall be My people: and walk ye in all the way
that I command you, that it may be well with you'. Here again,
Jeremiah has commonly been interpreted as denying the truth of

the Pentateuchal narrative. But there is a possibility that the prophets are using extreme language for the sake of emphasis. If we look back at Hosea 6. 6, we see that the words, 'I desire mercy, and not sacrifice', are followed by the parallel thought: 'and the knowledge of God *more than* burnt offerings'.[1] And this gives us the clue to what Hosea, as God's spokesman, was insisting on. God did not want sacrifice for its own sake; what He wanted was obedient men and women, receptive of His self-revelation and loyal to the covenant which He had established with them. They were making the mistake of thinking that God wanted sacrifices and burnt offerings in themselves, whereas God wanted these only in so far as they expressed the inward and practical holiness of the worshippers. It was the same thing that God emphasized when speaking through Jeremiah—that it was not for the sake of burnt offerings and sacrifices[2] that He gave them His law when He brought them out of Egypt, but in order that He might have a people responsive to His revealed character and will.

We have wandered a considerable distance from the technicalities of language with which the chapter opened, but these technicalities are not ends in themselves, any more than burnt offerings and sacrifices are; they are but means to enable us to understand something of the mode in which God's revelation was recorded, so that we may better appreciate for ourselves that revelation and the God who gave it.

---

[1] Some helpful thoughts on the meaning of this and similar passages are given by Professor H. H. Rowley in *The Unity of the Bible* (London, 1953), pp. 30 ff.

[2] It is possible that the words rendered 'concerning', in Jer. 7. 22, might be rendered 'for the sake of': so L. Elliott Binns, *The Book of Jeremiah* (1919), pp. 75-77; also O. T. Allis, *The Five Books of Moses* (1943), pp. 168-171, approved in a review by W. F. Albright, *Journal of Biblical Literature*, 62 (1943), p. 360, where C. von Orelli's commentary on Jeremiah is cited to the same effect. H. L. Ellison, *Men Spake from God* (London, 1958), pp. 85 f., prefers the rendering 'concerning details of'. But even if we keep the rendering 'concerning,' the interpretation given above may stand, considering the Hebrew emphatic usage of 'not' in the sense 'not only.'

CHAPTER IV

THE ARAMAIC LANGUAGE

IN one of the Rabbinical writings we meet the injunction: 'Let not the Aramaic be lightly esteemed by thee, seeing that the Holy One (blessed be He!) hath given honour to it in the Law, the Prophets, and the Writings'.[1] This means that certain portions of the Old Testament are written not in Hebrew but in Aramaic, and that these portions are distributed between the three great divisions of the Hebrew Bible.[2] The distribution, to be sure, is unequal; we find one Aramaic place-name in the Law (Gen. 31. 47), one verse in the Prophets (Jer. 10. 11), and two considerable sections in the Writings (Dan. 2. 4b—7. 28 and Ezra 4. 8-6. 18; 7. 12-26).

When Jacob and his father-in-law parted from each other in Transjordan, they made a mutual covenant and piled a cairn to mark the place and the occasion. Laban, we are told, called the cairn Yĕgar-sahădūthā, but Jacob called it Gal-'ēd. Both these names have the same meaning, 'The Cairn of Witness', but Laban named it in Aramaic and Jacob in Hebrew. Probably the cairn was near the linguistic frontier between the Hebrew and Aramaic-speaking peoples, and was known as Gal-'ed to the dwellers on the west of it but as Yegar-sahadutha to those on the east.

This is the first reference in the Bible to the Aramaic language. Aramaic, as we have seen, is, like Hebrew, a member of the Semitic family of languages. In Old Testament times it was spoken to the north and north-east of the Hebrew and Canaanite-speaking area. It was the language of the kingdom of Syria of which we read so much in the books of Kings, and was also spoken in the upper regions of the Euphrates valley. In view of the close relationship between the ancestors of the Israelites and Aramaic-speaking people, reflected in the patriarchal narratives of Genesis, it is not surprising to find Aramaisms in Old Testament Hebrew at quite an early date. One Aramaism has been detected in the Song of Deborah, which is thought to be practically contemporary with the victory it celebrates (c. 1125 B.C.); this is the word translated 'rehearse' in Judges 5. 11.

---

[1] Palestinian Talmud, tractate Sōtā, vii, 2.

[2] For these three divisions, the Law, the Prophets, and the Writings, see pp. 91 f.

An important stage in the history of the Aramaic language is reached in the eighth century B.C., when it came to be used as the language of diplomatic intercourse in the Assyrian Empire, for communication between the Assyrians and their subjects and tributaries in Western Asia. It is interesting to note that Akkadian, which had served as the language of diplomatic intercourse in Western Asia in the fourteenth century, was no longer used for that purpose, even when the dominant power spoke what was practically that very language. An interesting example of this use of Aramaic is found in 2 Kings 18. 17-37 (Isa. 36. 2-22). There we read how the king of Assyria in 701 B.C. sent a delegation of his principal officers to Jerusalem to demand the surrender of the city. The delegation from King Hezekiah went out to confer with the Assyrians outside the city wall, and several of the citizens watched the proceedings from the top of the wall. One of the Assyrian delegates, referred to as the Rab-shakeh (literally 'chief noble'; the word is a title and not a personal name), addressed Hezekiah's messengers so loudly in Hebrew that they became alarmed for the morale of the citizens on the wall, and requested him to follow the usual diplomatic conventions and address them in Aramaic, 'for', said they, 'we understand it; don't address us in the Jewish language, for then the people on the wall will know what you are saying'. But the Rab-shakeh retorted that that was exactly why he chose to speak in Hebrew, that the common people of Jerusalem might know the fate that lay in store for them if their king and government refused to submit to Sennacherib. And with that he ignored Hezekiah's delegates and addressed the people on the wall directly in Hebrew, in an attempt to seduce them from their allegiance to Hezekiah.

This diplomatic use of Aramaic was continued under the Assyrians' successors[1] until the overthrow of the Persian Empire by Alexander the Great in 331 B.C. Aramaic was the tongue in which the Persian king and his civil service corresponded with his subjects in Western Asia and Egypt. The form of Aramaic used for this official purpose did not correspond exactly to any dialect of the spoken language; it was a conventional form of the language specialized for diplomatic use, a form which German scholars have called *Reichsaramäisch*, i.e. 'Aramaic of the Empire', or, more simply, 'King's Aramaic'.

---

[1] For example, a letter written to Necho, king of Egypt, by one of his Palestinian vassals about 604 B.C., discovered in 1942, is in Aramaic. See D. W. Thomas (ed.), *Documents from Old Testament Times* (London, 1958), pp. 79 f.

In the light of this use of Aramaic under the Persian Empire
it is specially interesting to look at the Aramaic portions of the
book of Ezra. These portions contain a good deal of official
correspondence belonging to the reigns of Darius I (521-486 B.C.)
and Artaxerxes I (465-424 B.C.), kings of Persia. This correspondence is arranged according to subject-matter rather than in
chronological order, but taking the letters in the order in which
they come in our text we find the following five:

1. Letter to Artaxerxes from Samaritan officials (4. 11-16).
2. Letter from Artaxerxes to Samaritan officials (4. 17-22).
3. Letter to Darius from the governor of the province of Syria (5. 7-17).
4. Part of a letter (of which the beginning is lost) from Darius to the governor
   of Syria (6. 6-12).
5. Letter from Artaxerxes to Ezra (7. 11-26).

As such letters would in any case have been written in Aramaic,
it is at least conceivable that in the Aramaic text of these parts of
the Book of Ezra we are reading exact transcripts of the official
documents. It appears, indeed, that the Aramaic of the Book of
Ezra is the 'King's Aramaic' of the Persian Foreign Office. If we
could go so far as one German scholar, Professor H. H. Schaeder,
who has argued that Ezra's description as 'scribe of the law of the
God of heaven' (7. 12) is another way of saying 'Secretary of
State for Jewish Affairs', then the case for regarding the Aramaic
originals of these letters as replicas of the actual text preserved in
the imperial archives would be stronger still. The interest displayed
by the Persian king in Jewish religious affairs, to which the letter
of Artaxerxes to Ezra in particular bears witness, is not unparalleled,
as we shall see.

The single Aramaic verse in the Book of Jeremiah (10. 11) is
a brief denunciation of doom against false gods, addressed to Gentile
nations, and inserted in the midst of an address to Israel. It runs:
'Thus shall ye say unto them (i.e. to the nations mentioned in verse
10): The gods that have not made the heavens and the earth, these
shall perish from the earth, and from under the heavens'. It will
conveniently illustrate the similarity of Aramaic to Hebrew if we
give parallel transliterations of the Aramaic text of this verse
and of a Hebrew translation, together with the English rendering
word for word:

Aramaic	*Hebrew*	*English*
kidnāh	kōh	thus
tēmĕrūn	tōmĕrū	ye-shall-say
lĕhōm:	lāhem:	to-them:

Aramaic	Hebrew	English
'elāhayyā	hā-'elōhīm	the-gods
dī	'asher	that
shĕmayyā	ha-shāmayim	the-heavens
wĕ-'arqā	wĕ-hā-'āreç	and-the-earth
lā	lō	not
'ăbadū,	'ăbĕdū,	have-made,
yēbadū	yōbĕdū	shall-perish
mē-'ar'ā	mē-hā-'āreç	from-the-earth
u-min-tĕchōth	u-mit-tachath	and-from-under
shĕmayyā	ha-shāmayim	the-heavens
'ēlleh.	'ēlleh.	these.

An interesting point about the Aramaic of this verse is that the word for 'the earth' appears in two forms, 'arqā and 'ar'ā, the former being characteristic of earlier Aramaic. The use of both forms, found also in one of the Elephantine papyri (cf. p. 54), may imply a time when one was giving place to the other.

The Aramaic section of the Book of Daniel begins with the reply of the Babylonian astrologers to Nebuchadnezzar's demand that they should interpret his dream (Dan. 2. 4b), and goes on to the end of Daniel's vision of the four wild beasts in the first year of Belshazzar (7. 28). At the point where the Aramaic section begins, the English versions are misleading: A.V. has, 'Then spake the Chaldeans to the king in Syriack' (R.V. 'in the Syrian language'; R.V. margin, 'in Aramaic'). This implication that Aramaic was the language in which the Chaldeans addressed their king gave rise to the old-fashioned style of referring to the Aramaic language as 'Chaldee'. This was a natural, if mistaken, inference in the days when the very memory of the language actually spoken by the Babylonians was lost. But as a matter of fact the Hebrew word 'ărāmīth (in Aramaic) in this verse is simply a sort of marginal note to draw attention to the fact that the Aramaic portion of the book is just about to begin;[1] the narrative goes on immediately in literary Aramaic with the words malkā lĕ-'ālmīn cheyī, 'O king, live for ever' (the Hebrew for which would be ha-melek lĕ-'ōlāmīm cheyī).

Some well-known words in the Aramaic of Daniel are preserved untranslated in our English versions. These are the words which appeared on the wall at Belshazzar's feast: mĕnē mĕnē tĕqēl u-pharsīn. We are not to suppose that the words as they were written were illegible, or even that, taken as separate words, they were unintelligible. They are common Aramaic words, indicating various weights. The first, mĕnē, appears in various Semitic lan-

[1] So, rightly, in R.S.V. Fragments from Caves 1 and 4 at Qumran have preserved the two places in Daniel where the language changes (2. 4 and 8. 1).

guages (Heb. *māneh*; Akkadian *manu*, etc.), and from these it was borrowed at an early date by several Greek dialects in the form *mna* or *mina*. (In the parable of the pounds in Luke 19. 12-27 the word 'pound' represents Gk. *mna*, actually a weight of silver equivalent in value to about £4.) The next word of the inscription, *těqēl*, is the Aramaic equivalent of Heb. *sheqel* (*shekel*) and Akkadian *shiqlu*, which denoted a weight of about 0.4 oz. avoirdupois. In Babylonia and Assyria sixty shekels made a maneh; in Palestine, fifty shekels. As for *u-pharsīn*, this is made up of *u*, one of the forms taken by the conjunction meaning 'and', and *parsīn*, the plural of *pěrēs*, 'division' (the *p* becoming *ph* after the vowel *u*). So at first sight the inscription on the wall seemed to say: 'A mina, a mina, a shekel and half-minas' (for *pěrēs* is found in the sense 'half-mina'[1]). But it was difficult to make any sense of that. If the words were written in Aramaic, however, they would be written without vowels, and might also be derived from the verbs *měnā*, *těqal*, *pěras*—thus meaning 'numbered, weighed, divided'. And this was the sense which Daniel gave to them; in the last one he also found a word-play on 'Persia', which has exactly the same consonants. So he explained the words thus:

Měnē	God *has numbered* (*měnā*) your kingdom and brought it to an end.
Těqēl	*You are weighed* (*těqiltā*) in the balances and found to be under weight.
Pěrēs	Your kingdom *has been divided* (*pěrīsath*) and given to Media and Persia (*Pārās*).

When the Israelites were in captivity in the provinces of the Assyrian and Babylonian Empires, it would have been natural for them to pick up Aramaic as a convenient means of communicating with the other peoples among whom they found themselves, many of whom had also been uprooted from the territories west of the Euphrates. With the downfall of the Babylonian Empire, many of these exiles returned home in accordance with the new and enlightened policy of the Persian kings. But some of them, on their return to Palestine, found themselves no longer able to speak the Hebrew tongue of their forefathers. This may also have been so with some of the people who had remained in Palestine, as a result possibly of intermarriage with non-Jews. We may

[1] A. H. Sayce, following C. S. Clermont-Ganneau, gives a slightly different account: 'In the Babylonian language . . . the mysterious words which appeared upon the wall would have been *manî mana sikla u bar'si*, "Reckon a maneh, a shekel and (its) parts"' (*The Higher Criticism and the Verdict of the Monuments* [1895], pp. 530 f.). A number of scholars have suggested that there was once a form of the story in which the various units were understood to refer to successive kings of Babylon, e.g. the maneh to Nebuchadnezzar, the shekel to Evil-merodach, and the two half-minas to Nabonidus and his son Belshazzar.

remember how incensed Nehemiah was when he found the children of mixed marriages unable to speak Hebrew.[1] Hebrew by no means ceased after the exile; the prophets Haggai, Zechariah and Malachi uttered their oracles in Hebrew, and the fact that nearly all the post-exilic literature in the Old Testament is in Hebrew implies a Hebrew reading public. But from the time of the exile onwards Aramaic steadily spread as the Palestinian vernacular at the expense of Hebrew, until the situation became the reverse of what had obtained in Hezekiah's time. Then, the common people knew Hebrew, and Aramaic was known only to a few who had occasion to use it for special purposes; now, an increasing number of the general population used Aramaic as the language of daily life, and Hebrew became increasingly restricted to religious uses. There is a well-known scene in Nehemiah 8, where at the Feast of Tabernacles in 445 B.C. (though some would date it several years later) a great congregation is said to have assembled at Jerusalem 'into the broad place that was before the water gate' to hear Ezra and his assistants read 'the book of the law of Moses'. According to verse eight, 'they read in the book, in the law of God, *with an interpretation*, and gave the sense, so that they understood the reading'. The Hebrew word *mĕphōrāsh*, translated 'with (an) interpretation' in the R.V. and R.S.V. margins, is the exact equivalent of Aramaic *mĕphārash*, which was actually employed as a technical term in the diplomatic service of the Persian Empire to denote the procedure when an official read an Aramaic document straight off in the vernacular language of the particular province concerned. (The Aramaic term occurs in Ezra 4. 18, where R.V. margin rightly reads 'translated.') So, while opinions differ about the real meaning of Neh. 8. 8, it seems reasonable to infer that as the Law was read aloud in Hebrew, an oral interpretation in Aramaic was also provided for those to whom Hebrew was no longer familiar. If this is the right interpretation of the verse, then we have here the earliest recorded example of a *targum* or oral paraphrase of the Hebrew text of Scripture, of which we shall have more to say in Chapter XI.

Between the years 1893 and 1908 a remarkable collection of texts was found in the vicinity of the first cataract of the Nile, which proved to emanate from a Jewish colony which was settled in those parts in the time of the Persian Empire, particularly at the place now called Aswan and the river-island hard by which the ancient Egyptians called Yeb (known in Greek times as

[1] Neh. 13. 24.

Syene and Elephantine). These documents are for the most part papyri, and the language used is Aramaic. Their dates range over almost the whole of the fifth century B.C., during which Egypt was under Persian control.[1] The Jewish colony in question had originated with Jewish mercenary soldiers employed by Psammeti-chus II of Egypt (594-588 B.C.) in a war against Ethiopia, who at the end of the war were settled in the two southern fortresses of Syene and Elephantine. They actually had a temple of their own at Elephantine. This was technically a contravention of the law of the single sanctuary laid down in Deut. 12. 5ff.; but then Deuter-onomy did not envisage a Jewish community living far away from the Holy Land. Another surprising feature of their religious usage was the use of Canaanite religious terminology in con-junction with the name of Israel's God (which appears there in the form Yahu); we find such compound divine names as Anath-Yahu, Anath-Bethel, Ishum-Bethel, Herem-Bethel. But while these names reflect the tendency to religious syncretism so prevalent in the centuries following the Israelite conquest of Canaan, it is probable that at this late date they were little more than names under which various aspects of Yahu were hypostatized. Anath we know, for example, to have been an ancient Canaanite goddess (she appears in the Ras Shamra tablets as the sister of Baal), but it is unlikely that as late as the fifth century B.C. the Elephantine Jews still regarded her as the consort of Yahu.

The Jewish temple at Elephantine was already built when Cambyses of Persia conquered Egypt in 525 B.C. It stood for over a century, but was destroyed in 410 B.C. in an anti-Jewish pogrom instigated by the priests of the Egyptian god, Khnub, with the approval of Waidrang, the acting Persian governor of the pro-vince. The Elephantine Jews sent a latter to the high priest at Jerusalem, asking him to use his influence in their behalf, but no answer came. We can quite understand that the high priest would not approve of any temple but that at Jerusalem. It is interesting that this high priest was Johanan, the son of Eliashib who was high priest in the time of Nehemiah, in the preceding generation (cf. Neh. 3. 1; 12. 23). The Elephantine Jews waited for two years, and then, giving up hope of any help from Johanan, they sent a letter to Bagoas, Persian governor of Judaea, and one in similar terms to Delaiah and Shelemiah, the sons of Sanballat, governor of Samaria (cf. Neh. 2. 10, 19, etc.). The letter sent to

[1] They have been published in A. E. Cowley, *Aramaic Papyri of the Fifth Century B.C.* (Oxford, 1923) and E. G. Kraeling, *The Brooklyn Museum Aramaic Papyri* (Oxford, 1953).

Johanan is not extant, but two copies of that sent to Bagoas have been preserved, in which reference is made to the earlier and fruitless letter. The letter to Bagoas procured the desired reaction; a reply is preserved in another of the Elephantine papyri, which runs:

> Memorandum from Bagoas and Delaiah. They said to me: 'Let it be a memorandum to you in Egypt to speak to Arsames [Persian governor of Egypt] concerning the altar-house of the God of heaven, which was built in the fortress of Yeb formerly, before Cambyses, which Waidrang, that reprobate, destroyed in the 14th year of King Darius [i.e., Darius II, 423-404 B.C.], that it be rebuilt in its place as it was before, and let them offer meal-offerings and incense upon that altar as was done formerly'.

But the temple did not stand long after it was rebuilt; there was a successful Egyptian revolt against Persia in 400 B.C., and as the new native dynasty venerated the god Khnub, the cult of the 'God of heaven' was decisively suppressed.

The existence of this altar at Elephantine is connected by some scholars with the prophecy in Isa. 19. 19 of a coming day when 'there shall be an altar to the LORD in the midst of the land of Egypt'. Whether there is in fact any such connection is not certain; but what is certain is that the correspondence illustrates the generally liberal and tolerant policy of the Persian Empire with regard to the religious liberty of its subject peoples, which is also reflected in the Books of Ezra and Nehemiah. It has been questioned whether the Persian king would, in fact, have interested himself in such details of Jewish religious practice as are mentioned in the letter of Artaxerxes to Ezra (Ezra 7. 12-26). But we need not suppose that the terms of this letter imply a personal interest on the king's part; the letter is issued by the particular department of state dealing with these affairs, but bears the king's name because it is an official government document. As A. E. Cowley says: 'one can imagine the king, when once his consent had been obtained, saying, "Very well, then give the man an order for what he wants". The order would then be drawn up by the Minister for Foreign Affairs, probably advised by Ezra himself, and sealed by the king's seal-bearer. Granted the initial good-will of the king, there is nothing improbable about the rest'.[1] And an interesting parallel is found in one of the Elephantine papyri which contains instructions to the Jewish colony, sent from the king through Arsames the governor, with regard to the celebration of the Feast of Unleavened Bread from Nisan 15 to 21 in the year 419 B.C. The letter is written by a

---

[1] *Jewish Documents of the Time of Ezra* (1919), p. 17. Schaeder would say that the order was drawn up by Ezra himself, as Secretary of State for Jewish Affairs.

Jew named Hananiah, who had a position of some influence at the Persian court.

Aramaic remained the vernacular tongue of Palestine, as well as of Syria and other adjoining territories, until the Arab conquest of these lands in the seventh century A.D. It was thus the language commonly spoken in Palestine in New Testament times, the customary language of our Lord and His apostles and the early Palestinian church. Some Aramaic words and phrases from these first decades of Christian history have been taken over untranslated into the Greek New Testament. We have one or two short sentences preserved in Aramaic from the lips of Christ Himself, such as *talitha qumi*, in Mark 5. 41 (Little girl, get up), *ephphatha*, representing a dialect form of *'ithpattach*, in Mark 7. 34 (Be opened), and the cry of dereliction on the Cross, *Eloi Eloi lama sabachthani* (*'Elāhī 'Elāhī lĕmā shĕbaqtanī*), in Mark 15. 34. These last words are not the Hebrew original of Psa. 22. 1, which runs *'Elī 'Elī lāmā 'azabtanī*, but an Aramaic version.

Then we read in Mark 14. 36 how Jesus prayed in the Garden of Gethsemane, 'Abba, Father, all things are possible unto thee'. While *'Abbā* is an Aramaic word, it made its way into Hebrew use as well; to this day a Hebrew-speaking boy will address his father as *'Abbā*. But in addressing God, Jews did not and do not employ this form, the affectionate term for intimate use within the family, but the more formal *'Abī*, 'my father', or *'Abīnū*, 'our Father'. Jesus, however, of set purpose used the intimate and affectionate form *'Abbā* when addressing God, and His example was followed by the early Christians, who used the same Aramaic word. So Paul, in Rom. 8. 15 and Gal. 4. 6, reckons it a sign that God has sent the Spirit of His Son, 'the spirit of sonship', into the hearts of believers in Christ when they pray 'Abba, Father'.[1] Many grandiloquent phrases are often employed in addressing God in prayer and worship but none of them is so Christian as the simple *'Abba*, 'Father,' used by our Lord.

Another Aramaism which was current in some early churches, even those which were Greek speaking, was the phrase *Maranā thā*, 'Our Lord, come!' This is found in 1 Cor. 16. 22, and also in a document called *The Teaching of the Apostles*, recording the

---

[1] In Mark 14. 36; Rom. 8. 15, and Gal. 4. 6, 'Abba, Father,' represents *Abba, ho patēr* of the Greek New Testament, where *ho patēr* (the Father) is added to *Abba* as its Greek equivalent. It should be added that the simple form for 'a father' in both Hebrew and Aramaic is *'āb*; where Hebrew puts the definite article in front of the noun (*hā-'āb*), Aramaic, which has no definite article, uses instead what is called the 'emphatic state' of the noun, which is characterized by the suffix -*ā* (*'abbā*).

usage of a Christian community in Syria, probably, about the beginning of the second century A.D., where it comes at the end of the service of Holy Communion: 'Let grace come and let this world pass away. Hosanna to the God of David. If any is holy, let him come; if any is not, let him repent. *Marana tha.* Amen'.

The word 'mammon' found here and there in the Gospels is apparently an Aramaic word *māmōnā* from the same root as 'Amen' (Hebrew *'āmēn*), and meaning originally 'that in which one puts his trust'. Several of the place-names and personal names in the Gospels are also Aramaic, such as Golgotha (Aram. *gulgoltā*, 'the skull'), Gabbatha (literally 'elevated place' but used in John 19. 13 as the equivalent of Gk. *lithostrōton*, a tesselated pavement), Martha (mistress), Thomas (*těchōmā*, 'twin').

Besides the actual Aramaic words and phrases preserved in the New Testament, the Greek text itself, particularly of the Gospels and some sections of the Acts, is sometimes strongly marked by Aramaic idioms, and appears in places to have been translated from Aramaic. This is what we should expect, of course, in reports of the sayings of our Lord and of other speakers who spoke in Aramaic. But we should not accept uncritically theories which represent our Gospels as such as having originally been written in Aramaic.[1]

Within a very few decades Palestinian Aramaic gave place to Greek as the general language of Christianity, but there was one very important body of churches which continued to use Aramaic, though not the Palestinian dialect, and we shall have something more to say of them in Chapter XV.

[1] See pp. 71 f.

CHAPTER V

THE GREEK LANGUAGE

ALTHOUGH Aramaic appears to have been the common language of our Lord and of the earliest Christians, it is not the language of the New Testament. The revelation under the old covenant, which was in the first instance communicated to one particular nation, was appropriately expressed and recorded in the language of that nation. But the fuller revelation given under the new covenant was not intended to be restricted in this way. The words spoken by Simeon when he saw the infant Saviour (Luke 2. 30-32) had not long to wait for their fulfilment once that Saviour had accomplished His work of salvation:

> Mine eyes have seen thy salvation,
> Which thou hast prepared *before the face of all peoples*;
> A light *for revelation to the Gentiles*,
> And the glory of thy people Israel.

The Evangelist who narrates this incident closes his Gospel by telling how Jesus laid down a programme for His disciples 'that repentance and remission of sins should be preached in His name *unto all the nations*, beginning from Jerusalem' (Luke 24. 47).

The language most appropriate for the propagation of this message would naturally be one that was most widely known throughout all the nations, and this language lay ready to hand. It was the Greek language, which, at the time when the Gospel began to be proclaimed among all the nations, was a thoroughly international language, spoken not only around the Aegean shores but all over the Eastern Mediterranean and in other areas too. Greek was no strange tongue to the Apostolic Church even in the days when it was confined to Jerusalem, for the membership of the primitive Jerusalem Church included Greek-speaking Jews as well as Aramaic-speaking Jews. These Greek-speaking Jewish Christians (or Hellenists) are mentioned in Acts 6. 1, where we read that they complained of the unequal attention paid to the widows of their group by contrast with those of the Hebrews or Aramaic-speaking Jews. To remedy this situation seven men were appointed to take charge of it, and it is noteworthy that (to judge by their names) all seven were Greek-speaking.

Greek belongs to the Indo-European family of languages, as Hebrew and Aramaic belong to the Semitic family. That is to say,

Greek (in common with many other European and Asian languages) developed from a dialect of an original Indo-European language as the people who spoke that language spread out from a common centre. The Indo-European linguistic family comprises twelve groups, two of which are no longer represented by any spoken language. These two are Hittite,[1] spoken between 2,000 and 700 B.C. in Asia Minor and Syria, and Tocharian, the name popularly given to a few related languages[2] known from some texts of the second half of the first millennium A.D. which were found during the present century in Chinese Turkestan.

The ten groups which are still represented by living languages are (1) those languages of India which are akin to the ancient Sanskrit,[3] (2) Iranian, including the ancient and modern languages of Persia and some neighbouring territories,[4] (3) Slavonic, represented nowadays by Russian, Ukrainian, Polish, Czech, Slovak, and the languages of Yugoslavia and Bulgaria, (4) Baltic, represented nowadays by Latvian and Lithuanian, (5) Germanic, represented by English, German, Dutch, and the Scandinavian languages, (6) Celtic, (7) Italic, represented in antiquity chiefly by Latin and to-day by the Romance languages, (8) Illyrian, represented nowadays by Albanian, (9) Thraco-Phrygian, represented nowadays by Armenian, and (10) Greek.

Greek first appears in history as the language spoken by three successive waves of immigration into the southern part of the Balkan Peninsula. These waves belong to different periods in the course of the second millennium B.C., and they are known respectively as the Ionian, Achaean and Dorian waves. Down to 300 B.C. the various Greek dialects can be classified in three groups corresponding to these three immigrations. As the Ionians were the first body of Greeks to come south into Greece, they were pressed from behind by their successors, and most of them were pushed out of Greece proper to find a home across the Aegean Sea. There they came into contact with the peoples of Asia. As the Asian nations thus knew the Ionians before they knew any other Greeks, they used the term 'Ionians' as the general name for Greeks. In Hebrew the Greeks were called the bĕnē Yāwān, the sons of Yawan

---

[1] See the writer's Tyndale Lecture, *The Hittites and the Old Testament* (1947).

[2] In particular, two languages now called more accurately Agnean and Kutchean.

[3] Also Singalese and Romany. There are many other linguistic families represented in India, bearing no relation either to Indo-European or to each other. Of these the most important is Dravidian, represented by Tamil and Telugu.

[4] The Indo-Iranian groups of the Indo-European family of languages are also known as the Aryan languages. The word Aryan should not be used outside the Indo-Iranian field, and should be used only in a linguistic, never in a racial, sense.

or Javan, a name which is identical with Ion, the eponymous ancestor of the Ionians. One important group of Ionians remained on the Greek mainland, however, when their fellow-Ionians sought new homes overseas; these were the inhabitants of Attica, the district around Athens. At a later time not only the Ionians but the other Greeks as well went far afield founding colonies—in Asia Minor, Libya, Cyprus, Crete, Sicily, South Italy, Marseilles, and around the coasts of the Black Sea, including the Crimea. The Greek world was divided into a great number of small states, but wherever the Greek language was spoken, there was Greece. Greek, then, has been spoken in the Aegean world[1] for over 3500 years; it boasts a literature extending back from the present day to about 800 B.C. (The Greek documents in 'Linear B' are older than that, but those that have been deciphered thus far can scarcely be accorded the status of literature.) The oldest monuments of Greek literature—the Homeric epics, the *Iliad* and *Odyssey*—stand in the front rank of the world's classics. For delicate expressiveness and flexibility classical Greek stands unsurpassed among the languages of mankind. We cannot do better than quote the words of E. K. Simpson, written in his own inimitable style:

> No competent judge can dispute the claim of Greek to pre-eminence in any congress of languages, ancient or modern. In its golden prime it presents an unrivalled combination of elegance and vigour, of variety of style and precision of statement. 'The instrument responds', remarks Jebb, 'with happy elasticity to every demand of the Greek intellect'. And when we call to mind the felicities of its characteristic idioms, the repleteness of its syntax, the intricate harmonies of its prosody, and the sonorous cadences of its statelier prose, or reflect on the copious invention exhibited in its teeming vocabulary; and then bethink ourselves of the monumental longevity of the tongue, the siege of time it has sustained without capitulation; the title of Greek to homage in any symposium of the commonwealth of letters must be fully conceded.[2]

As Greek is better known than Hebrew, it seems unnecessary to mention some of the outstanding features of the language as was done in Chapter III for Hebrew. The information, for those who desire it, lies ready to hand in well-known introductions.[3] It is nowhere more sadly true than in the acquisition of Greek that 'a little learning is a dangerous thing'. The uses of the Greek article,[4]

---

[1] The Greek settlements in Asia Minor, maintained for 3000 years, came to an abrupt end in 1923 with the exchange of populations which followed the Græco-Turkish War.

[2] *Words Worth Weighing in the Greek New Testament* (Tyndale New Testament Lecture, 1944), p. 5.

[3] E.g., H. P. V. Nunn, *The Elements of New Testament Greek* (Cambridge University Press); W. E. Vine, *A New Testament Greek Grammar* (Pickering & Inglis Ltd.).

[4] Those people who emphasize that the true rendering of the last clause of John 1. 1 is 'the word was *a* god', prove nothing thereby save their ignorance of Greek grammar.

the functions of Greek prepositions,[1] and the fine distinctions between Greek tenses[2] are confidently expounded in public at times by men who find considerable difficulty in using these parts of speech accurately in their native tongue. But if the inevitable limitations of self-instruction be borne in mind, and the rare grace of humility be sedulously cultivated, even a little learning can be rendered less dangerous than it normally is and used to profit in the study of the New Testament. This profit will be all the greater if the study is pursued with the aid of such a work as W. E. Vine's *Expository Dictionary*.[3]

As we saw in Chapter II, the Greek alphabet was derived at a fairly early date from the Phoenicians.[4] This does not argue a close acquaintance on the part of the Greeks with the Phoenician coastland, as the Phoenicians were mariners and traders who for some centuries dominated the Mediterranean. The Greeks make but little appearance in the Old Testament. Some of their earlier settlements are listed among the 'sons of Javan' (*bĕnē Yāwān*) in Gen. 10. 4 and 1 Chron. 1. 7.[5] Joel (3. 6) upbraids the Phoenicians and Philistines for selling Jews as slaves to the Greeks; Zechariah (9. 13) alludes to an outbreak of strife between the Jews and the Greeks; Daniel refers to the Græco-Persian wars of the fifth century B.C. and to the fortunes of Alexander the Great and his successors (see especially 11. 2 ff.). In the list of musical instruments played when Nebuchadnezzar's great image was set up in the plain of Dura (Dan. 3. 5, etc.) three of the Aramaic words are probably Greek in origin: *qaithrōs* (harp) from Gk. *kitharis*, *pĕsantērīn* (psaltery) from Gk. *psaltērion*, and *sūmpōnyā* (dulcimer; R.V. m. and R.S.V., bagpipe) from Gk. *symphōnia*.

A Greek (or a Hellene, to use the name by which they called themselves) was a man whose native language and culture were Greek; and Greece (or Hellas, to use the Greek word) extended as far as the Greek language and culture did, with no implication of political unity. The Greeks were politically the most disunited of peoples. At one period the majority of the Greek states did succeed in combining for a common aim, and that was when they

---

[1] The non-local senses of prepositions cannot be learned from a diagram illustrating their local senses; and even the local senses of prepositions in Biblical Greek differ somewhat from the usages of classical Greek.

[2] This is particularly to be noted in the theological inferences which have been unwarrantably drawn from the uses of the aorist tense.

[3] W. E. Vine, *Expository Dictionary of New Testament Words* (4 vols., Oliphants, 1939-41).

[4] See pp. 18 ff.; it is the Ionic alphabet of twenty-four letters that became the standard Greek alphabet.

[5] See p. 41.

were in imminent danger of being forcibly incorporated in the
Persian Empire by Darius I in 490 B.C., and again by his son,
Xerxes, ten years later. After the defeat of the Persians, the
Athenians made an attempt to found a maritime empire, consisting
chiefly of the Greek islands of the Aegean, but this empire collapsed
in 404 B.C. Further attempts at some degree of co-operation in
the following century were short-lived, until political unity was
imposed on the states of Greece proper by Philip of Macedon in
338 B.C. Philip's intention was to lead a united Græco-Macedonian
empire against the Persians, but he was assassinated in 336, and left
his ambitions together with his newly-won empire to his son,
Alexander the Great. Alexander's conquests in Asia and Africa
spread Greek civilization still further afield; from his time onward
Greek was established for many centuries as the common language
of the lands bordering the Eastern Mediterranean. The conditions
attending and following the Macedonian conquest tended to break
down the older difference between the Greek dialects, and the
last three centuries B.C. witnessed the rise of 'Hellenistic' Greek,
frequently called the 'common speech' of Greek—the *koinē dialektos*
—because it was the form of Greek in widest commonalty spread.
The *koinē* drew upon several of the older Greek dialects for its
distinctive features, but chiefly upon Attic (the dialect of Athens
and the neighbouring territory).

Hellenistic Greek became the official language of the empires
into which Alexander's domain was divided after his death (323
B.C.), including those which one after the other dominated the
Holy Land—the Ptolemaic Empire in Egypt, which dominated it
until 198 B.C., and the Seleucid Empire in Syria, which won
Palestine from Egypt as a result of the Battle of Panion in that year,
and controlled it until the Hasmoneans established their brief age
of Jewish independence about 142 B.C. and maintained it for nearly
eighty years.

When Palestine was incorporated into the Roman Empire in
63 B.C., as part of the province of Syria, Greek continued to be
the common language of those parts as in the eastern Roman
Empire generally. The Roman Empire was thoroughly bilingual.
In the Roman army Latin was the official language in all parts of
the Empire, but for the rest, Greek remained the official tongue
in the Eastern Mediterranean lands. In the city of Rome itself
Greek was spoken as much as Latin, in the highest and lowest
classes alike. To the highest classes Greek was a language of
education and culture; a man like Cicero wrote Greek as easily as

Latin. As for the lowest classes, slaves and freedmen were largely Greek-speaking by birth. The early Roman Christians were obviously Greek-speaking; when Paul wrote his letter to the Roman church, he wrote it in Greek, though he could no doubt have written Latin if necessary. When Clement wrote his letter on behalf of the Roman church to the church at Corinth about A.D. 95, Greek was again the language of communication. Indeed, up to the beginning of the third century Greek appears to have been the chief language used by the Roman Christians, although Latin was making headway and soon superseded it.

Until about eighty years ago the Greek of the New Testament stood almost alone in Greek literature as a peculiar form of Greek. Richard Rothe, a German theologian, explained its peculiarity by calling it 'a language of the Holy Ghost'—presumably devised specially for the occasion of writing the New Testament.[1] But others saw more clearly what the nature of New Testament Greek really was. It is recorded, for example, that Bishop Lightfoot, lecturing in 1863, referred to a Greek word occurring in the New Testament but not found in classical literature outside the fifth century B.C. writer, Herodotus, and said:

> You are not to suppose that the word had fallen out of use in the interval, only that it had not been used in the books which remain to us; probably it had been part of the common speech all along. I will go further, and say that if we could only recover letters that ordinary people wrote to each other without any thought of being literary, we should have the greatest possible help for the understanding of the language of the New Testament generally.[2]

It was not long before this remarkable prophecy was put to the test. From the 1880's onwards large numbers of the very sort of thing that Lightfoot desiderated—letters and other documents written by ordinary people, from the centuries immediately preceding and following the time of Christ—have come to light after two millennia of burial in the sands of Egypt. Many of these are written on scraps of papyrus, and others on pieces of pottery (ostraca). These vernacular documents, recovered from ancient rubbish-dumps, proved to be written in a kind of Greek strikingly similar to the Greek of the New Testament. The 'language of the Holy Ghost' turned out to be the language of the common

---

[1] *Zur Dogmatik* (1863), p. 238. Of course, in the providence of God, *koinē* Greek was available for this use when the Gospel came in the fulness of time; but this is not what Rothe meant.

[2] Quoted by J. H. Moulton, *Prolegomena* (1908), p. 242. In the General Introduction to Moulton and Milligan's *Vocabulary of the Greek Testament* (1930), pp. xii, xiii, similar hints are quoted from Masson (1859), Donaldson (1876), and Farrar (1884).

people—which is just what we should expect. (One still finds good people, all the same, who imagine that He has a decided preference for Elizabethan or Jacobean English!)

The person responsible for first pointing out the affinity between vernacular *koinē* Greek and the New Testament idiom was the great German scholar, Adolf Deissmann, who embodied his researches in this field in a monumental work entitled *Licht vom Osten*, translated into English under the name, *Light from the Ancient East*. While he was a pastor at Marburg, Deissmann was turning over in the University Library at Heidelberg a publication containing selections from recently discovered Greek papyri. As he looked at these texts he was suddenly impressed by the similarity between their language and New Testament Greek, and further study confirmed this first impression. In this country the study was taken up by some distinguished scholars, outstanding among whom were J. H. Moulton and G. Milligan, joint-editors of *The Vocabulary of the Greek Testament*, a great work in which the lexical information supplied by these papyri and other non-literary sources is arranged alphabetically.

Of course, there are wide differences of style within the New Testament, and we must not exaggerate the extent to which New Testament Greek resembles the idiom of the vernacular papyri, as has been done by some writers who have incautiously used language implying the New Testament Greek can nowadays be accounted for entirely in terms of these new discoveries. Much depends on the starting-point from which the student approaches New Testament Greek. 'Any man,' says Professor A. D. Nock, of Harvard, 'who knows his classical Greek authors and reads the New Testament and then looks into the papyri is astonished at the similarities which he finds. Any man who knows the papyri first and then turns to Paul is astonished at the differences'.[1]

Paul, we may say, comes roughly half-way between the vernacular and more literary styles. The Epistle to the Hebrews and the First Epistle of Peter are true literary works, and much of their vocabulary is to be understood by the aid of a classical lexicon rather than one which draws upon non-literary sources.[2] The Gospels contain more really vernacular Greek, as we might expect, since they report so much conversation by ordinary people. This is true even

[1] *Journal of Biblical Literature*, 52 (1933), p. 138; from an article on 'The Vocabulary of the New Testament.'

[2] We may wonder that a Galilæan fisherman of provincial speech should produce a work of such high literary quality as 1 Peter; Dean Selwyn and others have pointed to the mention of Silvanus in 1 Peter 5. 12 by way of explanation.

of Luke's Gospel. Luke himself was master of a fine literary style, as appears from the first four verses of his Gospel, but in both Gospel and Acts he adapts his style to the characters and scenes that he portrays. We may quote E. K. Simpson again for the kind of light that the vernacular papyri cast on New Testament Greek:

> In recent years we have been flooded with testifications to the vernacularity of the New Testament; so much indeed that methinks the balance needs to be somewhat redressed. Unquestionably we owe a debt to the Egyptian papyri and inscriptional lore that cannot be ignored. They have shed light on many incidental points in the sacred text and supplied parallels to many anomalous grammatical forms. When we wish to ascertain the exact sense of *logia* or *apographē*, or of a phrase like *synairein logon* (Matt. 18. 23), 'to square accounts', or *hoi anastatountes hymas* (Gal. 5. 12), 'your upsetters', the papyri stand us in good stead. They illustrate the language of the market-place or the courts of law, wherever such aspects of life crop out in the Gospels or Epistles. In wayside episodes popular diction suits the speakers. *Ti skylleis ton didaskalon?* (Mark 5. 35), 'Why do you bother the teacher?' matches with the lips in which the sentence is placed. It tallies perfectly with its popular environment, and, needless to say, can be plentifully paralleled from the papyri, so large a proportion of which are scribbled waste-papers, which betray by their misspellings the hand of illiterate scrawlers. As long as Scriptural writers hug the coast of mundane affairs, the Egyptian pharos yields a measure of illumination to their track, but when they launch out into the deeps of the divine counsels, we no longer profit by its twinkling cross-lights.[1]

It is not from the papyri and ostraca alone that we derive our knowledge of vernacular Greek. As far back as Plato, and even Herodotus, we find a strain of colloquial Greek present in the literature, especially in reports of ordinary people's conversation. We find this, for example, in some of Plato's simpler dialogues, in the mime-writers, in the fifteenth idyll of Theocritus, and in Menander, the outstanding poet of the New Comedy at Athens. We may be sure, too, that many of the words peculiar to the dialogue parts of Aristophanes, the great poet of the Old Attic Comedy (at the end of the fifth century B.C.), are not to be regarded as words peculiar to comedy, but simply as ordinary words of everyday speech which do not happen to be used by other writers because they were not of literary quality.

Again, *koinē* or Hellenistic Greek is not confined to the vernacular speech. There was a flourishing *koinē* literature in the centuries before and after the time of Christ. 'Those who are familiar with the Greek New Testament,' writes Dr. Basil Atkinson, 'will recognize that Polybius stands much nearer to it than he does to Thucydides or Plato. . . . The writings of Luke are in a direct

---

[1] *Words Worth Weighing in the Greek New Testament*, pp. 6 f. I have replaced the Greek script of the original by italics.

line of descent from those of Polybius'.[1] A study of New Testament Greek which concentrated on the parallels with the vernacular *koinē* of the papyri and ostraca, to the exclusion of the literary *koinē* of the Hellenistic writers, would be sadly unbalanced. The late E. K. Simpson, who for many years made a special study of the New Testament vocabulary from this last viewpoint, has at various times drawn attention to most remarkable and suggestive parallels in style and diction not only with the great Hellenistic writers, such as Polybius, Strabo, Epictetus, Lucian and Plutarch, and the Jewish writers, Philo and Josephus, but also with such obscure and (in themselves) unimportant people as Vettius Valens the astrologer and Philodemus the Palestinian rhetorician. Nor has Mr. Simpson been alone in pointing out the importance of this comparative study.

The study of Hellenistic Greek, both in its literary and in its vernacular form, has shown how older Biblical scholars sometimes drew unwarranted inferences from New Testament phraseology by interpreting it according to the strict rules of the classical Greek of the fifth and fourth centuries B.C. One frequently noted feature of Hellenistic Greek is its modification of the earlier senses of the prepositions. In this it represents a stage in the development from classical Greek to modern Greek. For example, the encroachment of *eis* (originally meaning 'into') upon *en* (originally meaning 'in'), which led in time to the complete disappearance of *en* from the Greek vocabulary, is abundantly evident in the New Testament. Attempts of earlier scholars, such as Bishop Westcott, to make fine distinctions between the senses of these two prepositions in such a passage as John 1. 18 (where '*in* the bosom of the Father' is expressed by *eis* and not by *en*) have been rendered superfluous in the light of the newer knowledge.[2]

It was not only prepositions that had their meanings modified in Hellenistic Greek. The conjunction *hina*, which in classical Greek introduces a clause denoting purpose (in order that . . .), has a considerably wider range of meaning in the New Testament. When it

---

[1] B. F. C. Atkinson, *The Greek Language* (1930), pp. 280 f.

[2] I think however (though this may be illogical conservatism on my part!) that a distinction is preserved in the New Testament between *eis* and *en* when followed by the noun *onoma* ('name'). While *en tō onomati* or *epi tō onomati* means 'in (or 'with') the name' or 'on the authority' of someone, I suggest that *eis to onoma* implies a transference of ownership, as when we to-day speak of paying money 'into someone's name.' This is noteworthy in the baptismal formulæ of the New Testament: baptism 'into the name' of the Triune God (Matt. 28. 19), or 'into the name of the Lord Jesus' (Acts 8. 16; 19. 5; cf. 1 Cor. 1. 13, 15), is the sign that He is Lord and that the baptized person belongs to Him; baptism 'in the name of Jesus Christ' (Acts 2. 38; 10. 48) probably refers to the pronouncing of His name by the baptizer (cf. Jas. 2. 7; Acts 15. 17) or the invoking of His name by the baptized person (Acts 22. 16).

appears in John 17. 3, for example ('this is life eternal, *that* they may know thee'), we need not infer that the knowledge of God is the purpose of eternal life, as we should if *hina* were used here with its classical force, but simply that eternal life consists in the knowledge of God—as an old hymn puts it, "'Tis eternal life to know Him'. And there is one remarkable saying in the Gospels where *hina* in one Gospel appears as the equivalent of the conjunction *hoti* in another. The Gospel where *hina* appears is Mark, where we read in 4. 11, 12; 'unto them that are without, all things are done in parables: *that* (Gk. *hina*) seeing they may see, and not perceive; and hearing they may hear, and not understand; lest haply they should turn again, and it should be forgiven them'. This looks at first sight as if our Lord's purpose in teaching by parables was to make it impossible for some of His hearers to repent and receive forgiveness. But in fact He was describing the attitude of heart which these people were already adopting. The parallel passage in Matt. 13. 13 runs: 'Therefore speak I to them in parables; *because* (Gk. *hoti*) seeing they see not, and hearing they hear not, neither do they understand'. We might, in fact, paraphrase the passage in Mark as follows: 'The revelation of the kingdom of God, which was formerly a secret, has been given to you; but all these things take the form of riddles to those who are outside, who[1] see, to be sure, but do not perceive the real meaning; who hear, to be sure, but fail to understand; and in consequence cannot return and receive forgiveness'. So much, indeed, did *hina* extend its range of meaning that in time the construction with *hina* followed by the subjunctive mood superseded the older infinitive forms of the verb, and *hina* (in a shortened form *na*) with the subjunctive is the regular form of the infinitive in modern Greek.

A good example of change of meaning between the classical and Hellenistic periods is afforded by the verb *laleō*, which in the earlier period means 'chat', 'babble', 'prattle' (as in child's talk), but in the New Testament appears as the ordinary verb meaning 'speak', be the speaker God or men.[2]

The word *parousia* is one whose New Testament meaning is better understood when we consider its usage in contemporary Hellenistic to denote the official visit of a king or some other dignitary to a place. Its ordinary Greek sense is 'presence', and it is used thus, for instance, in Phil. 2. 12: 'not as in my presence

[1] It is evident, on a consideration of the text of this passage in Mark, that the quotation from Isa. 6. 9, 10 is introduced according to the Targumic interpretation (see p. 138); this has suggested the use of 'who' in the paraphrase here.

[2] This question sometimes arises in connection with the use of this verb in 1 Cor. 14. 34.

(*parousia*) only, but now much more in my absence (*apousia*)'. Its characteristic New Testament usage, however, has reference to the second advent of Christ, and here it closely follows its idiomatic Hellenistic usage. It denotes, that is to say, the coming to earth of her Sovereign Lord, 'in power and great glory'. (Other words associated with this event are *apokalypsis*, 'revelation', as in I Cor. I. 7, etc., and *epiphaneia*, 'manifestation', as in I Tim. 6. 14; once we have the phrase 'the *epiphaneia* of His *parousia*', 2 Th. 2. 8, that is, 'the forthshining of His advent', emphasizing the brilliance or glory of the event.)

With this Hellenistic use of *parousia* is closely associated another word, *apantēsis*, which ordinarily means 'meeting', but in Hellenistic Greek 'seems to have been a kind of technical term for the official welcome of a newly arrived dignitary—a usage which accords excellently with its New Testament usage'.[1] When some distinguished personage was approaching a town to pay an official visit or *parousia*, a deputation of the leading citizens went out to meet him and escort him on the final stage of his journey. This sense of the Greek word *apantēsis* became so regular that it was even used as a technical term in Latin, instead of being replaced by a Latin equivalent. The Roman statesman, Cicero, for example, when writing to his friend, Atticus, inserts the Greek *apantēsis* more than once in a Latin letter. Referring to Julius Caesar in Italy in 49 B.C., he says: 'The municipalities are treating him as a god, without dissembling as when they offered prayers for him when he was sick. . . . Just imagine what *apantēseis* he receives from the towns, what honours are paid him'.[2] Five years later he says much the same thing about Caesar's adopted son, the future Emperor Augustus: 'The municipalities are showing remarkable favour to the boy. When he was on his journey to Samnium he came to Cales and stayed at Teanum. Wonderful *apantēsis* and encouragement! Would you have thought it?'[3] A good New Testament example of this use of *apantēsis* is found in Acts 28. 15. Paul and his companions are approaching Rome, and the Christians in the capital pay him the honours appropriate to a distinguished visitor by sending a deputation out along the Appian Way to meet him and escort him back to Rome: 'the brethren', says Luke, 'when they heard of us, came to meet us (*eis apantēsin hēmin*) as far as The Market of Appius [forty-three miles from Rome] and The Three

[1] Moulton and Milligan, *Vocabulary of Greek Testament*, p. 53.
[2] Cicero, *Letters to Atticus*, viii. 16. 2 (*apantēseis* is the plural of *apantēsis*).
[3] *Ib.* xvi. 11. 6.

Taverns [thirty-three miles from Rome]'. And it is interesting in
1 Thess. 4. 15-17 to find this same phrase *eis apantēsin* linked with
the term *parousia*. 'We that are alive', says Paul, 'that are left unto
the coming (*parousia*) of the Lord, . . . shall . . . be caught up in
the clouds, to meet the Lord (*eis apantēsin tou kyriou*) in the air'.
In other words, when Christ returns to pay His royal visit to earth,
His people will go forth to welcome Him and form His escort—
the thought that Frances Ridley Havergal expresses in a line of
one of her hymns: 'We shall meet thee on thy way'. For while
parousia and *apantēsis* separately need not have this special sense
unless the context warrants it, their collocation in this passage
strongly supports this interpretation.[1]

In the petition for 'our daily bread' (Matt. 6. 11; Luke 11. 3),
the rare adjective *epiousios* has been explained in many ways—of
Christ as the Bread of life, of the Lord's Supper, and so on—but
it occurs in a papyrus in the sense of 'daily rations', thus justifying
the old familiar rendering.

Hellenistic Greek marks a stage in the development from
classical Greek to Byzantine and modern Greek. And modern
Greek as well as classical Greek has a contribution to make to the
study of Hellenistic. The intermediate position of New Testament
Greek is evident not only in grammar but also in pronunciation
and vocabulary. The pronunciation of modern Greek is vastly
different from the pronunciation of Greek in the classical age, and
it is probable that that of New Testament Greek was nearer to the
modern pronunciation than to that in vogue in Athens in 400 B.C.
Sometimes, too, the modern Greek dictionary illumines the New
Testament use of certain words. This is so with the word *arrhabōn*,
used by Paul of the 'earnest' or 'pledge' which Christians have in
the Holy Spirit (2 Cor. 1. 22; 5. 5; Eph. 1. 14);[2] one of its meanings
in modern Greek is 'betrothal' or even 'engagement ring', which
suggests very clearly the kind of idea that Paul had in mind. And
much unnecessary trouble over the week-day on which the crucifixion took place might have been saved if the word *paraskeuē*
(Matt. 27. 62; Mark 15. 42; Luke 23. 54; John 19. 14, 31, 42) had
been looked up in a modern Greek dictionary and found to bear
the meaning 'Friday'. It is, in fact, the ordinary word for 'Friday'

---

[1] The same idea is found in Matt. 25. 1, 6, where the ten maidens are said to have gone
out to meet the bridegroom and escort him to the wedding feast; in verse 1 the better
attested expression is *eis hypantēsin*, though many authorities have *eis apantēsin*.

[2] The word, appearing in classical Greek with the meaning 'earnest-money', 'caution-
money', 'deposit', was borrowed from a Semitic source (probably Phoenician); it is akin
to Heb. *'ērābōn*, rendered 'pledge' in Gen. 38. 17, 18, 20 (cf. the cognate *'ărubbāh*, rendered
'pledge' in 1 Sam. 17. 18).

in modern Greek, and it bears the same sense in ecclesiastical Latin, with the spelling *parasceve*. In the passion narrative it means 'the day before the sabbath', and is the equivalent of the Hebrew phrase '*ērebh shabbāth*.

Although the *koinē* obliterated most of the earlier dialect distinctions in Greek, it was not devoid of dialect distinction within itself, nor could it have been, for it was a living language. Jerome claimed to find Cilician provincialisms in Paul's Greek; and while scholars of a bygone day may have exaggerated the extent of what they called 'Jewish Greek' in the New Testament, it would indeed be surprising if speakers whose linguistic background (whether more or less remote) was Semitic did not betray in their use of Greek some Semitic turns of thought and modes of speech.

There is, in fact, a good deal of Semitic idiom in certain parts of the New Testament, and this Semitic idiom takes two clearly differentiated forms. We have on the one hand the influence of the 'translation-Greek' of the Septuagint, and on the other hand the influence of the Aramaic vernacular of Palestinian Jews. (Even Paul, though not a Palestinian Jew but brought up in Tarsus, belonged to a family which spoke Aramaic, not Greek, at home.[1] It was in his original tongue that the heavenly voice addressed him, according to Acts 26. 14.)

The Septuagint is the name commonly given to the translation of the Old Testament from Hebrew into Greek made by Alexandrian Jews in the third and second centuries B.C., of which we shall have more to say in Chapter XII. This translation was practically the 'Authorized Version' of the Bible for Greek-speaking Jews (until the end of the first century A.D.) and for Greek-speaking Christians (throughout the whole Christian era). Among Greek-speaking Christians in the early days of Christianity it was as well-known as our Authorized Version is to English-speaking Christians, and exercised a comparable influence on their style. We know, for example, how deeply indebted a writer like John Bunyan was for his prose style to the English Bible. In this case the influence was wholly admirable, for (quite apart from 'the heavenliness of the matter') the Authorized Version is written in magnificent English. But the Septuagint was not written in magnificent Greek. The first five books of the Bible had special attention paid to them, and their Greek style is tolerable; but many of the books were translated very indifferently, and the Hebrew idioms were imported

---

[1] This is probably what Paul means by calling himself 'a Hebrew of Hebrews' (Phil. 3. 5)—the Aramaic-speaking son of Aramaic-speaking parents.

bodily into Greek. To one accustomed to reading good Greek, Septuagint Greek reads very oddly; but to a Greek reader acquainted with Hebrew idiom, Septuagint Greek is immediately intelligible. The words are Greek, but the construction is Hebrew. This was the version, then, in which so many early Christians knew the Old Testament, and for those of them who became 'men of one book' it influenced their style, Hebrew idioms and all. So, when we find Hebrew idioms in the Greek of the New Testament, we may put it down to the influence of the Septuagint. This is true even in a writer like Luke, who, as we have said, commanded a good, idiomatic Greek style. Even in the English translation it is difficult to miss the transition in style which takes place between the fourth and fifth verses of his Gospel. From the fifth verse of his first chapter to the end of his second chapter we might be reading a continuation of the Old Testament, so reminiscent is the style of his nativity narratives of the characteristic phraseology of the Old Testament. Some scholars have supposed that for these nativity narratives Luke was dependent on a Hebrew document. This is possible—indeed, it seems to the writer more likely—but it is also possible that Luke was simply composing deliberately in 'Septuagint' style because he judged that most appropriate for the subject-matter of these two chapters.

But apart from Hebrew idioms which came into New Testament Greek through the influence of the Septuagint style upon the New Testament writers, we should consider the Septuagint influence upon the New Testament vocabulary. The most important kind of influence exercised by the Septuagint on New Testament Greek is in the meaning of certain theological and ethical terms. The Greek outlook on religion and morals differed from that of the Jews, and the Greek terms were of course devised and used to reflect the Greek outlook. But the Septuagint translators used these terms to represent Hebrew words which reflected the Jewish outlook, and thus gave these Greek terms a new connotation. And it is this new connotation which regularly attaches to these words when they are used in the New Testament. We shall have more to say about this in our chapter on the Septuagint.[1]

As for the influence of Palestinian Aramaic on the Greek of the New Testament, this is found particularly in the conversations and discourses recorded in the Gospels and the earlier chapters of Acts, and in the book of Revelation. Some scholars have argued that our Gospels were actually written in Aramaic and then turned

[1] See pp. 159 ff.

into Greek.[1] The evidence, however, is against this. There were no doubt Aramaic summaries of the story of Jesus and collections of His sayings in circulation in the primitive Palestinian Church, but while our Gospels may have drawn upon these, they are not in themselves translations. It is only to be expected, of course, that we should find traces of Aramaic idiom in works which record the sayings of people who spoke in Aramaic and some of which were written by authors whose native tongue was Aramaic. A writer's native idiom will come out in spite of himself. Dr. Moffatt's modern version of the Bible has been called 'the translation of the Bible into Scots' by some critics because of the Scotticisms which it contains—like the use of 'factor' for 'steward' in the first parable of Luke 16!

The study of the Aramaic background of the language of the Gospels and some other parts of the New Testament is an interesting and illuminating one, though it has its limitations and is not, as some imagine, the key to unlock all mysteries.

These Semitic elements in New Testament Greek—the Hebraisms derived from the Septuagint and the Aramaisms derived from contemporary Palestinian speech—distinguish it from other forms of vernacular and literary *koinē*: 'in the vulgar Greek of the Levant there was nothing corresponding to the Semitic flavour of the early Christian writers'.[2]

Although Latin was not, except in the Roman army, the language used in the Eastern Empire, the Greek spoken in those parts was not untouched by Latin influence. Indeed, several Latin loanwords made their way even into Rabbinical Hebrew and spoken Aramaic. In New Testament Greek there are several Latin words and a few Latin idioms. The chief Latin borrowings in the vocabulary of New Testament Greek are these:

Gk. *assarion* (Lat. *assarius*), 'farthing' (better 'halfpenny', 'cent'): Matt. 10. 29; Luke 12. 6.

Gk. *dēnarion* (Lat. *denarius*), 'penny' (Amer. R.V. better, 'shilling'): Matt. 18. 28, etc.

Gk. *kentyriōn* (Lat. *centurio*), 'centurion': Mark 15. 39, 44, 45.

Gk. *kēnsos* (Lat. *census*), 'tribute': Matt. 17. 25; Mark 12. 14, etc.

Gk. *kodrantēs* (Lat. *quadrans*), ¼ *assarion*: Matt. 5. 26; Mark 12. 42.

Gk. *kolōnia* (Lat. *colonia*), 'colony': Acts 16. 12.

Gk. *koustōdia* (Lat. *custodia*), 'watch': Matt. 27. 65, etc.

Gk. *legiōn* (Lat. *legio*), 'legion': Matt. 26. 53, etc.

Gk. *lention* (Lat. *linteum*), 'towel': John 13. 4, 5.

[1] C. F. Burney, *The Aramaic Origin of the Fourth Gospel* (1922); C. C. Torrey, *The Four Gospels* (1933), *Our Translated Gospels* (1936), *Documents of the Primitive Church* (1941).
[2] A. D. Nock, *loc. cit.*

Gk. *libertinos* (Lat. *libertinus*), 'freedman': Acts 6. 9.

Gk. *makellon* (Lat. *macellum*), 'shambles': 1 Cor. 10. 25.

Gk. *membrana* (Lat. *membrana*), 'parchment': 2 Tim. 4. 13.

Gk. *milion* (Lat. *mille* [*passus*]), 'mile' (1000 paces): Matt. 5. 41.

Gk. *modios* (Lat. *modius*), 'bushel': Matt. 5. 15; Mark 4. 21; Luke 11. 33.

Gk. *praitōrion* (Lat. *prætorium*), 'government house': Matt. 27. 27, etc.

Gk. *sikarios* (Lat. *sicarius*), 'dagger-man', 'assassin': Acts 21. 38.

Gk. *simikinthion* (Lat. *semicinctium*), 'apron': Acts 19. 12.

Gk. *soudarion* (Lat. *sudarium*), 'sweat-rag', 'napkin': Luke 19, 20. etc.

Gk. *spekoulatōr* (Lat. *speculator*), 'executioner': Mark 6. 27.

Gk. *tabernē* (Lat. *taberna*), 'tavern': Acts 28. 15.

Gk. *titlos* (Lat. *titulus*), 'title', 'inscription': John 19. 19, 20.

Gk. *phailonēs* or *phelonēs* (Lat. *pænula*), 'cloak': 2 Tim. 4. 13.

Gk. *phoron* (Lat. *forum*), 'marketplace': Acts 28. 15.

Gk. *phragellion* (Lat. *flagellum*), 'a scourge': John 2. 15.

Gk. *phragelloō* (Lat. *flagello*), 'to scourge': Matt. 27. 26; Mark 15. 15.

THE GREEK ALPHABET.

	Capital	Minuscule	Name of letter	Equivalent in Roman script	Approximate Pronunciation
1	A	α	alpha	a	*a* as in *father*
2	B	β	bēta	b	*b*
3	Γ	γ	gamma	g	*g* as in *gas*
4	Δ	δ	delta	d	*d*
5	E	ε	epsilon	e	*e* as in *get*
6	Z	ζ	zēta	z	*dz* as in *adze*
7	H	η	ēta	ē	*ea* as in *bear*
8	Θ	θ	thēta	th	*th* as in *thin*
9	I	ι	iōta	i	*i* as in *machine*
10	K	κ	kappa	k	*k*
11	Λ	λ	lambda	l	*l*
12	M	μ	mu	m	*m*
13	N	ν	nu	n	*n*
14	Ξ	ξ	xi	x	*x*
15	O	ο	omikron	o	*oa* as in *oak*
16	Π	π	pi	p	*p*
17	P	ρ	rhō	rh	*r*
18	Σ	σ: final ς	sigma	s	*s* as in *ass*
19	T	τ	tau	t	*t*
20	Υ	υ	upsilon	y, ü	*ü* (modified *u*)
21	Φ	φ	phi	ph	*f*
22	X	χ	khi	ch, kh	*ch* as in *loch*
23	Ψ	ψ	psi	ps	*ps*
24	Ω	ω	ōmega	ō	*oa* as in *oar*

The sign ' over an initial vowel indicates that the word begins with the aspirate sound (*h*); the sign ' over an initial vowel indicates that there is no aspirate sound. These signs are called the rough breathing and the smooth breathing respectively. Every initial vowel carries either the one or the other. Initial υ (*upsilon*) always carries the rough breathing: so also does initial ρ (*rhō*), probably indicating a pronunciation like that of Welsh *rh* in *Rhyl*.

CHAPTER VI

THE TWO TESTAMENTS

IF someone who was previously quite unacquainted with the Bible were suddenly introduced to an ordinary copy of the English Bible and looked rapidly through it in an attempt to size up its character and contents, he would soon discover that it falls into two unequal parts, called respectively 'The Old Testament' and 'The New Testament'. But he might be at a loss to discover just why these two parts are called 'Testaments'. The natural sense in which we use the word 'testament' in English is when we refer to someone's 'last will and testament'; but there is not much about the two parts of the Bible that bears any relation to 'testament' in this sense. It is, in fact, unfortunate that the word 'testament' was ever applied to the two parts into which the Bible is divided, especially as there is a much more suitable English word which might be used, and a perfectly familiar word at that—the word 'covenant'.

We have derived the English word 'testament' from Latin *testamentum*, which also has the sense of a 'last will and testament'. In the standard Latin version of the Bible, the two parts are called respectively *Vetus Testamentum* and *Novum Testamentum*. This word *testamentum* was chosen as a translation of the Greek word *diathēkē*, which is similarly used in copies of the Greek Bible, where Part I is called *hē palaia diathēkē* (the old *diathēkē*) and Part II is called *hē kainē diathēkē* (the new *diathēkē*). So we have to consider this Greek word *diathēkē*. It is, we discover, a word which can bear more meanings than one. It may mean 'testament' (in the sense of 'last will and testament'), but it may also mean 'covenant'. It is used frequently in the Greek Bible—both in the Greek (Septuagint) translation of the Old Testament and in the original Greek of the New Testament—and its regular Biblical meaning is 'covenant'. There was, indeed, another Greek word, *synthēkē*, which the Septuagint translators might have used to render the Hebrew word for 'covenant' (*běrīth*); but they avoided it, because it might have suggested that a covenant between God and men was concluded as an agreement between equals, whereas *diathēkē* is better suited to the Biblical idea of a covenant or 'settlement' which

God initiates by His saving grace and freely bestows upon His people.

In the Authorized Version, unfortunately, *diathēkē* is often translated 'testament' in the New Testament, but this has the effect of obscuring its real force. For example, in Heb. 9. 20 the Authorized Version says that when Moses had delivered the original summary of the law to Israel he sacrificed various animals and sprinkled their blood and said: 'this is the blood of the testament which God hath enjoined unto you'. But of course, Moses said something rather different, as we can see even in the Authorized Version by turning up the passage quoted, Exod. 24. 8, where we are told that Moses said: 'Behold the blood of the *covenant*, which the LORD hath made with you concerning all these words'. The fault does not lie with the writer to the Hebrews, who used the Greek word *diathēkē* quite properly in its sense of 'covenant' (as he found it used in the Greek Septuagint version of Exod. 24. 8); the mistake lies with the English translation 'testament', following the Latin translation *testamentum*.[1] In the earlier days of Latin-speaking Christianity, indeed, another word than *testamentum* was frequently used to represent Greek *diathēkē*. This was the Latin word *instrumentum*, which in this connection was much more suitable. If the use of *instrumentum* had prevailed, and its English derivative 'instrument' had been employed in the titles of the two parts of the Bible, it would have been more satisfactory, for 'instrument' can be used in the sense of 'agreement'. So far as English is concerned, however, 'covenant' is an even better word than 'instrument', for 'covenant' is a perfectly well-known word meaning a particularly solemn and binding form of agreement. Indeed, the special Bible sense of 'covenant' goes still farther: it conveys the idea of mutual 'belonging', of incorporation into the family, of a marriage-bond,[2] solemnly ratified by the shedding of blood (whence the Hebrew term for making a covenant literally means '*cutting* a covenant').

[1] The Revised Version regularly gives 'covenant' for *diathēkē* in the New Testament. But in Heb. 9. 16, 17, in spite of using 'covenant' elsewhere in the same passage, both before and after, the Revisers felt themselves compelled to use 'testament': 'For where a testament is, there must of necessity be the death of him that made it. For a testament is of force where there hath been death: for doth it ever avail while he that made it liveth?' Similarly the R.S.V., which elsewhere translates *diathēkē* by 'covenant', translates it by 'will' in these two verses. The reason is that *diathēkē*, which has the wider sense of 'settlement', can include the idea of 'bequest' or 'testament', and this is the particular kind of *diathēkē* meant in these two verses, because this is the only kind of settlement whose validity depends on the death of the person who makes it. The New English Bible marks the transition from the general sense of 'covenant' to the special sense of 'testament' by beginning verse 15: 'And therefore he is the mediator of a new covenant, or testament.'

[2] The idea of the covenant as a marriage-union between God and His people is specially emphasized in the Book of Hosea; cf. Jer. 2. 2; Ezek. 16. 8.

We may, therefore, replace the word 'Testament' by the word 'Covenant' in the titles of the two parts of the Bible, and call them respectively, 'The Books of the Old Covenant,' and 'The Books of the New Covenant'. If we think of the Bible as comprising these two collections, we shall be well on our way to understanding what the Bible is and what it contains.

To take the second and smaller collection first: in what sense may we call the New Testament books 'The Books of the New Covenant'? What is this 'New Covenant'? For the answer to that we must remind ourselves of the solemn act performed by Jesus in the Upper Room at Jerusalem on the evening before His death. We remember how He instituted the Holy Communion, in which, after giving His disciples bread as the token of His body, He gave them the cup of wine, saying: 'This is my blood of the (new) covenant, which is shed for many'.[1] To one who remembers the Old Testament background, the significance of these words is immediately evident. As we have just mentioned, it was Moses who, when he gave the law to the people of Israel, offered sacrificial victims and sprinkled their blood, saying: 'This is the blood of the covenant which the LORD hath made with you'. By that act and these words Moses, acting as mediator, solemnized the covenant between Jehovah and Israel, by which He undertook to be their God and they promised to be His people. Now Jesus takes upon His lips words reminiscent of those used by Moses so long before, and, acting as Mediator, inaugurates a *new* covenant between God and men, a covenant to be ratified by the blood of no ordinary sacrificial victims, but by His own:

> A sacrifice of nobler name
> And richer blood than they.

But why was a new covenant necessary? Why did not the Mosaic covenant remain in force? Because the Mosaic covenant was defective. It was an undertaking solemnly entered into by Jehovah and Israel; its continued validity depended upon both sides honouring their agreement. There was no doubt about this on Jehovah's part, of course; but what about the people? They intended to keep the covenant, it is true. When they listened to Moses reading the divine law, 'the book of the covenant', they

---

[1] Mark 14. 24. Here, as in Matt. 26. 28, R.V. and R.S.V. omit 'new' in the text but supply it in the margin. In any case, it is implied if not expressed. Matt. 26. 28 adds 'unto remission of sins' after 'many'. Luke 22. 20 reads: 'This cup is the new covenant in my blood, even that which is poured out for you.' But some early authorities omit Luke 22. 19 after 'This is my body' and the whole of verse 20. The earliest written account of the Institution is in 1 Cor. 11. 23-25; here the words spoken over the cup (verse 25) are: 'This cup is the new covenant in my blood: this do, as oft as ye drink it, in remembrance of Me.'

said: 'All that the LORD hath spoken will we do, and be obedient' (Exod. 24. 7). But, when they were put to the test, they found it difficult, and indeed impossible, to keep their agreement. There lay the defect. But although the people of Israel failed to keep their side of the covenant, the God of Israel continued to keep His. And the first covenant, inadequate though it was, was used by Him to prepare the way for another covenant which should replace the first and succeed where it failed. So we go on to the time of Jeremiah, roughly midway between Moses and Jesus, and hear him announcing the purpose of God:

'Behold, the days come, saith the LORD, that I will make a new covenant with the house of Israel, and with the house of Judah: not according to the covenant that I made with their fathers in the day that I took them by the hand to bring them out of the land of Egypt; which my covenant they brake, although I was an husband unto them, saith the LORD. But this is the covenant that I will make with the house of Israel after those days, saith the LORD; I will put my law in their inward parts, and in their heart will I write it; and I will be their God, and they shall be my people; and they shall teach no more every man his neighbour, and every man his brother, saying, Know the LORD: for they shall all know me, from the least of them unto the greatest of them, saith the LORD: for I will forgive their iniquity, and their sin will I remember no more' (Jer. 31. 31-34).

The significance of our Lord's words, then, is that in Him the new covenant, predicted by Jeremiah, became effective. The implications of His inaugurating the new covenant to take the place of the old are drawn out in particular by the writer to the Hebrews in the eighth and ninth chapters of his epistle. The same teaching is emphasized, though in different language, by the Apostle Paul when he describes how the purpose of the sacrifice of Christ was 'that the ordinance of the law might be fulfilled in us, who walk not after the flesh, but after the spirit' (Rom. 8. 4). For the superiority of the New Covenant lies partly in this, that those who enter into it receive into their own lives the life of Christ and the power of the Holy Spirit, a life which knows and desires the will of God and a power which is able to do it.

The Books of the Old Covenant, then, tell how God made the necessary preparation for the sending of His Son to inaugurate the New Covenant. The books of the New Covenant tell how the Son of God came to do this and set forth the implications of this New Covenant. Both collections alike speak of Christ; it is He who gives unity to each and to both together. The former collection looks forward with hope to His appearance and work; the latter tells how that hope was fulfilled.

The books of the Old Covenant open with a summary of the early days of men in Western Asia which forms an introduction to the story of Israel, the people whom God chose for Himself and with whom He entered into covenant-relationship. God's choice of Israel was no act of favouritism—He is no respecter of persons (or of nations, either)—but He selected this particular nation in order that the knowledge of Himself and of His will, revealed to them, might be communicated by them to other nations; and He chose them most of all in order that they might be prepared as the nation in which, when God's time was ready, the Saviour of the world might be born.

The history of this preparation is the chief concern of the books of the Old Covenant. God prepared this nation to be the vehicle of His purpose by revealing Himself to them in mighty works and by the words of His spokesman the prophets. Throughout this period prophets and righteous men in Israel looked forward to the accomplishment of God's purpose in the promotion of which they played their allotted parts, and they 'died in faith, not having received the promises, but having seen them and greeted them from afar' (Heb. 11. 13). The promise was carried out and the period of fulfilment dawned when Christ came. So He could say to His disciples: 'Blessed are your eyes, for they see; and your ears, for they hear. For verily I say unto you, that many prophets and righteous men desired to see the things which ye see, and saw them not; and to hear the things which ye hear, and heard them not' (Matt. 13. 16, 17).[1] The books of the New Covenant tell how the divinely-implanted hopes and aspirations of these ancient men of God were realized in Christ.

A question which naturally arises here is this. Since the New Covenant fulfilled and, indeed, superseded the Old, and since we now have in our hands the books of the New Covenant, why should we trouble any more about the books of the Old Covenant? Does not the New Testament render the Old obsolete? As it introduces a covenant of grace and not a covenant of works, does it not, indeed, contradict the Old Testament? Why, then, does the Christian Church continue to include the Old Testament among her sacred books?

The general belief of the Christian Church is expressed in the opening words of Article VII (in the Thirty-Nine Articles of Religion of the Church of England):

---

[1] The parallel passage in Luke (10. 23, 24) has 'prophets and kings' instead of 'prophets and righteous men.'

'The Old Testament is not contrary to the New; for both in the Old and New Testament everlasting life is offered to mankind by Christ, who is the only Mediator between God and Man, being both God and Man. Wherefore they are not to be heard, which feign that the old Fathers did look only for transitory promises . . .'

From time to time, however, men have risen in the Church to argue that the Old Testament is so thoroughly superseded by the New that it should no longer be ranked among the canonical writings of the Church. One of the earliest of these was Marcion, who flourished in the second century A.D. Marcion, a native of Sinope in Asia Minor, came to Rome about A.D. 140, and there founded a sect which persisted for many years. His distinctive doctrine was that the Old Testament was inferior to the New and had been rendered obsolete by Christ. Marcion stressed the contrast between the two Testaments so far as to say that the God revealed in the one was quite a different being from the God revealed in the other. The righteous God, the Creator, Israel's Jehovah, revealed in the Old Testament was a different and inferior deity to the good God revealed by Jesus under the name 'Father'. This, Marcion thought, was rendered sufficiently obvious by the fact that it was the worshippers of the righteous God of the Old Testament who sent the Revealer of the good God to His death. Marcion, therefore, repudiated the authority of the Old Testament, and defined the Christian canon as consisting of one Gospel and a collection of ten Pauline epistles. (We shall have more to say about Marcion's canon in Chapter VIII.) Paul, to Marcion's way of thinking, was the only real apostle of Christ, who had remained true to His mind and revelation. The Church, as a whole, he maintained, had followed in the error of the Judaizers, among whom the original apostles of Christ were to be reckoned—Peter, John and the rest. Marcion stated his view of the opposition between the two Testaments in a work called the *Antitheses*, where he collected a number of contrasts between the revelation of the Old Testament and that of the New.

Marcion's dualism between the righteous God and the good God has often been reproduced, though not usually in such a thorough-going form. We still find people drawing a contrast between the God of the Old Testament and the God of the New, although they do not, like Marcion, regard the God of the Old Testament as having an independent existence, but regard Him as a developing idea in the minds of His worshippers, which reached full growth when it attained the measure of the stature of the God and Father of our Lord Jesus Christ. Others make the contrast between the attributes of God—His righteousness and His mercy—as though the former were characteristic of the Old Testament revelation and the latter of the New Testament revelation, whereas in fact both coexist in harmony throughout the whole Bible.

One illustrious Marcionite of comparatively recent times was the great German church historian Adolf von Harnack, who was himself no mean authority on Marcion. 'The rejection of the Old Testament in the second century,' said Harnack, 'was a mistake which the Great Church rightly refused to make; the retention of it in the sixteenth century was a fate which the Reformation was not yet able to avoid; but that Protestantism since the nineteenth century should continue to treasure it as a canonical document is the result of a paralysis which affects both religion and the Church'.[1]

Practical difficulties in the use of the Old Testament arise in various places and times, but these difficulties are to be surmounted by further teaching about the preparatory character of the Old Testament revelation, not burked by throwing the Old Testament overboard. Gibbon[2] reports that when Ulfilas, the apostle to the Goths, translated the Bible into the Gothic language about A.D. 360, 'he prudently suppressed the four books of Kings,[3] as they might tend to irritate the fierce and sanguinary spirit of the Barbarians'. Whether this was so or not, we are told that similar difficulties arise in Africa, where converts to Christianity find in the Old Testament too much that reminds them of their ancestral practices and beliefs—too much, for example, to confirm them in their polygamous customs. How far this representation is exaggerated can be ascertained from missionaries.

On the other hand, the contrary difficulty is experienced in India, one hears, where the Old Testament is uncongenial to the intellectual heritage of educated Hindus. Hindu thought is abstract, impersonal and static, whereas the Old Testament outlook is concrete, personal and dynamic. The Indian sometimes says that the Old Testament reflects a morality and a conception of God which is lower than that of the best Indian religion, and asks why the ancient literature of his own people should not play for him the rôle of Gospel-preparation which the Old Testament plays for others. A cursory comparison of even the earliest and purest

---

[1] *Marcion* (1921), p. 217.

[2] *Decline and Fall of the Roman Empire*, chap. 37 (Chandos Classics edition, Vol. II, p. 516).

[3] The 'four books of Kings' are those which we know as 1 and 2 Samuel and 1 and 2 Kings. Gibbon's information came from the Arian historian Philostorgius. Probably Ulfilas did not live to complete his translation. See p. 216.

literary monuments of Indian religion with the Old Testament may well fill one with surprise that such an idea could ever be entertained; but it certainly has been and still is entertained, and not by Indians only. Perhaps it all depends on what one means by 'morality' and 'religion'.

The sect of 'German Christians' which flourished in Germany under the Hitler régime urged a similar argument. Why should Nordic Christians cherish a volume of Jewish religion and history when they had the sagas and beliefs of their own pre-Christian ancestors? These latter should serve as the proper introduction to 'German Christianity' as they understood it, instead of the Hebrew Scriptures. An adapted edition of the book of Psalms appeared in these circles during the thirties of the present century, entitled *Divine Songs for Germans*, where the historical and personal references in the Psalms were replaced by others drawn from Germanic and Indo-European history and mythology: for example the place-names of Psa. 87 were replaced by the geographical landmarks of Indo-European migrations from the Ganges to Scandinavia.

In the early days of the Church difficulties were felt in connection with the Old Testament even among those who repudiated Marcionism and maintained the apostolic faith. The Greek Fathers, especially those of Alexandria, found the concrete realism of the Old Testament uncongenial to their heritage of Greek philosophic thought, and they had large recourse to the method of allegorization. In this they had a predecessor in the Jewish scholar, Philo of Alexandria (*c.* 20 B.C.-A.D. 50), who himself followed the pagan scholars who applied similar methods to the poems of Homer and Greek mythology in general. The allegorical treatment was carried to absurd lengths, but the Alexandrian Fathers held, as some Christians do even to-day, that where the literal sense is plainly impossible (that is to say, impossible in their eyes), the text must be interpreted allegorically. The fact of the matter is that very little indeed of the Old Testament was originally intended to be understood allegorically.

The fact that books are still published professing to deal with *Moral Difficulties of the Old Testament* suggests that some readers even to-day find difficulties in the acceptance of the Old Testament as part of the Church's canon.

Yet we must ever bear in mind that the Old Testament was the Bible of our Lord and His apostles, and its authority was fully acknowledged by them. That some of its provisions were of the nature of a temporary accommodation was recognized; Jesus, for example, said that the provision which the Mosaic law made for divorce and remarriage was introduced because of the men's 'hardness of heart'; but it was from the Old Testament that he took the fundamental and abiding principle in the light of which the Mosaic provision was seen in its true character. 'Have ye not read, that He which made them from the beginning made them male and female, and said, For this cause shall a man leave his father and mother, and shall cleave to his wife; and the twain shall become one flesh? So that they are no more twain, but one flesh. What therefore God hath joined together, let not man put asunder. . . . Moses for your hardness of heart suffered you to put away your wives: but from the beginning it hath not been so' (Matt. 19. 4-8).

The Old and New Testaments, in fact, cannot be dissociated; while on the one hand we cannot understand the preparatory revelation of the Old apart from its fulfilment in the New, it is also true, on the other hand, that we cannot understand the New apart from the Old. The Old Testament is to the New as the root is to the fruit. It is a grave mistake to think that the fruit of the Spirit in Christianity will grow and ripen better if the plant is severed from its roots in the Old Covenant.

A few years ago Professor A. M. Hunter wrote an excellent little book called *The Unity of the New Testament*. He found the unity of the New Testament to lie in its presentation of the history of salvation, a history which is like a cord made up of three strands —the Bringer of salvation; the way of salvation; the saved people. We might say very much the same thing in terms of the covenant-idea if we speak of the three strands as being: the Mediator of the covenant; the basis of the covenant; the covenant-people. In the New Testament, of course, the Bringer of salvation or the Mediator of the Covenant is our Lord Jesus Christ; the way of salvation or the basis of the covenant is 'by grace alone through faith alone'; the heirs of salvation or the covenant-people are the Church. But what Professor Hunter says of the New Testament is equally true of the Bible (as he would be the first to agree). The Bible—Old Testament and New Testament together—has a unity of its own; and that unity is to be found in the fact that the Bible tells the story of salvation—the story of God's covenant-mercy. This explains what the Bible is. It is the record of God's revelation of Himself as a righteous God and a Saviour.

This record has a threefold theme. As for the first strand, it is God Himself who is the Saviour of His people; it is He who keeps covenant and mercy for ever. All through the Old Testament

He points His people forward to a day when He will vindicate His character, establish His covenant, set up His kingdom, and bring near His salvation. We turn the page into the New Testament, and find Him doing just this, in the person of Jesus Christ His Son.

This Bringer of salvation, the Son of God, does not appear suddenly in the New Testament as a visitant on earth from another realm, having no connection with the course of prior events down here. As touching His eternal relationship with the Father, He is 'without genealogy, having neither beginning of days nor end of life'; but as touching His Manhood, He is indissolubly bound up with all previous history. Marcion, in editing Luke's Gospel to make it a suitable Gospel for his Canon, cut out the genealogy of Christ which we find in Luke 3. 23-38; but the genealogy is there of right, as is also the companion genealogy in the first chapter of Matthew's Gospel. In Matthew, Christ is introduced as a true son of Abraham and heir to the throne of David; in Luke, He appears as a true son of man, the Saviour of mankind. But both genealogies emphasize the link binding Christ and the New Covenant to the age of the Old Covenant. The genealogy of Christ is the culmination and explanation of the many genealogies which almost seem to form the skeleton round which Old Testament history is built up. The words of Mr. Robert Rendall express this truth illuminatingly:

'It is in retrospect from Christ that the common genealogies reveal their primary spiritual value. When being written, the exact course and issue of the divine purpose could not have been foreseen. True, here and there, a particular branch was singled out for special notice, and, as time passed, a main interest developed, but in general no one could say certainly from which line the Messiah would come. The documents were a plain straightforward transcription of genealogical data: it was only afterwards that God's action therein began to be seen. Thus the genealogy of Christ was not isolated as such from the common genealogical tables, but was embedded in the general register of names. This accounts for the seeming irrelevance of a large mass of names in these genealogies, and proves beyond question that the Messianic element is there, not through human foresight, but through a dispensation of divine providence. This hidden development in the long succession of Hebrew generations is that from which Old Testament history derives its substance and completeness'.[1]

This means that the Saviour is bound up with His people—bone of their bone and flesh of their flesh. So we may take this strand next in the history of salvation—the people of God, the elect community—as one which runs through the whole Bible. This continuity is obscured for us in the English Bible because

[1] *History, Prophecy and God* (London, 1954), p. 61.

it uses for this community in the New Testament a word which it does not use in the Old Testament—the word 'church'. But in the Bible of the early Christians—the Greek Bible—the continuity was plain, for the Greek New Testament word *ekklēsia*, which is translated 'church' in the English Bible, is also used in the Greek (Septuagint) translation of the Old Testament to denote Israel as the community ('assembly' or 'congregation') of Jehovah. Indeed, we find it used twice in this sense in the New Testament: in Stephen's speech in Acts 7. 38, where he says that Moses 'was with the church in the wilderness' (where the whole people of Israel is meant), and in a quotation from Psa. 22. 22 in Heb. 2. 12: 'in the midst of the church will I sing praise unto Thee' (where a particular local community of Israelites appears to be meant).[1]

The Christian Church was, of course, a new beginning: Christ used the future tense when He said: 'upon this rock I will build My church' (Matt. 16. 18). But the very word that He used for His new community (*ekklēsia*) pointed to its connection with the *ekklēsia* of Old Testament times.[2] For He Himself forms the organic link between the two and embodies the continuity of both. He is the Messiah-Saviour to whom the old community—the ancient covenant-people—looked forward; He is Saviour and head over all things to His Church—the new covenant-people. He belongs to both and both belong to Him, and in Him they are not two but one. Abraham had the Gospel proclaimed to him[3] and is the spiritual father of all believers;[4] Moses esteemed the reproach of Christ greater riches than the treasures in Egypt.[5] Of these and all other believers under the Old Covenant it is written that 'these all, having had witness borne to them through their faith, received not the promise, God having provided some better thing concerning us, that apart from us they should not be made perfect'.[6] The first followers of Christ were at one and the same time the last believing remnant of the old community and the first believing nucleus of the new. The New Jerusalem has the names of the twelve tribes of the children of Israel written on its gates and the names of 'the twelve apostles of the Lamb' inscribed on the foundation-stones of its wall.[7] Neither in the Old Testament nor in the New is solitary salvation envisaged: the salvation

[1] In these two New Testament passages A.V. uses 'church'; R.V. has 'church' in Acts 7. 38 ('congregation' in margin), and 'congregation' in Heb. 2. 12 ('church' in margin); R.S.V. has 'congregation': the word in both cases is Greek *ekklēsia*. See p. 244.

[2] This is true no matter what language our Lord was speaking on the occasion. Probably He used the Aramaic term *kĕnishtā*.

[3] Gal. 3. 8.   [4] Rom. 4. 16 ff.   [5] Heb. 11. 26.
[6] Heb. 11. 39, 40.   [7] Rev. 21. 12, 14.

of God is enjoyed in the membership of the saved community.

When we consider the third strand, the way of salvation, too, is a theme common to both Testaments. In both salvation results from the exercise of God's free electing love. God chose Abraham that he might be the father of many nations, that through his seed blessing might be brought to all the families of the earth. He set His love on Abraham's descendants when they were slaves in the land of Egypt and wrought their deliverance that they might come to know Him as their God and spread that knowledge to others. And the New Testament believers are taught to regard themselves as having been chosen in Christ before the world's foundation that they should be holy and blameless before Him. It is of grace alone, that it might be of faith alone. Abraham believed God, and it was reckoned to him for righteousness, and thus he became the father of all who by similar faith receive God's righteousness. The covenant at Sinai might be a covenant of works so far as Israel's undertaking was concerned; but it was a covenant of grace so far as God's fulfilling it was concerned, for He continued to treat Israel as His people even when Israel forgot that He was their God. Paul's insistence on justification by faith is no innovation in Biblical doctrine; he turns to the Old Testament to confirm and illustrate it. In the New Testament the focus of our faith and the declaration of God's grace is the self-offering of Christ upon the cross; but when Christ Himself wished to make plain the significance of His death He did so in language drawn from the Old Testament—in particular from the picture of the obedient Servant of Jehovah in Isa. 53, whose suffering is endured for the sake of others, whose sin He bears Himself. 'The Son of man came not to be ministered unto, but to minister, and to give His life a ransom for many' (Mark 10. 45).

Apart from the organic unity of the Old Testament with the New, which makes it an indispensable part of the Christian canon, the Old Testament makes in various ways its own distinctive contribution to the volume of revelation.

The supreme *religious* value of the Old Testament is the way in which it presents God as the Living God, One who is dynamically alive and active in self-revelation, not simply the Prime Mover or Pure Actuality of certain schools of philosophy, nor yet merely the Self-Existent Being. He is that, of course, but He is much more. He is the God of creation, providence, and redemption; He is the God who makes Himself known in the mighty acts with which He breaks into the course of history. And this picture of God in the Old Testament prepares us for the supremely redemptive mighty act which He wrought in sending His Son into the world for our deliverance and in raising Him from the dead. The God of the Old Testament is not aloof from the world, which He created and maintains; He is not disinterested in His creatures, but satisfies their need. Nor is He partial; He has no 'respect of persons'. The nation to which He reveals Himself and with which He enters into covenant-relationship cannot presume on that privilege; if it abuses His goodness, His judgment is all the more severe on it just because it is peculiarly *His* nation. 'You only have I known of all the families of the earth: therefore I will visit upon you all your iniquities' (Amos 3. 2). True, His providence is not restricted to Israel: He brought up the Syrians from Kir in the desert and the Philistines from Crete just as He had brought up the Israelites from Egypt, but He had not revealed Himself to those others as He had to Israel, and therefore Israel is more responsible than the Syrians and Philistines. How different this God is from such a nature-deity as Chemosh, the god of the Moabites! Chemosh had no independent existence; his fortunes rose and fell with the fortunes of Moab, and when Moab disappeared, so did Chemosh. Unlike Chemosh and all gods of that order, Jehovah is the living God, who freely chooses His people and makes ethical demands on them; He is 'a God with a character', and that character of holiness and truth, righteousness and mercy, He desires to see reproduced in His people.

This brings us to the *ethical* value of the Old Testament. The Old Testament is introduced by the Books of the Law, in which the holy requirements of God's will are made known. 'The law', says Paul, 'was our custodian until Christ came' (Gal. 3. 24, R.S.V.). The law is the preparation for the Gospel; the Gospel offers forgiveness of sins, but the law makes us conscious of our sinfulness and of our need for forgiveness. Above the religions of the nations which surrounded Israel the Old Testament revelation towers high in its insistence that God, who is Himself holy, requires holiness in His people. 'Ye shall be holy: for I, Jehovah your God, am holy' (Lev. 19. 2; cf. 1 Peter 1. 16). Thus we are prepared for the supreme demand made by Christ in the Sermon on the Mount: 'Ye therefore shall be perfect, as your heavenly Father is perfect' (Matt. 5. 48). And if, in face of such an uncompromising ethic, we feel utterly unable even to begin to attain it, we are ready to hear the Gospel note: 'What the law could not do . . . God has done, by sending His own Son in the likeness of sinful flesh and

as an offering for sin, . . . in order that the law's righteous require-
ment might be fulfilled in us who do not order our lives according
to the flesh but according to the Spirit' (Rom. 8. 3, 4, free
translation).

And the Old Testament is distinctive in its presentation of the
historical process. This process is not illusion, as it is to certain
phases of Indian thought; it is not an indefinite series of cycles,
as some Greek schools held; it is the steady unfolding of God's
one increasing purpose. We have to await the New Testament
record of the coming of Christ to see the consummation of that
purpose in Him, but the broad view of its outworking is found in
the Old Testament. The Old Testament writers had a philosophy
of history long before Herodotus, who among secular historians
is rightly hailed as the father of history. They were not mere
annalists, as their contemporaries in Egypt and Assyria were for
the most part; they selected and presented the facts which they
recorded in accordance with a guiding principle which we find
fully embodied in Christ. The Old Testament has been compared
by Dr. Emil Brunner to the first part of a sentence and the New
Testament to its second and concluding part. This comparison is
all the more forceful if we think of a complex sentence in Dr.
Brunner's native German tongue, where the sense of the whole
cannot be comprehended until the last word is spoken. So God,
to the fathers through the prophets, spoke the first part of His
salvation-bringing sentence; but the last word, completely revealing
and redeeming, was spoken in His Son.

That is why the Old Testament prophets did not know clearly
the full import of their words: they 'searched and inquired about
this salvation; they inquired what person or time was indicated
by the Spirit of Christ within them when predicting the sufferings
of Christ and the subsequent glory' (1 Peter 1. 10, 11, R.S.V.). But
the apostles, in whose days Christ Himself came, had no such
questionings: taught by their Master, they knew that He was the
One of whom Moses and the prophets had spoken, and that it was
to their own days that those men of old had looked forward.
'This is that which was spoken by the prophet', Peter claimed
when interpreting the strange events of the first Christian Pentecost.
For Christ was the key to the problem and the answer to the
questionings of the prophets. The New Testament, as Augustine
declared, lies hidden in the Old; the Old Testament is revealed in
the New.

CHAPTER VII

THE FORM OF THE BIBLE

WE have already discussed the main feature of the structure of the Bible—its division into the books of the Old Covenant and the books of the New Covenant. We are now to look more particularly at the way in which these two bodies of covenant-literature are built up.

The Bible, at first sight, appears to be a collection of literature —mainly Jewish. If we enquire into the circumstances under which the various Biblical documents were written, we find that they were written at intervals over a space of nearly 1400 years. The writers wrote in various lands, from Italy in the west to Mesopotamia and possibly Persia in the east. The writers themselves were a heterogeneous number of people, not only separated from each other by hundreds of years and hundreds of miles, but belonging to the most diverse walks of life. In their ranks we have kings, herdsmen, soldiers, legislators, fishermen, statesmen, courtiers, priests and prophets, a tentmaking Rabbi and a Gentile physician, not to speak of others of whom we know nothing apart from the writings they have left us. The writings themselves belong to a great variety of literary types. They include history, law (civil, criminal, ethical, ritual, sanitary), religious poetry, didactic treatises, lyric poetry, parable and allegory, biography, personal correspondence, personal memoirs and diaries, in addition to the distinctively Biblical types of prophecy and apocalyptic.

For all that, the Bible is not simply an anthology; there is a unity which binds the whole together. An anthology is compiled by an anthologist, but no anthologist compiled the Bible. Somehow or other it *grew* in the course of these many centuries until at length it attained full stature as the Bible which we know. And it grew under the hand of Him who makes all living things grow, 'the Holy Spirit, the Lord and giver of life, who spake by the prophets'. The unifying principle which makes the Bible a living whole has already been pointed out: it is Christ Himself, the Bringer of salvation. The Holy Scriptures in their entirety were given to make us wise unto salvation through faith in Him and to teach us how, in the divine fellowship which links all the heirs of salvation together in Christ, we ought to direct our ways according to the will of God.

Any part of the human body can only be properly explained in reference to the whole body. And any part of the Bible can only be properly explained in reference to the whole Bible. We have mentioned the genealogies of the Bible in the previous chapter.[1] The first nine chapters of 1 Chronicles, for example, are full of genealogies and similar lists. Take these chapters by themselves, out of their context in the continuous history of salvation, and what have we? Little more than genealogies and similar lists—the sort of thing that can be paralleled from any secular record-office. We shall not understand why these chapters are in the Bible if we look at them in isolation. But as part of the whole Bible they have a definite and valuable function. They may not make us wise unto salvation in the way that Isaiah 53 can; but it would be a strange body all of whose members discharged the same functions. The genealogies of 1 Chronicles, as has already been indicated, are part of the story which leads up to Christ, part of the context in which the divine revelation is given; Christ is their goal as He is the goal of all the Old Testament.

But now let us look at the structure of the Bible, taking each of its two component parts separately.

(I) The Old Testament

The Old Testament as we know it in our ordinary editions of the English Bible falls into four sections: (1) the Pentateuch, or five books of Moses (Genesis to Deuteronomy); (2) the historical books (Joshua to Esther); (3) five books of poetry and ethics (Job to the Song of Songs); (4) the books of the prophets (Isaiah to Malachi). One of the books in the last group, the Book of Lamentations, might have been included in the third group, so far as its literary type is concerned, but as it is concerned with the fall of Jerusalem in 587 B.C., it is appended to the Book of Jeremiah, who lived and prophesied at that time. (The tradition that Jeremiah was the author of Lamentations is not supported by the contents of the book.)

One thing that strikes us as we consider this division of the Old Testament is the important part which is devoted to history. Not only are there the books properly called historical, but the Law in the Pentateuch is also set in an historical framework. In fact, from the beginning of Genesis to the end of 2 Kings we have

[1] See p. 83.

a continuous history from Adam down to the middle of the Babylonian captivity (562 B.C.). This is followed by another historical corpus, Chronicles-Ezra-Nehemiah, which covers the same ground, and carries the narrative on to the period following the return from the Babylonian captivity, although it covers the period from Adam to David only in the skeleton-form of genealogies (1 Chron. 1-9).[1] Whereas the former group of historical books looks at the history from what may be called a prophetic point of view, the latter group looks at it from a more 'institutional' point of view, with a dominant interest in the rise and progress of the worship at the Temple in Jerusalem.[2] Both the prophetic and institutional elements were essential and complementary in the religion of Israel.

There is, however, nothing surprising in the amount of history contained in the Old Testament when we reflect that the God of the Bible is the God who reveals Himself in history, both by the general overruling providence which He exercises as Lord of history, and the mighty works by which He breaks into the historical process, such as the redemption of Israel from Egypt and the greater redemption wrought in Christ for all mankind.

This arrangement of the books of the Old Testament is one that the English Bible has taken over from the Latin Vulgate version, and the Latin Vulgate in turn took it over from the Greek Septuagint translation, which belongs to the third and second centuries B.C. The early copies of the Septuagint do not agree altogether in the arrangement of the books; sometimes the poetical and ethical books are put after the prophets instead of before them, and there are variations in the arrangement of individual books. But they do present this fourfold arrangement of Pentateuch, Historical Books, Poetical and Ethical Books, and Prophetical Books; and in particular, Chronicles-Ezra-Nehemiah regularly take their place immediately after the books of Kings (in the Septuagint the two books of Samuel and two of Kings are called the four books of the Kingdoms; in the Vulgate they are called the four books of Kings).[3]

The Septuagint arrangement may not have been new; it was possibly one of the arrangements current among the Jews at the

---

[1] The books of Ruth and Esther, the two remaining narrative books of the Old Testament, belong to neither of these groups.

[2] This is only a rough distinction; it is noteworthy that while the author of 1 and 2 Kings judges the kings of Judah largely by an 'institutional' test (their attitude to the local worship at the 'high places'), the Chronicler judges them largely by their response to prophetic messages.

[3] The presence of the Apocryphal books in the Septuagint and Vulgate is not discussed here, but is left over to Chapter XIII.

time, but it was not the arrangement which prevailed among the
Jews of Palestine and Babylonia, where the Hebrew Bible was
preserved and edited. In some respects the Septuagint arrangement
reflects the chronological order of certain books better than the
arrangement which prevailed in the Hebrew Bible does; for
example, Chronicles-Ezra-Nehemiah is the chronological order
and not Ezra-Nehemiah-Chronicles, which we find in the Hebrew
Bible. The book of Daniel is not included among the prophetical
books of the Hebrew Bible, but in the Septuagint it appears as
fourth of the Major Prophets (Isaiah, Jeremiah, Ezekiel, Daniel),
and this has led some writers to suggest that it may have originally
been reckoned among the Prophets and only later removed to
another section of the Hebrew Bible.

What, then, is this arrangement of the Hebrew Bible which
differs so much from the arrangement which has come down to
us from the Septuagint? It is a threefold arrangement. The three
parts of the Hebrew Bible are the Tōrāh (Law), the Nĕbhî'îm
(Prophets), and the Kĕthûbhîm (Writings). The various books are
divided between these three groups as follows:

1. Tōrāh (Law): Genesis, Exodus, Leviticus, Numbers, Deuteronomy.[1]
2. Nĕbhî'îm (Prophets):
    (a) Nĕbhî'îm Rîshōnîm (Former Prophets): Joshua, Judges, 1 and 2
        Samuel, 1 and 2 Kings.
    (b) Nĕbhî'îm 'Achărōnîm (Latter Prophets): Isaiah, Jeremiah, Ezekiel, and
        the Book of the Twelve Prophets.[2]
3. Kĕthûbhîm (Writings): Psalms, Proverbs, Job; Song of Songs, Ruth, Lamen-
        tations,[3] Ecclesiastes, Esther;[4] Daniel, Ezra-Nehemiah,[5] 1 and 2
        Chronicles.[6]

[1] These names of the first five books were given to them by the Septuagint translators
to indicate their contents: Genesis (Origin, Generation); Exodus (Departure); Leviticus
(pertaining to the tribe of Levi); Numbers (translation of Greek Arithmoi, Latin Numeri,
so called from the two census-records in this book); Deuteronomy (Second Law, at first a
misunderstanding of the phrase 'a copy of this law' in Deut. 17. 18, but acceptable because
the Deuteronomic code is a repetition and expansion of the earlier 'Book of the Covenant',
Exod. 20-23). In the Hebrew Bible, however, these books are named by the first words or
first significant words that they contain: Genesis is Bĕrēshîth (In the Beginning), Exodus is
Shĕmōth (Names), Leviticus is Wayyiqrā (And [He] Called), Numbers is Bĕmidhbār (In the
Desert), Deuteronomy is Dĕbārîm (Words) or 'Elleh ha-Dĕbārîm (These are the Words).
[2] In the Hebrew Bible the Twelve (or Minor) Prophets are reckoned as constituting
one book. The common epithet 'Minor' applied to them concerns their length, not their
importance.
[3] In the Hebrew Bible Lamentations is denoted by the first word of the book, the
sorrowful interjection 'Ekhāh (translated 'How!' in the English Bible).
[4] The five books, Song of Songs, Ruth, Lamentations, Ecclesiastes, and Esther form a
smaller group within the 'Writings'; they are known as the five Mĕgillōth (Rolls).
[5] Ezra and Nehemiah are reckoned as one book in the enumeration of the books of
the Hebrew Bible.
[6] The arrangement of the books varied somewhat within the three main groupings;
the above is the arrangement found in all printed copies of the Hebrew Bible.

The most noteworthy feature of the arrangement of the books in the Hebrew Bible is that several of the books which we regard as historical are there placed among the Prophets—Joshua, Judges, and the books of Samuel and Kings. The reason for this has been suggested already; these books are not simply concerned with recording events, but with using events to illustrate the great principles on which the prophets insisted. They teach prophetic lessons and are therefore listed among the prophetic books, along with those books which we recognize in a more literal sense as the books of the prophets.

We might, of course, have expected *a priori* that if God wished to communicate the knowledge of His nature and will to mankind He might have done so in a series of propositions, after the manner of theological summaries, bodies of divinity and confessions of faith which are drawn up article by article in logical sequence. Doubtless God might have done so, but doubtless He never did. These doctrinal statements may be firmly based upon the Bible, and if so they have their place in religious life and teaching, but the Bible itself does not take this form. What we have just said with regard to the form of the Old Testament suggests that God chose to reveal Himself as the God of living action, revealing Himself in mighty acts of mercy and judgment and interpreting His ways to men through His spokesmen the prophets. He is no impassive Deity, detached from the world and wrapped up in His self-existent Being. The very *form* of the Old Testament reveals the God He is, and prepares us for His incarnation in One who should both accomplish the greatest of all God's mighty self-revealing acts and speak as His supreme Spokesman. And so we turn expectantly to the form assumed by the literature of the New Covenant.

(II) The New Testament

The New Testament falls into three easily-distinguished sections: (*a*) narrative books; (*b*) epistles, and (*c*) the single book of Revelation, which belongs to the literary type which we describe by the epithet 'apocalyptic'.

(*a*) The first section, comprising five narrative books, is further divided between the four Gospels and the book of Acts.

The four Gospels—or rather the four records of the one and only Gospel, which is the good news of God's salvation brought near in Jesus Christ—are not, as is sometimes imagined, biographies of Christ, not in the proper sense of the word at any rate. They are rather the written deposit of the early apostolic preaching and teaching, the burden of which was the works and words of Christ. The first three Gospels are commonly called the 'Synoptic' Gospels, because the amount of material common to all three or to two of them makes it convenient to view them synoptically, for example in three parallel columns where their common and special material may be taken in at a glance. Not that this is the only way to study these Gospels; some students have got so used to the synoptic approach that they have almost forgotten that each Gospel is a work by itself with a unity and emphasis of its own. The fourth Gospel was probably written after the first three. The testimony of this Gospel is that it preserves the witness of John the Apostle, and this finds corroboration in our earliest external evidence bearing on the subject, according to which it was written at the dictation of John, the last survivor of the apostles, shortly before his death at the end of the first century A.D. Each of the four Gospels, with its distinctive picture of Christ, seems to have circulated at first in the churches of a particular area, but shortly after the appearance of the fourth the four appear to have been bound up together and acknowledged by the churches at large as the authoritative fourfold Gospel of Christ.

The book of the Acts of the Apostles was the second part of a history of Christian origins written by Luke the physician of Antioch, the friend and travel-companion of Paul. It takes up the story at the point where Part I of Luke's history (the third Gospel) ends, the ascension of Christ, and tells how the Gospel spread along the road from Jerusalem to Rome in the first thirty years after the death and resurrection of Christ. When the Gospel of Luke was bound up with the other three Gospels, its sequel, the book of Acts, was left by itself; it was as a matter of convenience very frequently thereafter bound up with the General or Catholic Epistles.

(b) The second section of the New Testament comprises twenty-one letters or epistles. Thirteen of these bear the name of Paul, two bear the name of Peter, one of James and one of Jude. Then there are three which do not bear the writer's name, but their close affinity with the fourth Gospel bears out the tradition which ascribes them to the same author and so entitles them the 'Epistles of John'. (In two of them the writer introduces himself as 'The Elder'—a title by which he appears to have been familiarly known because of his great age and his being the sole survivor of the original disciples of Jesus.) There is one other anonymous epistle—The Epistle to the Hebrews—to which it is, perhaps, wiser not to try to assign any known personage as author. Seventeen hundred years ago the learned Church Father, Origen of Alexandria, had to confess: 'Who really wrote it, God only knows'—and that is the position still.

The Pauline Epistles fall into two groups—those written before the end of Paul's two years' imprisonment in Rome recorded in Acts 28. 30, and the Pastoral Epistles (those to Timothy and Titus) which were written later. The earlier group, dating between A.D. 48 and 61, forms our earliest extant Christian literature (with the possible exception of the Epistle of James), for our Gospels did not begin to circulate in writing until about the end of this period.

(c) The book of Revelation, though not the last book of the New Testament to be written, is fittingly placed at the end of the Bible, because in the pictorial and symbolical language of the apocalyptic literature to which it belongs it gathers up all the threads of previous revelation and—against the background of a day of fierce persecution—portrays the triumph of Christ and His people and the advent of the day when 'the kingdom of the world is become the kingdom of our Lord, and of His Christ: and He shall reign for ever and ever' (Rev. 11. 15).

CHAPTER VIII

THE CANON OF SCRIPTURE

OUR English word 'canon' goes back through Latin to the Greek *kanōn*, which in its turn was borrowed from a Semitic word which in Hebrew takes the form *qāneh*. The root meaning of the word is 'reed' (it is also the word from which our 'cane' is derived). It then acquires a number of derivative senses; since a reed might be used as a measuring rod *kanōn* is found with this meaning, and also with the meaning of a rule or standard in a metaphorical sense. It is in this last sense that a Greek Father like Origen used the word *kanōn* to denote what we call the 'rule of faith', the standard by which we are to measure and evaluate everything that may be offered to us as an article of belief. In this sense the word is closely linked with the authority of Scripture, because Scripture is the rule both of faith and of practice; it was given to teach us (in the words of the *Westminster Shorter Catechism*) 'what man is to believe concerning God and what duty God requires of man'. Then there is a further use of *kanōn* in the sense of a list or index (this sense is probably derived from the series of marks on a measuring rod). This is the sense which lies behind the expression 'the canon of Scripture'; the canon of Scripture is the list of books which are reckoned as Holy Scripture. But since the books which are reckoned as Holy Scripture are those which are reckoned as supremely authoritative for belief and conduct, the sense of 'rule' or 'standard' is never far away when we speak of the canon of Scripture.[1]

There is a distinction between the canonicity of a book of the Bible and its authority. Its canonicity is dependent upon its authority. For when we ascribe canonicity to a book we simply mean that it belongs to the canon or list. But why does it so belong? Because it was recognized as possessing special authority. People frequently speak and write as if the authority with which the books of the Bible are invested in the minds of Christians is

---

[1] Origen (184-254) uses the word *kanōn* in the sense of the 'rule of faith' but not in the sense of the 'canon of Scripture'. It appears that this later sense, 'the list of writings acknowledged by the Church as documents of the divine revelation,' is not earlier than Athanasius (296-373). (See H. Chadwick, *Journal of Theological Studies*, 49 [1948], pp. 17-27.)

the result of their having been included in the sacred list. But the historical fact is the other way about; they were and are included in the list because they were acknowledged as authoritative.

For example, when Moses came down from Mount Sinai and told the people all the words that he had received from God, reading them from the 'book of the covenant' in which he had written them, the people answered: 'All that the Lord hath spoken will we do' (Exod. 24. 7). That is to say, they acknowledged that the words they heard from Moses' lips were the words of God, and therefore absolutely authoritative and binding. But we can hardly say that they recognized these words as *canonical*, for the idea of a list or collection of such writings lay still in the future. Or when, in New Testament times, Paul wrote to the Christians in Corinth, 'If any man thinketh himself to be a prophet, or spiritual, let him take knowledge of the things which I write unto you, that they are the commandment of the Lord' (1 Cor. 14. 37), no doubt those members of the Church whose spiritual sense was alert acknowledged the written words of Paul as the commandments of Christ Himself. But the idea of a New Testament canon was still to take shape. Both logically and historically, authority precedes canonicity.

In this chapter, then, we are not dealing so much with the recognition of the Biblical oracles as authoritative as with the formation of a canon of those writings which had already the stamp of authority upon them. And in making our investigation, we must take the two Testaments separately.

(I) *The Old Testament*

When our Lord appeared to His disciples in the upper room in Jerusalem on the evening of His resurrection, He impressed on them the fact that all that had happened to Him was in exact accord with what had been prophesied in Old Testament Scripture. He reminded them how, even before His crucifixion, He had told them 'that all things must needs be fulfilled, which are written in the law of Moses, and the prophets, and the psalms, concerning Me' (Luke 24. 44). In these words He indicated the three sections into which the Hebrew Bible was divided—the Law, the Prophets, and the 'Writings' (here probably called 'the Psalms' because the Book of Psalms is the first and longest book in this third section). We have already discussed the contents of these three sections in Chapter VII. Here what we must notice particularly is that our Lord refers to the threefold body of Old Testament writings not only as divinely authoritative but also as canonical, for the authoritative writings had been gathered together into one collection, and the distinctive feature of this collection was that all the writings within it were Holy Scripture, and all the writings outside it were not.

It can be taken for granted that by this time the first two sections—the Law and the Prophets—contained all the books which they contain in the Hebrew Bible we know. But did the third section—the 'Writings' (or the Psalms, as our Lord said) —contain all the books which it now contains? Probably it did. It is almost certain that the Bible with which He was familiar ended with the books of Chronicles, which come right at the end of the 'Writings' in the Hebrew Bible. The evidence for this is that when He wished to sum up all the martyrs whose blood had been shed in Old Testament times He used the expression: 'from the blood of Abel unto the blood of Zachariah, who perished between the altar and the sanctuary' (Luke 11. 51; cf. Matt. 23. 35). Now Abel is obviously the first martyr of the Bible, but why should Zachariah come last? Because in the order of books in the Hebrew Bible he is the last martyr to be named; in 2 Chron. 24. 21 we read how he was stoned while he prophesied to the people 'in the court of the house of the LORD'.

The chief reason for asking if the 'Writings' section was complete in our Lord's time is that we have records of discussions that went on among the Rabbis after the Fall of Jerusalem in A.D. 70 about some of the books in this section. When the destruction of the city and temple was imminent, a great Rabbi belonging to the school of Hillel in the Pharisaic party—Yochanan ben Zakkai by name—obtained permission from the Romans to reconstitute the Sanhedrin on a purely spiritual basis at Jabneh or Jamnia, between Joppa and Azotus (Ashdod). Some of the discussions which went on at Jamnia were handed down by oral transmission and ultimately recorded in the Rabbinical writings. Among their debates they considered whether canonical recognition should be accorded to the books of Proverbs, Ecclesiastes, the Song of Songs and Esther. Objections had been raised against these books on various grounds; Esther, for example, did not contain the name of God, and Ecclesiastes was none too easy to square with contemporary orthodoxy. But the upshot of the Jamnia debates was the firm acknowledgment of all these books as Holy Scripture. Some disputants also asked whether the Wisdom of Jesus the son of Sira (Ecclesiasticus), and the *gilyonim* (Aramaic Gospel-writings) and other books of the *minim* (heretics—probably Jewish Christians), should be admitted, but here the answer was uncompromisingly negative.

We should not exaggerate the importance of the Jamnia debates for the history of the canon. The books which they decided to acknowledge as canonical were already generally accepted, although questions had been raised about them. Those which they refused to admit had never been included. They did not expel from the canon any book which had previously been admitted. 'The Council of Jamnia, as J. S. Wright puts it, 'was the confirming of public opinion, not the forming of it'.[1]

In fact, one of the books which was debated most keenly in the first century A.D. was one whose presence in the second section of the Hebrew canon must have been settled long before—the book of Ezekiel. The chariot-vision of Ezekiel gave rise to a great deal of mystic speculation (some of it very unprofitable), and then there was a difficulty in reconciling the prescriptions for worship in Ezek. 40-48 with those in the Pentateuch. 'When Elijah comes', one said, 'he will explain the difficulty'. But fortunately it was not necessary to wait so long. 'Blessed be the memory of Hananiah, son of Hezekiah: if it had not been for him, the Book of Ezekiel would have been "hidden" (i.e., withdrawn from public reading), because its words contradict the words of the Law. What did he do? They brought him 300 measures of oil, and he sat down and explained it.' The spectacle of Hananiah burning the midnight oil to the tune of 300 measures until he reconciled Ezekiel and Moses is an affecting one; but there is little likelihood that the expulsion of Ezekiel from the canon, or even its withdrawal from the lectionary, was a practical possibility at that late date. The Rabbis of the early centuries A.D., like disputants of all centuries, enjoyed a really tough subject for debate.[2]

Philo, the learned Jew of Alexandria, whose life overlapped the life of Christ by about twenty years at either end, seems to have known and accepted the Hebrew canon. The Law to him is pre-eminently inspired, but he also acknowledges the authority of the other books of the Hebrew canon (although, as an Alexandrian, he used only the Greek version). He does not regard the

---

[1] *The Evangelical Quarterly*, April, 1947, p. 97. So also A. Bentzen, *Introduction to the Old Testament*, i (1948), p. 31, insists that the Jamnia 'discussions have not so much dealt with acceptance of certain writings into the Canon, but rather with their right to remain there'.

[2] This fascinating question of the early rabbinical debates on canonicity is treated very perfunctorily above. For a fuller and authoritative treatment see G. F. Moore, *Judaism*, Vol. I (1927), pp. 238 ff.

apocryphal books as authoritative, and this suggests that, although these books were included in the Septuagint, they were not really accorded canonical status by the Alexandrian Jews.[1] We cannot however, be sure about Philo's attitude to some of the Old Testament books, especially a few in the 'Writings', because he does not refer to them. We cannot say dogmatically that he accepted all the books of the Hebrew canon, though he may very well have done so.

We are on firmer ground when we come to Josephus, another eminent Jew who wrote in Greek. For he tells us much more precisely what books were accounted specially authoritative by his nation. 'We have not 10,000 books among us', he says, 'disagreeing with and contradicting one another, but only twenty-two books, which contain the records of all time, and are justly believed to be divine. Five of these are by Moses, and contain his laws and traditions of the origin of mankind until his death. . . . From the death of Moses till the reign of Artaxerxes, king of Persia, who reigned after Xerxes, the prophets who succeeded Moses wrote down what happened in their times in thirteen books; and the remaining four books contain hymns to God and precepts for the conduct of human life'.[2] Josephus, of course, knew and used other Jewish writings, such as 1 Maccabees, but of these later writings he says: 'Our history has also been written in detail from Artaxerxes to our own times, but is not esteemed equally authoritative with the books already mentioned, because there was not then an exact succession of prophets'. His explanation of the exclusion of these latter books from the canon is in line with the rabbinic belief that scriptural inspiration ceased along with the gift of prophecy soon after the return from the Babylonian exile. In any case, Josephus echoes the prevailing opinion about what books were canonical and what were not. And though he uses the Septuagint freely, he does not regard the Apocrypha as canonical.

But what are the twenty-two books to which he accords canonicity? The number of the books is probably arranged to agree with the number of letters in the Hebrew alphabet. The Pentateuch, of course, occupies a place by itself. As for the thirteen books written by the prophets, these will include the eight books in the 'Prophets' section of the Hebrew Bible and also probably Daniel, Chronicles, Ezra, Nehemiah, Esther. If Ezra and Nehemiah were reckoned as one book, as in the Hebrew Bible, then Job might be included here as well. It has at least as much claim to be regarded as a 'prophetic' writing as Chronicles, Ezra, Nehemiah

[1] See p. 164.   [2] Josephus, *Against Apion* i. 8.

and Esther. Why Josephus should have included these among the books written by the prophets is not easy to understand. Possibly he felt he had to accommodate his theory that all the canonical books belonged to the prophetic era to the fact that these books were accepted in his time as canonical. The arrangement of the twenty-two books, $5 + 13 + 4$, may be his own idea. The four books of hymns and practical precepts may have been Psalms, Proverbs, Ecclesiastes and the Song of Songs (though it is just possible that he omitted the Song of Songs, in which case Job will have been one of these four, and Ezra and Nehemiah in the middle section will have been separated). Probably, too, he reckoned Ruth as an appendix to Judges, and Lamentations to Jeremiah. The treatise *Against Apion*, in which this passage about the canon occurs, was written by Josephus towards the end of the first century A.D.

The earliest dateable Christian list of Old Testament books was drawn up by Melito, bishop of Sardis, about A.D. 170; he said he had obtained it by accurate enquiry while travelling in Syria. It has been preserved by Eusebius in the fourth book of his *Ecclesiastical History*.[1] 'Their names are these', writes Melito in a letter to his friend, Onesimus: 'five books of Moses: Genesis, Exodus, Numbers, Leviticus, Deuteronomy. Jesus Naue,[2] Judges, Ruth. Four books of Kingdoms, two of Chronicles. The Psalms of David, Solomon's Proverbs (also called Wisdom), Ecclesiastes, Song of Songs, Job. Of the Prophets: Isaiah, Jeremiah, the Twelve in a single book, Daniel, Ezekiel, Ezra.' It is likely that Melito included Lamentations with Jeremiah, and Nehemiah with Ezra (though it is curious to find Ezra counted among the prophets). In that case, his list contains all the books of the Hebrew canon (arranged according to the Septuagint order), with the exception of Esther. Esther may not have been included in the list he received from his informants in Syria.[3]

From about the same time as Melito's list, or slightly later, comes a list preserved in a manuscript in the Library of the Greek Patriarchate in Jerusalem, and reproduced in a somewhat later form in a treatise by the late fourth-century writer Epiphanius, bishop of Salamis in Cyprus. In this list the name of each Old Testament book is given twice, first in Hebrew or Aramaic transcribed into

---

[1] Eusebius, *Hist. Eccl.* IV. 26.

[2] *Nauē* is an early corruption of *Naun* (Gk. NAYN misread as NAYH) and appears generally in the Septuagint as the form for Nun, Joshua's father.

[3] See G. F. Moore, *Judaism*, Vol. I, pp. 238, 244 f. Esther is the only Old Testament book of which no trace has been found in the Qumran library. Athanasius (A.D. 367) does not include Esther along with the canonical books of the first rank, but places it along with some of the apocryphal books in a secondary list.

Greek characters, and then in the Greek Septuagint form. The total of the books listed is twenty-seven, but these twenty-seven correspond to our thirty-nine, except that Lamentations is not included by name. The omission of Lamentations, however, may be only apparent; probably it was reckoned as an appendix to Jeremiah.[1]

Origen, the greatest Biblical scholar among the Greek Fathers (A.D. 185-254), gives a list of canonical Old Testament books, which he enumerates as twenty-two, and names in their Hebrew as well as their Greek titles.[2] According to his reckoning the five books of Moses are followed by (6) Joshua, then (7) Judges and Ruth (which are reckoned as one among the Hebrews, he says), (8 and 9) the four books of Kingdoms (which among them count as one book of Samuel and one—our 1 and 2 Kings—which they call after its opening words, 'And King David'). Then (10) Chronicles, reckoned as one, (11) Ezra and Nehemiah as one; (12) Psalms, (13) Proverbs, (14) Ecclesiastes, (15) Song of Songs; (16) Isaiah; (17) Jeremiah with Lamentations and the 'Epistle of Jeremiah',[3] reckoned as one; (18) Daniel, (19) Ezekiel, (20) Job, (21) Esther. The book of the Twelve Prophets has been omitted from his list—accidentally, of course, because it is required to make up the twenty-two. 'Outside these', he adds, 'are the books of Maccabees'.

Athanasius, bishop of Alexandria, who discussed the Canon of Scripture in his Easter Letter for A.D. 367, arranged the Old Testament books so as to yield a total of twenty-two. These twenty-two correspond to our thirty-nine, except that Esther is omitted and Jeremiah has appended to it not only Lamentations but also Baruch (including the 'Epistle of Jeremiah'). Then he adds: 'There are also other books outside this list which are not canonical, but have been handed down from our fathers as suitable to be read to new converts . . . the Wisdom of Solomon, the Wisdom of Sirach, Esther, Judith and Tobias'.[4]

Jerome, the greatest Biblical scholar among the Latin Fathers (A.D. 347-420), says in the Preface to his commentary on Daniel: 'I point out that Daniel is not reckoned among the prophets by the Hebrews, but among those who wrote the Hagiographa (the sacred Writings). As a matter of fact they divide all Scripture into three parts—the Law, the Prophets, and the Hagiographa, consisting of five, eight and eleven books respectively'. But in his

---

[1] Cf. J. P. Audet, 'A Hebrew-Aramaic List of Books of the Old Testament in Greek Transcription', *Journal of Theological Studies*, new series 1 (1950), pp. 135-154.
[2] Quoted by Eusebius, *Hist. Eccl.* VI. 25.
[3] See p. 170.   [4] See p. 112, n. 3, and pp. 163 ff.

Prologue to the Books of Samuel and Kings, Jerome remarks that in some Jewish circles the number of books was reduced to twenty-two to correspond with the number of letters in the Hebrew alphabet, by counting Ruth along with Judges and Lamentations along with Jeremiah; while in others the number was raised to twenty-seven (to allow for those letters of the alphabet, five in number, which have two forms each),[1] by dividing Samuel, Kings, Chronicles, Ezra-Nehemiah and Jeremiah-Lamentations into two books each.

It is frequently said that among the Jews before A.D. 70 the Alexandrian Canon (represented by the Septuagint) was larger than the Palestinian. But it is not at all certain that we ought to think of an Alexandrian Canon at all,[2] as distinct from that accepted in Palestine. People who talk about a larger Alexandrian Canon are thinking of the inclusion of apocryphal books in the Septuagint translation. But it is remarkable that even Jewish writers who used the Septuagint, like Josephus and (what is more to the point) the Alexandrian Philo, do not attach divine authority to the Apocrypha. The question of the apocryphal books is, of course, very relevant to this whole subject of the canon of Scripture, but we have dealt with it in a separate chapter (Chapter XIII).

In the prologue which the Greek translator of Ecclesiasticus (the grandson of the Hebrew author) prefaced to the book about 132 B.C., he refers more than once to the threefold division of the Jewish sacred books. He calls them variously 'the law and the prophets and the others that have followed in their steps', 'the law and the prophets and the other books of our fathers', and ' the law itself and the prophecies and the rest of the books'. It is sometimes thought that the rather indefinite way in which he seems to refer to the third section of the Hebrew canon, the 'Writings', implies that this section was not yet closed. This, however, is not a certain inference; it is equally permissible to deduce from the words used that the Hebrew canon was already complete in its present form, and indeed we might deduce from the context in which these words are used that all these books had been translated into Greek by 132 B.C. However this may be, the language used by the translator of Ecclesiasticus does show that the threefold division of the Hebrew canon was known in his day.

Does this threefold division throw any further light on the

---

[1] See pp. 40 f. Compare the total of 27 in the Jerusalem list mentioned on pp. 100 f.

[2] Unless we think of the authorized Greek version of the Pentateuch as an Alexandrian Canon (see p. 149).

history of the Hebrew canon? It is commonly said to reveal the three stages by which the Old Testament books achieved canonical recognition. All scholars are not agreed on this point, however; it is denied, for example, by Professor E. J. Young, who says that 'there certainly is no evidence to support the view that there were three canons, that the Pentateuch was first accepted as canonical, then, at a later time, the Prophets and, finally, the Writings'.[1] But while there is no direct evidence, it is a very reasonable view. We should not speak of three canons, but that the Pentateuch was first accepted as canonical is a proposition which should commend itself even more to those who believe that the complete Pentateuch antedated the prophetical writings than to those who accept more or less the conclusions of the Wellhausen school,[2] which Professor Young is more particularly concerned to refute in the article to which we refer. The book of the Law was acknowledged as the very word of God from its earliest existence.

As for the second division, the 'Prophets', both its sub-divisions as such (the Former and the Latter Prophets), while they contain much pre-exilic matter, must date after the fall of the southern kingdom. The last event in the Former Prophets is dated in 562 B.C. (the first year of Evil-merodach's reign over Babylon), and the Latter Prophets cannot have been complete before the fourth century B.C.[3] But this is not to deny that the words of the prophets were divinely authoritative from the moment of utterance, and that the documents in which they were recorded were canonical in principle, if not in a technical sense, from the first.

The third division, the 'Writings', belongs as a completed corpus to a date somewhat later in the post-exilic age than the 'Prophets'. But this does not necessarily mean that the individual books in the 'Writings' are all later in date or lower in authority than the component parts of the 'Prophets'. Many of the Psalms and Proverbs, for example, are no doubt earlier than anything in the 'Latter Prophets'. It has been suggested in the previous chapter that the Septuagint preserves an order of the Old Testament books which may antedate the canonical order of the Hebrew Bible, as in some respects it keeps books in their original relationship, which

[1] In an essay on 'The Authority of the Old Testament', in the symposium *The Infallible Word* (ed. N. B. Stonehouse and P. Woolley, 1947), p. 85.

[2] A school which holds that the Pentateuch did not reach its final form and arrangement until after the Babylonian exile.

[3] L. Finkelstein (*The Pharisees* [1940], pp. 577 f.) holds that the 'Prophets' were finally canonized by the 'Great Synagogue' late in the 3rd century B.C.

has been dislocated in the Hebrew Bible. Thus in the Septuagint Chronicles precedes Ezra and Nehemiah, whereas it follows them in the Hebrew Bible. It may be inferred from this fact that Ezra and Nehemiah were accepted as canonical before Chronicles.

For Christians, however, it suffices that the Hebrew canon of the Old Testament was accepted as divinely authoritative by our Lord and His apostles. The apostles, no doubt, found in their Master's attitude to these writings sufficient warrant for theirs, and He accepted them, not because their canonicity had been handed down by tradition, but because He recognized their divine quality. In many points He condemned the Jewish tradition, but not with respect to the canonicity of Scripture. His complaint, indeed, was that by other traditions they had invalidated in practice the Word of God recorded in canonical Scripture. But in point of the canonicity of Scripture He confirmed their tradition, not because it was tradition, but because He knew on independent grounds that it was right. And in this as in all else we are safe when we follow Him. 'What was indispensable to the Redeemer', it has been well said, 'must always be indispensable to the redeemed'.[1]

(II) The New Testament

A once famous series of lectures, delivered before Yale University in 1899, began with the startling words: 'Few realize that the Church of Christ possesses a higher warrant for her Canon of the Old Testament than she does for her Canon of the New'.[2] For, as the lecturer went on to point out, the Old Testament is accredited by the authority of our Lord Jesus Christ in a way which, in the very nature of the case, does not apply to the New. For it was the Old Testament Scriptures that constituted Christ's Bible. 'He accepted its history as the preparation for Himself, and taught His disciples to find Him in it. He used it to justify His mission and to illuminate the mystery of His Cross. He drew from it many of the examples and most of the categories of His gospel. He re-enforced the essence of its law and restored many of its ideals. But, above all, He fed His own soul with its contents, and in the great crises of His life sustained Himself upon it as upon the living and sovereign Word of God'.[3] Obviously (as it must appear to every Christian) no body of literature ever had its credentials confirmed by a higher authority.

Does this mean that we receive the New Testament on lower

---

[1] Sir G. A. Smith, *Modern Criticism and the Preaching of the Old Testament* (1901), p. 11.
[2] G. A. Smith, *op. cit.*, p. 5.   [3] *Op. cit.*, p. 11.

authority than the Old? Not really; it only means that the impar-
tation of Christ's authority to the New is less immediately apparent.
But when we look into the matter we find that He who accredited
the Old Testament retrospectively accredited the New Testament
prospectively. The fourth Evangelist relates how Jesus, on the
eve of His crucifixion, promised His disciples to send them the
Holy Spirit, His Other Self, of whom He said among other things:
'He shall teach you all things, and bring to your remembrance all
that I said unto you. . . . He shall guide you into all the truth . . .
and He shall declare unto you the things that are to come' (John
14. 26; 16. 13). The New Testament, Christians believe, is the
written deposit of the special fulfilment of these words of Christ
in the life and witness of His apostles. But are Christians justified
in believing this?

The New Testament, as it lies before us now, consists of
twenty-seven documents—five narrative records, twenty-one letters,
and a book of visions. It appears, from a consideration of internal
and external evidence, that nearly all of these were in existence by
the beginning of the second century A.D. But how did they come
to form one collection? Who made the collection, and why? And
what was the nature of the authority by which they were accepted
by Christians as the complement of the dominically-ratified Old
Testament corpus, so that both together make up the Church's
rule of faith and life?[1]

It goes without saying that, to all who acknowledged our
Lord as Messiah and Son of God, His utterances could be no less
authoritative than those of the prophets through whom God had
spoken in Old Testament times. 'God, having of old time spoken
unto the fathers in the prophets by divers portions and in divers
manners, hath at the end of these days spoken unto us in His Son'
(Heb. 1. 1). The divine message through the prophets was partial
and intermittent; it found fulfilment and finality in the revelation
which came in Jesus Christ. The prophets were the vehicles of
divine inspiration in varying degrees and from time to time; in
Jesus the Holy Spirit dwelt in permanent fulness, and He Himself
was the Word of God incarnate. The written record of His words
must therefore inevitably receive a meed of veneration at least
equal to that accorded to the Old Testament oracles.

But just as in Old Testament times God revealed Himself by
saving acts as well as in prophetic words, so the crowning revelation

---

[1] I have dealt more fully with this subject of the New Testament Canon in *The Spreading
Flame* (London, 1958), pp. 221-237.

of God in Christ was conveyed not only through the words He said but also through the deeds He performed, and supremely in the great saving acts of His death and resurrection. The records of God's preparatory saving acts in Old Testament times were reckoned as prophetic writings; how much more the record of His full salvation brought near to mankind in His Son? So the Gospels contain not only the teaching of Jesus, but the narrative of His mighty works, leading up to the mightiest of all. The twofold contents of the Gospels are the written deposit of the twofold witness of the apostles. The apostles were commissioned by Christ not only to make known throughout the nations the good news of the salvation which God had accomplished in Him, but also to make disciples of all the nations by teaching them all that He Himself had commanded. In discharge of this commission the apostles bore a twofold testimony—to 'all that Jesus began both to do and to teach'. The apostles proclaimed from place to place the good news of what Christ had done, and to those who believed the good news and became members of the new Christian communities which the apostles founded they communicated further the teaching of Christ—both by word of mouth and by letter. The earliest documents in the New Testament are letters written by apostles to their converts and other Christians imparting this teaching and applying it to the various situations that arose in the infant churches. As the apostles did this, we believe, they experienced the fulfilment of their Lord's promise that His Spirit would lead them into all the truth. But it is a remarkable fact that there is no teaching in the New Testament which is not already present in principle in the teaching of Jesus Himself. The apostles did not add to His teaching; under the guidance of the promised Spirit they interpreted and applied it. And therefore their teaching, whether delivered orally or in writing, was intended to be received as the message of Christ Himself, just as the official communications made by an ambassador are intended to be received not as his personal observations but as the words of the sovereign whom he represents. Long before the apostolic letters were recognized as elements in a canonical collection, they were recognized as authoritative by most of those for whom they were written; as we said before, authority is the necessary precedent of canonicity.

Until about the sixties of the first century A.D. the need for written Gospels does not appear to have arisen. So long as the eye-witnesses of the great salvation-bringing events were alive to tell the tale, it was not so necessary to have a formal written record.

But the apostles were not going to live on earth for ever, and it was obviously desirable that their message should be preserved after they had gone. So we find Mark, the companion and interpreter of Peter, committing to writing in Rome the Gospel as Peter habitually proclaimed it; shortly afterwards we have Matthew's Gospel appearing in the East, based largely upon a collection of the sayings of Jesus probably written down first by Matthew himself; and Luke, the companion of Paul, writes in two books for Gentile readers a narrative of the beginnings of Christianity from the birth of John the Baptist up to Paul's two years' residence in Rome (A.D. 61-62). Towards the end of the century, John, perhaps the last surviving companion of Jesus in the days of His flesh, records his reminiscences of his Master's life and teaching, together with his meditations on them, in such a way as to supplement the earlier Gospels. The Gospels are not simple biographies—they are rather written transcripts of the Gospel preached by the apostles.

But we have not yet a canon in the sense of a collection of these writings. Towards the end of the first century, however, we find the beginnings of a movement in this direction. Not long after the writing of the fourth Gospel, the four Gospels appear to have been brought together in one collection. Thus, whereas previously Rome had Mark's Gospel, and Syria had Matthew's, and a Gentile group had Luke's, and Ephesus John's, now each church had all four in a corpus which was called *The Gospel* (each of the components being distinguished by the additional words *According to Matthew, According to Mark*, and so on). About the same time, or possibly a few years earlier, came a movement to gather together the letters which Paul had written to various churches and individuals, and thus a further collection began to circulate among the churches, bearing the title *The Apostle* (the various components being distinguished by the sub-headings *To the Romans, First to the Corinthians*, and so on).

When the four Gospels were gathered together in one collection this meant that the two parts of Luke's history of Christian beginnings must be separated from each other. Part I, which carried the story on to the appearances of the risen Christ to His disciples, was included in the fourfold Gospel with the caption *According to Luke*; Part II, which carried the record on from that point for a further thirty years or so, was left by itself, and in course of time received the title *Acts of Apostles*. But Acts naturally shared the authority and prestige of the third Gospel, being the work of the same author; and besides, it was a very important book. Not only

did it provide the sequel to the Gospel story, but it was an indispensable companion to the Pauline collection. Who was this
Paul? What were the grounds for the apostolic authority which
he claimed for himself (as he was manifestly not one of the Twelve
whom Jesus had appointed to be with Him)? Such questions as
these must have occurred to readers of the group of letters entitled
The Apostle. But Acts made the source and quality of Paul's
apostolic commission and service very plain. It therefore served
as a link between the fourfold Gospel and the Pauline corpus, and
thus well merits Harnack's description of it as the 'pivotal' book
of the New Testament.[1]

The letters of other apostles and 'apostolic men', and the
Apocalypse of the prophet, John, which he had received from
Christ to communicate to the churches, were for similar reasons
recognized to bear divine authority.

Now, about A.D. 140, a teacher from Asia Minor came to
Rome and introduced a novel form of teaching. This was the
heretic Marcion,[2] and he soon had a following large enough to
cause the ecclesiastical leaders in Rome and elsewhere considerable
concern. In accordance with his views about the supersession of
the Old Testament, he rejected the Bible of our Lord and the
Apostles and drew up a canon to take its place. This canon consisted of two sections—*The Gospel* and *The Apostle*. Marcion's
Gospel consisted of an expurgated edition of the Gospel of Luke,
which he probably regarded as the least Jewish of the Gospels,
as its author was a Gentile; his *Apostle* consisted of the Pauline
letters (excluding those to Timothy and Titus). Even the books
which he did accept as canonical Scripture were edited in accordance
with what he believed to be pure Christian doctrine. No doubt
he believed that by this process of editing he was removing inter-
polations introduced by those who followed the teaching of the
Twelve, as distinct from Paul, who in Marcion's eyes was the only
faithful apostle. Thus anything even in Paul's epistles which
seemed to recognize the authority of the God of Israel or to identify
Him with the God and Father of our Lord Jesus Christ was cut
out; it could not, on Marcion's premises, be genuine. All Old
Testament references were likewise excised. And in accordance
with his belief that Jesus was a supernatural being who appeared
suddenly among men in the mere semblance of humanity, his
Gospel began with the words: 'In the fifteenth year of Tiberius

---

[1] A. Harnack, *The Origin of the New Testament* (1925), pp. 64 f.
[2] See p. 79.

THE CANON OF SCRIPTURE

Caesar, in the times of Pontius Pilate, Jesus came down to Caper-naum, a city of Galilee, and taught in the synagogue'. This state-ment is based on Luke 3. 1; 4. 31, but it deliberately omits Luke's birth-narratives, the ministry of John the Baptist, the baptism of Jesus, His genealogy (according to Marcion, He had no human descent), and His temptation.

Marcion's followers formed quite an influential group for a considerable time, and looked like attracting many others from the orthodox churches. The church leaders saw the necessity of defining the canon of New Testament Scripture more explicitly by way of countering Marcion's canon. It is not correct to say, as is some-times said, that Marcion was the first to draw up a New Testament canon, and that the orthodox party thereupon drew up theirs as a reply to his. The canon was well on its way to taking clear shape before Marcion's activity began. But his activity certainly pro-vided the church leaders, especially in Rome, where he chiefly propagated his views, with an incentive to state the orthodox position regarding the canon more clearly. The main points of this position were that the canon contained four Gospels, not one; thirteen Pauline epistles, not only ten; the book of Acts, which vindicated the apostolic commission of Paul, but also related some-thing of the doings of other apostles, and thus refuted Marcion's depreciation of those; and (in addition to the writings of Paul) writings of some other apostles and 'apostolic men'.

One orthodox writer whose evidence is specially important in this connection is Irenaeus. The importance of his evidence lies in his link with the apostolic age and in his ecumenical associations. Brought up in Asia Minor at the feet of Polycarp, the disciple of John, he became bishop of Lyons in Gaul, A.D. 180. His writings attest the canonical recognition of the fourfold Gospel and Acts, of Rom., 1 and 2 Cor., Gal., Eph., Phil., Col., 1 and 2 Thess., 1 and 2 Tim., and Titus, of 1 Peter and 1 John, and of the Revelation. In his treatise, *Against Heresies*, III, 11, 8, it is evident that by A.D. 180 the idea of the fourfold Gospel had become so axiomatic throughout Christendom that it could be referred to as an established fact as obvious and inevitable and natural as the four cardinal points of the compass (as we call them) or the four winds.

An early list of New Testament books, drawn up in the church at Rome later in the second century, is called the Muratorian fragment, after the antiquarian, L. A. Muratori, who discovered it in manuscript and published it in 1740. It is pretty obviously an orthodox counterblast to Marcion. The fragment is mutilated at the beginning, but seems to have mentioned Matthew and Mark, because it goes on to mention Luke as the 'third' Gospel; then it mentions John, and gives a curious account of the circumstances under which his Gospel was composed. Acts is next named, and called the 'Acts of *all* the apostles'—an obvious misnomer, but equally obviously a reminder that *all* the apostles were to be recognized, and not Paul only. Then it enumerates Paul's nine letters to churches and four to individuals, Jude's epistle, two epistles of John, and the Apocalypse of John and that of Peter.[1] The *Shepherd* of Hermas (an allegory written by a member of the Roman church early in the second century) is then said to be worthy to be read in church but not to be included among the apostolic writings. Its character might have entitled it to a place among the *prophetic* writings, but its date was too recent for that to be possible.

It is sometimes said that the criterion which the early Christians applied in deciding whether a book was to be regarded as canonical or not was that of apostolic authorship. Now, it is certain that apostolic authorship counted for very much. It was for this reason that such a flood of apocryphal literature appears in the second century bearing the names of various apostles—Gospels, Acts, Epistles, and Apocalypses. The intention certainly was to win respect for these books by putting them forth under such authoritative names. And there is no example of a certainly apostolic writing being refused canonical recognition, except among people like the Marcionites. But apostolic authorship, though an important factor, was not the only ground of canonicity. It is probably a mistake to think that we owe the presence of the Epistle to the Hebrews in our Bibles entirely to the happy accident that it was popularly ascribed to Paul. For, after all, two of the Gospels bear the names of men who were not apostles, and yet that did not stand in the way of accepting Mark and Luke as equally inspired with Matthew and John. True, Mark and Luke were 'apostolic men'—close companions of the apostles—but their Gospels won such early and widespread acceptation just because they bore the convincing marks of real authority. When our Lord asked the Pharisees whether John's baptism was carried out by divine or human authority and they professed themselves unable to answer, He would not tell them the source of His own authority. In other words, if they could not tell divine authority when they saw it, no argument or sign would convince them of it. The early Christians were not

---

[1] See p. 261. It also adds the Wisdom of Solomon (see p. 169).

exceptionally intelligent people, but they did have the capacity to recognize divine authority when they saw it. And that they judged wisely in distinguishing the canonical writings from the uncanonical will be apparent to anyone who compares the New Testament with other early Christian literature.

In the case of some books the apostolic or quasi-apostolic authorship was disputed, but there was a tendency to give the benefit of the doubt to a book whose contents were in keeping with the apostolic faith. The fact that a book received general canonical recognition among the churches in various parts of the Christian world was also a point in its favour.

One important practical question may be noticed here; some direction had to be given about the public reading of books in church. It is plain that the number of books that might be read in church was larger than the number of those which were to be accounted canonical. Just as the sixth Anglican Article of Religion permits the Old Testament Apocrypha to be read 'for example of life and instruction of manners' but not as part of the rule of faith, so in the Early Church several books were read for public edification which were never really regarded as divinely authoritative. In days when books were few and each copy had to be reproduced separately by hand, it was natural that some books would, for general convenience, be read at public gatherings of Christians which would nowadays be read at home. This may help to explain why early manuscript copies of the Scriptures have such books bound in with the canonical ones. Thus the *Codex Sinaiticus* included the Epistle of Barnabas and the *Shepherd* of Hermas; the *Codex Alexandrinus* had the letter which Clement wrote on behalf of the Roman church to the Corinthian church about A.D. 95, the ancient Christian homily conventionally called the Second Epistle of Clement, and the 'Psalms of Solomon', a collection of Jewish hymns of the first century B.C. A work called the 'Gospel of Peter' was read in a church near Antioch about A.D. 190 in all innocence until the bishop of Antioch discovered that it was an heretical document. Possibly the readers and hearers honestly imagined that it was really a narrative by the Apostle Peter himself.

It is evident that at an early time New Testament books were read in church meetings along with the books of the Old Testament. Justin Martyr, about the middle of the second century, says that the 'memoirs of the apostles' were read in Christian gatherings on Sundays along with the 'writings of the prophets'.[1]

[1] *First Apology*, chap. 67.

Another practical consideration grew out of the disputes with heretics. In these disputes what books could be appealed to as undoubtedly authoritative? And yet another arose when the last great persecution of Christians under the Roman Empire broke out in A.D. 303. In this persecution an attempt was made to destroy the Christian Scriptures, and church officials were visited by the imperial police and ordered to hand over their sacred books. To hand over copies of Holy Scriptures for destruction was, in the Christians' eyes, as bad as outright apostasy; but it was tempting to hand over other Christian books in the belief that the police would not know the difference. In this way a practical distinction might be made between books which must not be handed over on any account and books which perhaps *might* be handed over. But this had no practical importance for the fixing of the canon; by this time there was general agreement about the limits of the canon. It merely served to make those limits more widely known among the generality of Christians.

Origen,[1] about A.D. 230, enumerates in the list of New Testament books the four Gospels, Acts, Paul's thirteen epistles, 1 Peter, 1 John and Revelation, as those which are acknowledged by all Christians; he adds that Hebrews, 2 Peter, 2 and 3 John, James and Jude, with the 'Epistle of Barnabas', the *Shepherd* of Hermas, the *Didachē*, and the 'Gospel according to the Hebrews' were disputed by some. This means simply that all the churches by his time were in agreement about the canonical quality of most of the New Testament books, but that a few doubted some of the less well-known epistles, while others were inclined to include some books which did not secure a permanent place in the canon. Eusebius,[2] early in the fourth century, mentions all the books of the New Testament as generally acknowledged except James, Jude, 2 Peter, 2 and 3 John. These, he says, were still disputed by some Christians, but recognized by the majority. The first known list of the twenty-seven books which we recognize appears in the Festal Letter written by Athanasius, bishop of Alexandria, to the churches when announcing the date of Easter in A.D. 367.[3] Shortly afterwards we find Jerome and Augustine in the west defining the canon by listing these same twenty-seven books.

What is particularly important to notice is that the New Testament canon was not demarcated by the arbitrary decree of any

---

[1] Quoted by Eusebius, *Hist. Eccl.* VI. 25.   [2] *Hist. Eccl.* III. 25.
[3] Athanasius classes the *Didachē* (or *Teaching of the Twelve Apostles*) and the *Shepherd* of Hermas along with Wisdom, Ecclesiasticus, Esther, Tobit and Judith as outside the canon but useful for edification. See p. 101.

Church Council. When at last a Church Council—the Synod of Hippo in A.D. 393—listed the twenty-seven books of the New Testament, it did not confer upon them any authority which they did not already possess, but simply recorded their previously established canonicity.[1] As Dr. Foakes-Jackson puts it: 'The Church assuredly did not make the New Testament; the two grew up together'.[2] We may well believe that those early Christians acted by a wisdom higher than their own in this matter, not only in what they accepted, but in what they rejected. Divine authority is by its very nature self-evidencing; and one of the profoundest doctrines recovered by the Reformers is the doctrine of the inward witness of the Holy Spirit, by which testimony is borne within the believer's heart to the divine character of Holy Scripture. This witness is not confined to the individual believer, but is also accessible to the believing community; and there is no better example of its operation than in the recognition by the members of the Early Church of the books which were given by inspiration of God to stand alongside the books of the Old Covenant, the Bible of Christ and His apostles, and with them to make up the written Word of God.

[1] The ruling of the Synod of Hippo was re-promulgated four years later by the Third Synod of Carthage.

[2] *A History of Church History* (1939), p. 21.

CHAPTER IX

THE TEXT OF THE OLD TESTAMENT

EARLY in 1948 there was announced the discovery of several ancient manuscripts in Palestine, a discovery to which sober and distinguished scholars applied adjectives like 'sensational' and 'phenomenal'—words not generally employed in the world of scholarship. Of these manuscripts the one which excited greatest interest was a complete parchment scroll of the book of Isaiah in Hebrew. When this roll was examined by experts of the American Schools of Oriental Research, it was seen at once to be older by far than any roll of Hebrew scripture hitherto known. Professor Millar Burrows of Yale University assigned it to the first century B.C.;[1] Professor W. F. Albright, of Johns Hopkins University, put it even earlier, 'about the second century B.C.'[2] Professor Albright seems at first to have based his estimate on a comparison between the scripts of this newly discovered roll and of an early copy of the Ten Commandments in Hebrew, the Nash Papyrus, belonging to Cambridge University Library.[3] He holds that the Nash Papyrus is 'late Maccabaean, from the first century B.C.', and the script of the Isaiah roll is 'materially older than that of the Nash Papyrus.' Further evidence has confirmed his dating of the Isaiah scroll.

In the following years further manuscript discoveries were made in the same area, the district known as Qumran, north-west of the Dead Sea. These manuscripts have come to be known popularly as the 'Dead Sea Scrolls'.[4] This is not the place to enter into details about them; suffice it to say that they represent the surviving fragments of the library of a Jewish community—probably a community of Essenes—which had its headquarters in that region for about two centuries, roughly from 130 B.C. to A.D.

---

[1] As reported in *The Biblical Archæologist*, May, 1948, pp. 21 ff.

[2] Professor Albright gives his account in the *Bulletin of the American Schools of Oriental Research*, April, 1948, pp. 2 f.

[3] The Nash papyrus contains the Decalogue (Deut. 5. 6-21) followed by the words: 'The statutes and the judgments which Moses commanded the [children of Israel] in the wilderness when they came out of the land of Egypt: "Hear, O Israel, YHWH our God is one YHWH, and thou shalt [love YHWH] thy God with all thy heart, and with all thy soul, and with all thy might".' (Cf. Deut. 6. 1, 4, 5.)

[4] See my *Second Thoughts on the Dead Sea Scrolls*, 2nd edition (London, 1961).

70. From the forty thousand inscribed fragments recovered from caves in the Qumran region, some five hundred books have been reconstructed (many of them in a sadly incomplete condition); of these five hundred books about one hundred are books of the Old Testament in Hebrew. Some of the Old Testament books are represented several times over; the only Old Testament book not represented at all is Esther.

Much work of the highest importance for Biblical studies remains to be done on these manuscripts. Our business is to consider why scholars were so excited when they began to be discovered. Simply stated, the reason for their excitement was that these Biblical manuscripts were a thousand years older than the oldest Hebrew Biblical rolls or codices previously known.

The New Testament, of course, was written when the Old Testament was already complete. But we had extant copies of the Greek New Testament far older than any extant copies of the Hebrew Old Testament. We had copies of the Greek New Testament written in the fourth century A.D., very substantial fragments dating from the third century, and some pieces which had survived from the second century. But when we turned to our earliest copies of the Hebrew Bible, we found them separated by a much greater space of time from the autographs. The Revisers' Preface to the Old Testament (1884) mentions in a footnote that 'the earliest MS. of which the age is certainly known bears date A.D. 916.' This is a codex of the Prophets at Leningrad. Another very early Hebrew MS. at Leningrad (very early, that is to say, as Hebrew MSS. go) is a codex of the whole Old Testament belonging to the first decade of the eleventh century. Oxford possesses an almost complete codex of the Hebrew Old Testament nearly as old as this. In a synagogue at Aleppo there was, until 1948, a codex of the whole Hebrew Bible written probably early in the tenth century. This codex was lost, and it was feared that it had been destroyed, in disturbances attendant upon the establishment of the State of Israel and the fighting in Palestine in that year. However, it was announced in 1958 that, although it had suffered some damage, it had survived its adventures and was in safe keeping. This was indeed good news because, of all the Hebrew Biblical manuscripts produced just before and after A.D. 900, the Aleppo codex is regarded as the most valuable. Scholars of the Hebrew University of Jerusalem have launched an ambitious 'Bible project' which has as its first assignment the preparation of a critical text of the Hebrew Bible on the basis of this codex. Older still is a codex of the Hebrew Pentateuch in the British Museum, usually dated in the ninth century, and a Cairo codex of the Prophets, completed in A.D. 895.

The reason for the relatively late date of these very important Hebrew MSS is not far to seek. It is largely bound up with the almost superstitious veneration with which the Rabbis regarded the actual copies of Holy Scripture. When these were too old and worn to be of any further use for ordinary reading purposes, they were reverently interred. It was better, they thought, to give them honourable burial than to allow the risk that the name of God inscribed upon them might be profaned by the improper use of the material. Before they were taken to consecrated ground for burial they were stored for a shorter or longer time in what is called a *genizah*—a room attached to the synagogue where documents no longer in use were stowed away or hidden (*genizah* literally means a 'hiding place').

One such *genizah*, by some happy chance, continued to house its literary contents for hundreds of years, until they were discovered and made available to Hebrew scholars in the second half of last century. This was the *genizah* of a synagogue in Old Cairo, which has in recent years formed the subject of a fascinating book by Dr. Paul Kahle—*The Cairo Geniza* (the British Academy Schweich Lectures in Biblical Archæology for 1941).[1] Among the other treasures which this old store-room contained were many portions of Hebrew Scripture belonging to a period older than those already mentioned. These and other documents found in the *genizah* have greatly added to our knowledge of the condition of the text of the Old Testament in the centuries before A.D. 900.

It was not only wear and tear, however, that led to the removal of old copies of the Hebrew Bible. We know that in the centuries preceding A.D. 900 Jewish scholars were at work on the Hebrew Bible, doing their best to safeguard the purity of the text. They set themselves to consider variant readings found in the manuscripts at their disposal and to decide between them. About A.D. 100 they produced a standard edition of the consonantal text of the Old Testament. Then, in order to safeguard the proper understanding and interpretation of this text, succeeding generations of editors affixed to it a large number of signs calculated to guide readers in the synagogues in the right enunciation of the sacred writings—punctuation marks as well as vowel points, since Hebrew

---

[1] A second and much enlarged edition appeared in 1959. It is to the second edition that reference is made in this book, except where otherwise indicated.

ISAIAH SCROLL COL. 33 = ISA. 40. 2-28
(Page 114)

was no longer a living vernacular. They further supplied a large body of notes on the text, the longer notes being placed at the beginning and end of the MSS., and the shorter notes written in the margins.

These editors did not carry out their work according to the strict canons of what we nowadays call Textual Criticism. Their business rather was to study and edit the text of the Hebrew Bible found in the copies available to them in the light of the authoritative traditions which had been handed down to them through successive generations of teachers. It is from this concern with tradition that these editors received the name by which they are generally known—Masoretes. This name is derived from the Hebrew word *māsōrāh*, 'tradition'; and the text which the Masoretes established on the basis of their studies is similarly known as the 'Masoretic' text.[1]

It must not be thought that in their devotion to traditional interpretation these Masoretes took liberties with the sacred text. On the contrary, they treated it with the greatest imaginable reverence, and devised a complicated system of safeguards against scribal slips. They counted, for example, the number of times each letter of the alphabet occurs in each book; they pointed out the middle letter of the Pentateuch and the middle letter of the whole Hebrew Bible, and made even more detailed calculations than these. 'Everything countable seems to be counted', says Dr. Wheeler Robinson;[2] and they made up mnemonics by which the various totals might be readily remembered.

When the Masoretic text was finally established by these means, it appears that previous copies of the Scriptures were withdrawn from use and consigned to *genizoth* as a preliminary step to interment. The final recension of the Masoretic text became the standard for all subsequent copies of the Hebrew Bible, whether in manuscript form or in printed editions. Of course, with the best care in the world a few variations have crept into the text in the course of its being copied and recopied by hand and at the press during the last thousand years. For centuries printed editions of the Hebrew Bible followed the text of an edition printed in 1524-5 under the editorship of a Hebrew Christian called Jacob Ben Chayyim. But Dr. Kahle has pointed out that Ben Chayyim's text depended on manuscripts not earlier than the fourteenth

---

[1] From *massōrāh*, a variant spelling of the Hebrew word, the English words are also frequently spelt 'Massoretes' and 'Massoretic'.

[2] *Ancient and English Versions of the Bible* (1940), p. 29.

century. The third edition of R. Kittel's *Biblia Hebraica* (published at Stuttgart in 1937) shows a text prepared by Dr. Kahle on the basis of the Leningrad copy of the complete Old Testament dated 1008-9. This copy is closely related to the Aleppo copy already mentioned (which was not available to Dr. Kahle). In addition to this Leningrad copy Dr. Kahle availed himself of photographs of the ancient codex of the Pentateuch in the British Museum and the Cairo codex of the Prophets, both of which date from the closing years of the ninth century. These copies, together with the Leningrad codex of the Prophets, represent the text established by members of a Masoretic family of Tiberias in Palestine—the Ben Asher family. On the basis of these early copies a more accurate edition of the Masoretic text was produced than any previously printed.

More recently the British and Foreign Bible Society has published a new edition of the Hebrew Bible, edited by Dr. Norman H. Snaith of Leeds (1958). Dr. Snaith's aim was to reproduce as far as possible the Ben Asher text. The manuscripts which he chiefly used, however, were manuscripts of Spanish provenance in the British Museum; the resultant text, however, is substantially the same as Dr. Kahle's. The measure of agreement between the two editions is reassuring when we consider that the two editors worked along different lines. The treasures found in the Cairo *genizah* included portions of the Hebrew Bible antedating this final Masoretic recension, and these revealed something of the lengthy process of Masoretic work on the text of the Old Testament. There were Masoretes at work in Babylonia as well as at Tiberias in the centuries preceding A.D. 900, although the form which ultimately prevailed was the form established at Tiberias. There is reason to think that the Masoretes were stimulated in their activities in the eighth and ninth centuries by the example of Muslim scholars who had already done similar work for the text and pronunciation of the Qur'an.

Of the signs or 'points' added by the Masoretes to the consonantal text of the Hebrew Scriptures, some denoted the vowel-sounds, since the Hebrew alphabet contained only consonants. Others indicated the punctuation, and others showed the reader when he had to pronounce something different from the text which lay before him. There are several places in the Old Testament where one word is written (*kĕthībh*, as it is called) and quite another word publicly read (*qĕrē*). For example, we are told in Judges 18. 30 that the priest who functioned at the sanctuary in Dan,

where there was a graven image, was a grandson of Moses (see
R.V.). But, centuries before the time of the Masoretes, this was
felt to be such a scandalous state of affairs that those who revered
the name of Moses preferred not to draw public attention to it.
The synagogue reader was therefore directed to say 'Manasseh'
instead of 'Moses' when he came to this verse. And lest he should
forget, the letter N was inserted between M and S—not actually
on the line, but suspended. We might represent the resulting
appearance of the Hebrew consonantal text מנשה by the English
letters MNSH. The consonants of 'Moses' are משה MSH; those
of 'Manasseh' are מנשה MNSH; and by inserting the suspended
N into MSH these pious scribes spared the embarrassment of
readers and hearers. It was not that they wanted these people to
think that the idolatrous priest in question was really the son of
Manasseh and not of Moses; in that case they would have written
the inserted N on the line instead of suspending it. But they did
suggest that this priest's behaviour made him a fitter associate of
the wicked king Manasseh, or of the Manasseh who built the
schismatic temple on Mount Gerizim, than of Moses, the man of
God. When the Masoretes came to affix vowel points to this
word, the vowels which they added were those of 'Manasseh', not
of 'Moses'—that is to say, in accordance with their regular procedure, they added the vowels of the word which the synagogue
reader had to pronounce.

One permanent differentiation of the kĕthībh (the written
text) from the qĕrē (the word to be read) concerns the Divine
Name which we know as Jehovah. In the consonantal text of the
Hebrew Bible this word is written with four consonants יהוה
which we may represent by YHWH. In the later centuries B.C.
this name came to be regarded with such veneration that it ceased
to be used. The Third Commandment enjoins: 'Thou shalt not
take the name of YHWH thy God in vain, for YHWH will not
hold him guiltless that taketh His name in vain'. Primarily this
may be a warning against perjury, though we need not limit its
scope to perjury in the technical sense. The *Westminster Shorter
Catechism* is no doubt right in affirming that this Commandment
'requireth the holy and reverent use of God's names, titles, attributes,
ordinances, word, and works' and 'forbiddeth all profaning or
abusing of any thing whereby God maketh himself known'. The
ancient Jews felt something like this, and decided that the best
way of avoiding the unworthy use of the Divine Name was not to
use it at all. At first, probably, they gave up using it in ordinary

conversation; then they even gave up using it when reading the
Scriptures aloud, and substituted a term like 'Lord' or 'God' in
its place. This was already the custom when the Hebrew Scriptures
began to be translated into Greek in the third century B.C., for in
that translation (the Septuagint) the name YHWH is not rendered
as a proper name but represented by the Greek word for 'Lord'
(kyrios) or 'God' (theos).[1] It is said that the only occasion on which
it was actually pronounced in those days was when the High Priest
uttered it on his annual entry into the Holy of Holies in the Temple
on the Great Day of Atonement; and that practice came to an end
with the destruction of the Temple in A.D. 70. So the original
pronunciation seems to have been forgotten among the Jews.
At any rate, when the editors of whom we have been speaking
affixed vowel signs to the Hebrew consonants for the guidance
of readers, there would have been no point in any case in attaching
the proper vowel signs to the consonants YHWH, as the word
was not to be pronounced. What they did was to attach to the
consonants YHWH the vowel signs of the word that was to be
read in its place, whether of 'Adōnāy ('Lord') or of 'Elōhīm ('God').
When the knowledge of Hebrew was revived in Western Europe
from the twelfth century onwards, it was not realized at first
that the consonants YHWH were accompanied by the vowels of
another word, and an attempt was made to read the consonants
YHWH or JHVH along with the vowels of 'Adōnāy; the result
was the hybrid form 'Jehovah', which was introduced by William
Tyndale into English,[2] where it has become thoroughly naturalized.
What the original Hebrew vowels of the name were is a matter
of some debate, although it is usually considered that they were
a and e, the word being pronounced Yahweh. There is adequate
evidence that this was how it was pronounced in the early Christian
centuries among the Samaritans and others who did not share the
Jewish scruples about uttering it. There is further evidence in the
Old Testament that it was also current in the abbreviated forms
Yahu and Yah (cf. Psa. 68. 4, R.V.; 'His name is JAH').

Some of the divisions which appear in copies of the Hebrew
Bible were fixed by the end of the Masoretic period. The division
into verses is quite early; it can be traced back to the early centuries
of the Christian era. There were fluctuations of practice with

[1] In a fragmentary papyrus roll of the Greek Deuteronomy in Cairo (p Fouad 266),
dating from the second century B.C., the name YHWH is written untranslated in square
Hebrew characters. It was so written also in Aquila's Greek version (see p. 152). But the
instructed Greek reader knew to pronounce it kyrios or theos.

[2] Ancient and English Versions of the Bible, pp. 165 f.

regard to verse division in various centres; the standard division of the Old Testament into verses which has come down to our own day and is found in most translations as well as in the Hebrew original was fixed by the Masoretic family of Ben Asher about A.D. 900. This system divides the thirty-nine books of the Old Testament (as we reckon them) into 23,100 verses. The Hebrew text of the Bible is also divided into paragraphs which correspond to the natural sense; and the Pentateuch bears marks indicating the sections into which it was divided for the purpose of synagogue lessons. There were two such systems—an older one, used in Palestine, which divided the Pentateuch into 154 lessons, sufficient to last throughout a three years' cycle; and a later one, used in Babylonia, dividing the Pentateuch into fifty-four sections to serve as lessons for a one-year cycle. The former sections are called *sĕdārīm* (singular *sēder*) and the latter are called *pārāshiyyōth* (singular *pārāshāh*). The latter, Babylonian, system finally prevailed and is used to the present time in synagogues throughout the world.

The division into chapters on the other hand, is much later, and probably was first carried through by Cardinal Hugh of St. Cher in 1244.

It may be thought that we have a much slenderer guarantee of the accurate transmission of the Hebrew text of the Old Testament than of the Greek text of the New Testament, in view of the late date of our principal Hebrew MSS. But the conditions in which the Hebrew text was transmitted give us ground for greater confidence than might be supposed. We have already mentioned the meticulous care which the scribes and Masoretes took to avoid errors in copying. The Masoretes did not disturb the consonantal text which had been handed down to them; they simply added vowel-points, accents, and other signs and notes to aid in the interpretation of the consonantal text and to give guidance in reading it. Although there were no doubt some variations in the text of the MSS. which the Masoretes used, there cannot have been many. The available evidence suggests that there has been little change or variation in the consonantal text since the time of Rabbi Aqiba, early in the second century A.D. This is borne out by the Biblical quotations in the Mishnah (*c.* A.D. 200) and the Gemaras of Palestine (*c.* A.D. 350) and Babylonia (*c.* A.D. 500[1]), by the fragments of Origen's transliteration of the Hebrew in Column 2 of the Hexapla (*c.* A.D. 240[2]), as also by the character of the text

[1] See p. 37.   [2] See p. 155.

paraphrased or translated in the Aramaic Targums[1] and in the Greek version of Aquila.[2]

About A.D. 400 Jerome translated the Old Testament into Latin directly from Hebrew.[3] His translation, together with references made to the original text of Old Testament passages in some of his other writings, is thus a witness to the character of the Hebrew text 500 years before the Masoretes had concluded their work. Still earlier in the Christian era is the Syriac version of the Old Testament which we are to consider in Chapter XV. And from the last three centuries B.C. we have the Greek translation of the Old Testament called the Septuagint. Although, as we shall see in Chapter XII, the Septuagint text sometimes deviates from the Masoretic text and occasionally helps us to correct it, yet in general it confirms that no serious changes were introduced into the text of the Old Testament during the thousand years and more between the time when this translation was made and the time to which our chief Hebrew MSS. belong.

A still earlier witness, so far as the Pentateuch is concerned, is the Samaritan Bible, which is restricted to these five books. As we shall learn in Chapter X, the variations between the Samaritan Pentateuch and the Masoretic edition of these books are quite insignificant by comparison with the area of agreement.

The roll of Isaiah mentioned at the beginning of this chapter exhibits a text which is closer to the Masoretic text than to the Septuagint. It differs from the Masoretic text especially in matters of spelling[4] and grammatical forms, but also to some extent in wording. The variants in wording are due for the most part to the substitution of familiar for less familiar words. But this means that the newly discovered manuscript ('Isaiah A', as it is called) presupposes a text similar but inferior to the traditional consonantal text preserved by the Masoretes.

There are several places where the 1952 Revised Standard Version of the Old Testament adopts readings of 'Isaiah A.' One is in Isa. 21. 8, where the puzzling Masoretic reading (A.V., 'And he cried, A lion'; R.V., 'And he cried as a lion') is replaced by 'Then he who saw cried'—a reading hitherto known from no Hebrew manuscript, but frequently suggested as an emendation (the difference being between Heb. *haro'eh*, 'he who sees,' and *'aryeh*, 'a lion').

---

[1] See pp. 133 ff.   [2] See p. 152.   [3] See p. 205.

[4] It makes much more use of letters of the Hebrew alphabet to represent vowels (cf. p. 41) than the Masoretic text does.

An incomplete scroll of Isaiah, found along with the other in the first Qumran cave, and conveniently distinguished as 'Isaiah B', agrees even more closely with the Masoretic text. Both 'Isaiah A' and 'Isaiah B' agree with the Septuagint in reading the opening words of Isa. 53. 11 as 'Out of the travail of his soul shall he see light.'

As the Biblical manuscripts from Qumran have been studied, it has become possible to distinguish three main types of text among them. One is the ancestor of the consonantal text which formed the basis of the Masoretes' editorial work. Another is the type of text which must have lain before the men who produced the Greek translation commonly called the Septuagint in the last three centuries B.C. And a third type, confined to the first five books of the Old Testament, is closely related to the Samaritan Pentateuch. These three text types were probably of Babylonian, of Egyptian, and of Palestinian provenance respectively. In addition to manuscripts which can immediately be classified under one or another of these three, there are some which exhibit a mixed type of text, and others which may belong to textual traditions not yet identified.

A relatively well preserved manuscript of the books of Samuel from the fourth cave at Qumran is exceptionally interesting. It is generally recognized that the books of Samuel formed one of the principal sources used by the author of Chronicles in his later writing of the history of Israel. This particular manuscript from Qumran is said to exhibit a text of Samuel closer to that which the Chronicler must have known than it is to the Masoretic text.

We have now ample reason to recognize that when Rabbi Aqiba and his colleagues published a standard text of the Hebrew Bible at the beginning of the second century A.D., the one which they published—the ancestor of the Masoretic text—was the best one available to them. Before their time, as the Qumran evidence indicates, Biblical manuscripts of various text types were used indiscriminately by Palestinian Jews. From their time forth, the use of other Hebrew text types ceased. It is instructive to contrast the variety of text types represented at Qumran (belonging to the generations before A.D. 70) with the situation in other caves in the Wadi Murabba'at and the En-gedi region, farther south along the west shore of the Dead Sea. These caves have yielded manuscripts from the period A.D. 132-135, when they were used as hideouts by Jewish insurgent forces in the second revolt against the Romans. Like the Qumran manuscripts, these include pieces of Biblical texts, but unlike the Qumran Biblical manuscripts, these exhibit one uniform type of Hebrew Biblical text—the type recently established by Aqiba and his colleagues.

Before the discovery of the Qumran manuscripts Sir Frederic Kenyon asked what he called a 'great, indeed all-important question' with regard to the traditional text of the Hebrew Bible. It was this: 'Does this Hebrew text, which we call Masoretic, and which we have shown to descend from a text drawn up about A.D. 100, faithfully represent the Hebrew text as originally written by the authors of the Old Testament books?'[1] The Qumran discoveries have enabled us to answer this question in the affirmative with much greater assurance than was possible before 1948.[2]

---

[1] *Our Bible and the Ancient Manuscripts*, 4th edition (1939), p. 47.

[2] I have dealt with this subject more fully in 'Qumran and the Old Testament', *Faith and Thought* 91 (1959), pp. 9 ff., and in *Second Thoughts on the Dead Sea Scrolls*, 2nd edition (1961), pp. 61 ff.

CHAPTER X

THE SAMARITAN PENTATEUCH

THE rivalry between Jews and Samaritans was not a growth of yesterday in New Testament times. Its roots run far down into the earliest days of the Israelite settlement in Canaan. The Joseph tribes in Central Canaan were separated from the tribe of Judah in the south by a belt of Canaanite territory, and in particular by the Jebusite fortress of Jerusalem, which did not pass into Israelite hands until the reign of David. The northern and central tribes (collectively called Israel in the narrower sense which excludes Judah) had little to do with Judah until the reign of David. David, himself a member of the tribe of Judah, became king over Judah immediately after the death of King Saul (*c.* 1000 B.C.) and a few years later, on the death of Saul's son Ishbaal, he became king over Israel as well. From that time Israel and Judah formed a united monarchy until the end of Solomon's reign, but even so they were uneasy bedfellows. In David's reign we read of an abortive attempt by Sheba the son of Bichri to engineer a revolt of the northern portion of the kingdom. His rallying cry is very similar to that which gave the signal for the disruption of the united kingdom after Solomon's death: 'We have no portion in David, neither have we inheritance in the son of Jesse: every man to his tents, O Israel' (2 Samuel 20. 1). And at his call, we read, 'all the men of Israel went up from following David, and followed Sheba, the son of Bichri: but the men of Judah clave unto their king, from Jordan even to Jerusalem' (2 Sam. 20. 2). If Solomon let Judah off more lightly than Israel in the matter of taxation (1 Kings 4. 7-19), that will have helped to accentuate the feeling of cleavage; and when the tribes came to elect their new king after Solomon's death, it was no difficult matter for Jeroboam to detach Israel from Solomon's son, Rehoboam, who was left with Judah and the small tribe of Benjamin, which was easily controlled from Jerusalem. The breach remained unhealed. When Omri, king of the northern realm, made Samaria his capital, the name of the capital came to be extended to the country as a whole, which was thus called the kingdom of Samaria, while the term 'Samaritans' came to be applied not only to the population of the city but in a wider sense to the population of the whole northern kingdom. In the eighth century B.C. the northern kingdom was incorporated in two stages into the Assyrian Empire. In 732 the territory north of the Plain of Jezreel and east of Jordan was overrun by Tiglath-pileser III, and many of the inhabitants were deported to other parts of the Assyrian Empire; eleven years later a similar fate befell the remainder of the kingdom of Israel at the beginning of the reign of Sargon II.[1] Sargon tells how he removed 27,290 people from Samaria, and in 2 Kings 17. 24-41 we are told of the colonists whom the Assyrian kings sent to take the place of the deportees, and how they intermarried with the people left in the land, which was now organized as the Assyrian province of Samaria. Although these colonists at first worshipped their own gods, they ultimately gave up their idolatrous worship and worshipped Jehovah, as did the native Samaritans.[2] In the closing centuries B.C. the Samaritans were as free from idol worship as the Jews.

Later on, the kingdom of Judah was brought to an end (587 B.C.) by Nebuchadrezzar, king of Babylon, who deported the nobility and large sections of the population of Judah to Mesopotamia. When some of these returned by the permission of the kings of Persia and began to reorganize the Jewish polity, the Samaritans and others who had not gone into exile offered to co-operate with them, but their offer was turned down. Being refused a part in the temple-worship at Jerusalem, the Samaritans, about 400 B.C., built their own temple on Mount Gerizim, near the ancient sanctuary of Shechem. To this place the woman of Sychar referred when she said to Jesus: 'Our fathers worshipped in this mountain' (John 4. 20). The Samaritan worship was condemned by the Jews as schismatic, and though the Samaritans were worshippers of Jehovah, the Jews exaggerated the foreign element in their population by calling them Cuthaeans (Cuthah being one of the cities from which the Assyrians had sent colonists to Samaria). The Samaritans were confirmed in possession of their temple on Mount Gerizim under Alexander the Great and his successors.[3] When the Hasmonaeans[4] had established their

---

[1] The siege of Samaria (2 Kings 17. 5) was begun while Shalmaneser V of Assyria was on the throne, but by the time the city was stormed Sargon II (cf. Isa. 20. 1) had superseded him.

[2] After the fall of Samaria, the Judæan kings Hezekiah and Josiah attempted to reunite the northern population with Judah—in a religious unity, at any rate, which in those days could hardly be dissociated from political unity (2 Chron. 30. 1 ff.; 35. 17).

[3] To this period (c. 180 B.C.) belong the words of Jesus ben Sira (Ecclesiasticus 50. 25, 26):
'With two nations is my soul vexed,
And the third is no nation:
They that sit upon the mountain of Seir, and the Philistines,
And that foolish people that dwells in Shechem.'

[4] Judas Maccabæus and his successors, who ruled Judæa till the Romans added it to their empire in 63 B.C.

power in Judah in the middle of the second century B.C., they embarked on a policy of extension northwards. About 108 B.C., John Hyrcanus overran the province of Samaria, and demolished the hated temple on Mount Gerizim, but the Samaritans remained Samaritans, and their sentiments towards the Jews grew no more affectionate for the destruction of their temple.

The Samaritans were relieved of Jewish domination when the Romans established their power in Palestine. They survived as an Israelite group (though repudiated by orthodox Jewry) for many centuries in a variety of centres. To this day, a small remnant has survived in Palestine. They have preserved their ancient traditions and worship at the place called Nablus, near the ancient Shechem, where some 250 of them still live; another fifty or so live at Tel-Aviv.

The Samaritans regard the Pentateuch alone as canonical, and they have preserved a text of these five books in Hebrew which has been transmitted independently of the Masoretic text. This may suggest that the Samaritan Pentateuch has an independent history going back to the time when Israel and Judah had no canon apart from the five books of the Law. At any rate, we may safely take it that the Samaritan Pentateuch has come down along a separate line of transmission since the founding of the Gerizim temple about 400 B.C. It is obviously a most important early witness to the text of the Pentateuch.

The Samaritan Pentateuch was known to some of the Church Fathers, such as Eusebius and Jerome. Interest in it was revived after the Reformation, and first-hand knowledge of it was brought to Western Europe early in the seventeenth century, when a copy bought from the Samaritan community in Damascus was placed in the library of the Oratory at Paris. In our own islands that great Biblical scholar, Archbishop James Ussher, of Armagh, procured six manuscripts of the Samaritan Pentateuch from the East. Since those days a number of other copies have reached Western Europe. There are also several in Leningrad, which possesses the largest collection of Samaritan MSS. in Europe. But the most interesting, if not the most important, manuscript of the Samaritan Pentateuch is a parchment roll in the possession of the Samaritans. The Samaritans themselves ascribe to it a quite impossible antiquity, for they take literally the words of its colophon (or scribal tailpiece), which makes the remarkable claim:

'I Abisha‘,[1] son of Phinehas, son of Eleazar, son of Aaron the priest (to

[1] This Abisha‘ is the Abishua of 1 Chron. 6. 4, 5, 50; Ezra 7. 5.

them be the favour of the Lord and His glory)—I have written this holy scroll at the gate of the tent of assembly on Mount Gerizim the house of God, in the thirteenth year of the settlement of the children of Israel in the land of Canaan. I thank the Lord'.

The Samaritan community possesses other early copies of the Pentateuch, but this is regarded by them as their chief treasure. Of course, if the claim that it was written by Aaron's great grandson were true (as they believe), it would lend powerful support to their contention that they, and not the Jews, are in the true succession from Moses and Aaron, that Gerizim, and not Jerusalem, is the place chosen by Jehovah out of all the tribes of Israel to place His name there, and that their recension, and not the Masoretic text, is the true representative of the original copy of the Mosaic Law. Indeed, the colophon could have been composed in order to vindicate the authenticity of the Samaritan Pentateuch as against the Jewish edition.[1]

The Abisha' scroll is said to have been rediscovered about the middle of the fourteenth century A.D. For a long time it was difficult to come to any certain conclusion about it, as some of the scholars who were permitted to see it ascribed to it a date not much earlier than the fourteenth century (the time of its rediscovery), while others thought it might be several centuries earlier. At last, in 1952, the mystery was solved, when the complete scroll was photographed for a Spanish Hebraist, Professor F. Pérez Castro. It speedily became plain that it was not a homogeneous scroll— that the end of it (from Numbers 35 onwards) was certainly old, possibly, as Professor Castro thinks, as old as the eleventh century A.D., but that the remainder was a much later manuscript, attached to the older part. Then it was recalled that a marginal note in an early fourteenth-century Samaritan chronicle told how once, during an open-air ceremony, a scroll of the Pentateuch was torn from the hands of the priest who was holding it and blown away by a sudden gust of wind. This accident undoubtedly explains the condition of the Abisha' scroll; it was only the end of it, comprising the last two chapters of Numbers and the book of Deuteronomy, that was rediscovered. The remainder had, disappeared irretrievably, and so had to be replaced by a new copy.[2]

---

[1] Professor F. P. Castro, however, regards the colophon as a cryptogram, indicating to the initiated that the scroll was written not in the year 13 from the settlement in the land, but in the year 3013, that is to say, about A.D. 1045, according to the Samaritan reckoning. This would agree well enough with the palæographically probable dating of the older part of the manuscript (*Supplement to Vetus Testamentum* 7 [1960], p. 60).

[2] F. P. Castro, *Séfer Abisha'* (Madrid, 1960); Kahle, *The Cairo Geniza*, 2nd edn. (1959), pp. 67, 154.

The oldest known codex (as distinct from roll) of the Samaritan Pentateuch is in the University Library, Cambridge, and bears a note saying that it was sold in A.D. 1149-50. Dr. Kahle[1] says it may have been written some centuries earlier.

The Samaritan Pentateuch, it is interesting to note, is written in an older form of Hebrew script than that of the Masoretic Bible and Jewish-Hebrew literature in general. Somewhere about 200 B.C. this older, 'palaeo-Hebrew', script was superseded among the Jews by the Aramaic or 'square' character; some of the older Biblical manuscripts from Qumran still show it. The palaeo-Hebrew script is of the same general style as the script found on the Moabite Stone, the Siloam Inscription, and the Lachish Letters, but the script of the Samaritans is a rather more ornamental development of it.[2]

But interesting as the questions of the date and character of the extant MSS. and their script may be, the question of the actual text of the Samaritan Pentateuch is much more important. It has about 6,000 variations from the Masoretic text, and in nearly 2,000 of these it agrees with the Septuagint. Where the Samaritan and Septuagint texts agree against the Masoretic text, there is a *prima facie* case in favour of the former.[3] But most of these variations are of minor significance. The most important Samaritan variants are a few which reveal the fundamental points at issue between the Samaritans and the Jews. The Samaritans liked to emphasize the importance of Shechem and Mount Gerizim; the Jews preferred to tone it down. Thus, where Moses in Deut. 12. 5, etc., speaks of 'the place which Jehovah your God shall choose' (later identified by the Jews with Jerusalem), the Samaritan edition makes him say 'the place which Jehovah your God has chosen' (meaning Mount Gerizim, which has already been specified in Deut. 11. 29 as the place where the blessings are to be pronounced when the Israelites enter Canaan). In Deut. 27. 4-8, where Moses commands that the stones bearing the words of the Law and an altar of unhewn stones are to be set up on Mount Ebal (according to the Masoretic text), the Samaritan text has Gerizim for Ebal. After the statement of the Ten Commandments in Exod. 20. 2-17 and Deut. 5. 6-21 the Samaritan edition inserts a passage to this effect:

'And it shall be that when Jehovah thy God brings thee into the land of the Canaanite whither thou goest to possess it, thou shalt erect for thyself

---

[1] *Op. cit.*, p. 67.   [2] See pp. 32, 36 ff.
[3] Thus both Samaritan and Septuagint texts agree in reading in Gen. 4. 8: 'And Cain said unto Abel his brother, Let us go into the field.' (See p. 157.)

great stones and shalt plaster them with plaster. And thou shalt write upon the stones all the words of this law. And it shall be that, when ye cross over Jordan, ye shall raise up these stones concerning which I command you this day upon Mount Gerizim. And thou shalt build there an altar to Jehovah thy God, an altar of stones: thou shalt lift up no iron upon them. With whole stones shalt thou build the altar of Jehovah thy God and thou shalt offer upon it burnt offerings to Jehovah thy God. And thou shalt sacrifice peace-offerings and shalt eat there and rejoice before Jehovah thy God. That mountain is across Jordan in the direction of the going down of the sun in the land of the Canaanite that dwells in the Arabah over against Gilgal, beside the terebinth of Moreh, over against Shechem'.[1]

They made sure work that there should be no mistake about the identification of the mountain!

Very many instances of variation between the Samaritan and Masoretic texts have to do with matters of grammar and spelling. The Samaritan Pentateuch has a strong tendency to repetition and expansion. If Moses is told to do something, for instance, and the directions are given in detail, it is not enough for the Samaritan text to say that Moses did all that the Lord commanded him; it must be explicitly recorded that Moses carried out every detail, word for word in accordance with the directions. There are also a number of chronological statements where the Samaritan and Masoretic texts differ; in several of these the Septuagint agrees with the Samaritan account.[2]

Before anything was known about the Dead Sea Scrolls, Dr. Kahle expressed the view that 'the Samaritan text is in the main a popular revision of an older text, in which antiquated forms and constructions, not familiar to people of later times, were replaced by forms and constructions easier to be understood, difficulties were removed, parallel passages were inserted'.[3] This judgment was confirmed beyond all expectation with the discovery and study of Biblical manuscripts from Qumran. Some of these manuscripts exhibit a textual type in the Pentateuch which is closer to the Samaritan than to the Masoretic types of text. They do not contain

---

[1] This addition, taken from Deut. 27. 2-7 and 11. 30 (with the substitution of Gerizim for Ebal), is reckoned by the Samaritans as the Tenth Commandment. (What we call the First Commandment is included by them as part of the preamble.)

[2] It is noteworthy that the Samaritan text alone gives figures in connection with the age of Terah in Gen. 11. 26-32 which present *prima facie* agreement with the statement of Stephen in Acts 7. 4 (and of Philo in his treatise *On the Migration of Abraham*, para. 177) that Abraham left Haran after his father's death. There are a few other instances of Old Testament quotations or allusions in the New Testament which agree better with the Samaritan than with the Masoretic or Septuagint texts. This does not mean that the New Testament writers used the Samaritan Pentateuch, but that there were forms of the Greek Old Testament known to them which preserved readings similar to those in the Samaritan recension, but which have not survived.

[3] *The Cairo Geniza*, 1st edition (1947), pp. 147 f.

the passages which reflect the dogmatic Samaritan tendency, but in other respects they agree remarkably with the Samaritan Bible. For example, a fragmentary scroll of Exodus from the fourth cave at Qumran, written in palaeo-Hebrew script, shows all the characteristic Samaritan expansions for the part of the book which has been preserved, apart from the 'sectarian' addition at the end of the Ten Commandments (Ex. 20. 17). The Samaritan Bible is thus shown more clearly to be basically a popular Palestinian type of text, which the Samaritans edited here and there in their own theological interest.

When the knowledge of the Samaritan Pentateuch was first brought to Western Europe, the value of the new discovery was over-estimated. Morinus, for example, who first published the Samaritan text in 1632, regarded it as vastly superior to the Masoretic text. Further critical study, however, has established the definite superiority of the Masoretic text. For one thing, the Samaritan scribes do not appear to have exercised the meticulous care in copying and handing on the text that characterized the Masoretes. While in certain details the Samaritans have preserved a true reading lost by the Jewish text (in which case the true reading has usually been preserved by the Septuagint as well), the chief value of the Samaritan Pentateuch is the witness which it bears to the essential purity of the Masoretic text of the first five books of the Bible.

In addition to the Samaritan Pentateuch, which is an edition of the original Hebrew, the Samaritans have also preserved a version (or Targum) of the Pentateuch in the Samaritan dialect of Aramaic, dating from the early years of the Christian era, and an Arabic version of the Pentateuch, made about the eleventh or twelfth century. They have other literature as well, including a book of Joshua, based on the canonical Joshua, but not regarded as canonical by the Samaritans themselves, and a chronicle carrying their traditional history from Joshua's time down into the Christian era. They have preserved their traditional expectation of the Messiah, whom they call the *Taheb*, or 'Restorer'; they envisage Him primarily as a second Moses—the one of whom Moses said: 'Jehovah thy God will raise up unto thee a prophet from the midst of thee, of thy brethren, like unto me; unto him ye shall hearken' (Deut. 18. 15). They distinguish two main divisions of their history—the period of divine favour (*rahutha*) from Moses to Eli, and the period of divine displeasure (*panutha*) from Eli to the *Taheb*, through whom the divine favour will be restored. It was the *Taheb* that the woman at Jacob's well had in mind when she said, 'I know that Messiah is coming . . . when he comes, he will show us all things' (John 4. 25); and it was with the *Taheb* that Jesus identified Himself when He replied to her, 'I who speak to you am he' (John 4. 26).

CHAPTER XI

THE TARGUMS

IN Chapter IV we looked at an interpretation of Neh. 8. 8 which suggests that this passage is the oldest reference we have to the custom of giving an oral paraphrase or *targum* of the Old Testament Scriptures. The verse runs in the margin of the Revised Version: 'And they read in the book, in the law of God, with an interpretation; and they gave the sense, so that they understood the reading.'

Whether this is the true interpretation of this passage or not (and I believe it is) it is true at any rate that the practice of accompanying the public reading of the Scriptures in the synagogues by an oral paraphrase in the Aramaic vernacular grew up in the closing centuries B.C. Naturally, when Hebrew was becoming less and less familiar to the ordinary people as a spoken language, it was necessary that they should be provided with an interpretation of the text of Scripture in a language which they did know, if they were to understand what was read. The official charged with giving this oral paraphrase was called a *methurgeman* (translator or interpreter) and the paraphrase itself was called a *targum*.[1] It was probably more than a strict translation, embodying a certain amount of interpretative comment. The *methurgeman*, we are told, was not allowed to read his interpretation out of a roll, as the congregation might mistakenly think he was reading the original Scriptures. (Compare the way in which people even to-day attach greater authority to the written than to the spoken word: 'I saw it in black and white', they will say; 'I have it in print'.) With a view to accuracy, no doubt, it was further laid down that not more than one verse of the Pentateuch and not more than three verses of the Prophets might be translated at one time.

In due course these Targums were committed to writing. Considering their origin we might expect a high degree of variants among the various translations of any Biblical passage. In the centuries following A.D. 100, however, when the text and interpretation of the Hebrew Bible were more definitely fixed, two

---

[1] From an old Semitic root: cf. Akkadian *targumanu*, 'interpreter,' 'translator,' with modern *dragoman*.

authoritative Targums appeared, based on the official text and interpretation. One of these was a Targum to the Pentateuch called the Targum of Onqelos;[1] the other was a Targum to the Prophets (Former and Latter) called the Targum of Jonathan ben Uzziel. The former was the more important and authoritative, not only because the Pentateuch was invested with peculiar sanctity in the eyes of the Rabbis, but also because it was the only part of the Bible to be read through continuously in the synagogues; the Prophets were not read in their entirety, but only in selected lessons on sabbaths and festivals.[2]

In addition to these official Targums, which appear in written form among the Babylonian Jews in the fifth century A.D., others of an unofficial character, including a larger element of free comment on the text, circulated among the Jews in the following centuries. Such were the so-called Targum of Pseudo-Jonathan on the Pentateuch, the Palestinian Targum on the Pentateuch, and Targums on the 'Writings' or Hagiographa.[3]

But there were written Targums before those of Onqelos and Jonathan. When we are dealing with translations of sacred books, we regularly find that a fixed and authorized version is preceded by a number of varying and unofficial efforts. We are told of a written Targum of the book of Job which was in existence in the first century A.D.; when it was shown to Gamaliel (the teacher of Paul), he ordered it to be built into the Temple walls, which were not yet completed. As the Temple reached completion in A.D. 63, this gives us a lower limit for the date of this Targum, but we do not know how old it was at this time. Indeed, it was possibly in existence at the time when the Greek (Septuagint) translation of Job was made, for that translation has a note at the end of Job: 'This is translated from the Syrian book', which seems to indicate an Aramaic Targum. Special interest, therefore, was manifested when news was released about the manuscripts discovered in the eleventh cave at Qumran, early in 1956, for among them it was reported that an Aramaic Targum of Job had been identified (although, unfortunately, only the central portions of the scroll

---

[1] *Onqelos* seems to be a corrupt form of Aquila, the name of a Jewish translator of the Scriptures into Greek (see p. 152); it was attached to this Aramaic version through a misunderstanding. The error is the less serious, however, in that both Aquila's Greek translation and the Targum of Onqelos are excessively literal renderings of the Hebrew, carried out in the same spirit.

[2] The lessons from the Prophets are called *haphtārōth* (plural of *haphtārāh*); they followed the lessons from the Pentateuch. Cf. Acts 13. 15, 27.

[3] The Samaritans also had an Aramaic Targum of the Pentateuch; no official version of this was issued, however, so that nearly every manuscript of the Samaritan Targum has to some extent its own text.

had survived). When the text of this Targum is published, we may be able to judge whether this was the Targum which Gamaliel wished to be built into the Temple walls, or even the one used by the Septuagint editors.

The existence of this Targum on Job, for which we have adequate evidence, would in any case make it probable that there were other written Targums even in the pre-Christian period. Here too confirmation has come from Qumran; the fourth cave yielded fragments of a Targum of Leviticus, and the *Genesis Apocryphon* from the first cave certainly contains Targumic passages, and may even be 'an early specimen of a written Aramaic Pentateuch Targum from Palestine'.[1] When the official Targums were published, however, these older Targums would be regarded as obsolete, and their preservation would not be encouraged.

The Targums of Onqelos and Jonathan, while apparently committed to writing in the fifth century A.D., were authorized versions which conformed to the text of the Hebrew Bible established about A.D. 100 and to the official interpretations of the law codified in the Mishnah.[2] But they were not entirely new pieces of work; they would draw largely upon traditional material, while checking and revising it according to the established doctrine of the contemporary leaders in Israel.

Evidence has been forthcoming in recent years, however, of a Targum on the Pentateuch which circulated in Palestine till as late as the tenth century A.D.[3] For some time it was accessible only in fragments (especially from the Cairo *genizah*), but in 1957 its complete text was identified in a manuscript in the Vatican Library (MS. Neofiti 1), which is being edited for publication by a Spanish scholar, Dr. A. Diez Macho. Its language is Palestinian Aramaic of the first century, and therefore excellent evidence for the form of that language known to our Lord and His apostles. It presupposes a Hebrew text of the Pentateuch different in details from the text established at the beginning of the second century, and some of its legal interpretations deviate from those which were fixed in the Mishnah. That this Targum persisted so long in Palestine suggests that the authoritative Targum of Onqelos, which was published in

---

[1] M. Black, *The Scrolls and Christian Origins* (Edinburgh, 1961), p. 193, quoting a suggestion made by Dr. Kahle. J. T. Milik, on the other hand, says that it is 'no true Targum' (*Ten Years of Discovery in the Wilderness of Judæa* [London, 1959], p. 31); but so peremptory a judgment is premature, since most of this scroll is as yet unpublished.

[2] See p. 37.

[3] See M. Black, *An Aramaic Approach to the Gospels and Acts* (1946), pp. 18 ff.; P. E. Kahle, *The Cairo Geniza*, pp. 200 ff.; A. Diez Macho, 'The Recently Discovered Palestinian Targum', *Supplement to Vetus Testamentum* 7 (1960), pp. 222 ff.

Babylonia, may not have been introduced into Palestine long before the tenth century.[1]

The Targum of Onqelos contained little more than straight translation, and very literal translation at that. The old Palestinian Pentateuch Targum contained a good deal of traditional commentary and expansion over and above the bare translation of the Hebrew text. This additional material was not allowed to disappear; the later Targums on the Pentateuch consist of the Targum of Onqelos expanded by much of this old material.

One marked feature of the Targums is their avoidance of the anthropomorphisms which characterize some references to God in the Hebrew text. One frequent device is the use of the phrase 'the word of God' instead of simply 'God'. Thus in Gen. 3. 8, instead of 'they heard the voice of the LORD God walking in the garden', the Targums of Onqelos and Pseudo-Jonathan have 'they heard the voice of the word of the LORD God walking in the garden'. Where the Hebrew text says of Ishmael, 'God was with the lad' (Gen. 21. 20), the Targumic equivalent is: 'the word of God was in aid of the lad'. Edersheim counted 179 occurrences of this Targumic idiom in Onqelos, in 82 of which he considered that the term 'word' bore 'undoubted application to the Divine Personality as revealing Himself'.[2] In fact it has often been thought that this Targumic use of the phrase 'the word of God' lies behind the concept of the divine Word (Gk. logos) which we find in the opening verses of John's Gospel. This is doubtful, however. The Aramaic term used in this kind of context (mēmrā) is not that used by the Targums in places where the Hebrew text itself refers to the activity of the Word of God, such as Psa. 33. 6; 107. 20; Isa. 55. 11. These and similar passages certainly provide a background of thought to the Johannine doctrine.[3] The mēmrā of God in the Targums, on the other hand, is held by some competent scholars to be simply a verbal expedient for avoiding the ascription of anthropomorphic activity or experience to God. But even if this was the original purpose of this expression, its very use was bound to lead to other interpretations. A Jewish scholar, J. Abelson, has declared that the idea of the mēmrā 'has a deep and real theological import', and he quotes the philosopher, Nachmanides (1194-1270), as saying of expressions containing the term mēmrā

[1] By this time Arabic, and no longer Aramaic, was the vernacular of the Palestinians, but the Targum of Onqelos retained its value as an authoritative interpretation of the Pentateuch.

[2] Life and Times of Jesus the Messiah (1883), Vol. II, pp. 659 ff.

[3] As also does the personified Wisdom of God in such a passage as Prov. 8. 22 ff.

that 'their secret is known to students'.[1] Where experts disagree
it is wise not to be dogmatic, but the Targums provide a remarkable
verbal background, at least, to the statement of John 1. 14 that 'the
Word became flesh and dwelt among us, and we beheld his glory'.
For in that statement we have three terms, and not only one,
which are used in the Targums as substitutes for the bare name of
God. One is the term 'Word' (Gk. *logos*), corresponding verbally
at any rate to *mēmrā*. Then when the Word is said to have 'dwelt
among us', the expression used (Gk. *eskēnōsen*) is closely connected
with the thought of the divine presence which was manifested
in the tabernacle in the wilderness—the *shĕkhīnā* (from a Semitic
root meaning 'to dwell', 'to abide'). And thirdly we have the
word 'glory' (Gk. *doxa*), corresponding to Aramaic *yĕqārā*. As
mēmrā, *shĕkhīnā* and *yĕqārā* are all used in the Targums in connection
with the divine activity, it looks as if John is insisting that all the
forms or expressions of divine manifestation in Old Testament
times—Word, Abiding Presence, Glory—are summed up and
fulfilled in Jesus.

Some examples of the circumlocutionary use of *shekhina* may
be given here. Gen. 9. 27 ('let him dwell in the tents of Shem',
understood of God) runs in Onqelos: 'The *shekhina* will dwell in
the tents of Shem'. 'Is the LORD among us or not?' (Exod. 17. 7)
becomes 'Is the *shekhina* of the LORD among us or not?' Deut.
3. 24 ('what god is there in heaven or in earth?') becomes 'Thou
art God; Thy *shekhina* is in heaven above and reigns on earth
below'. 'The good will of Him that dwelt in the bush' (Deut.
33. 16) is expanded to 'the good will of him whose *shekhina* is in
heaven and who revealed Himself in the bush to Moses'.

The term 'glory' is similarly used, and may be illustrated by
the following quotations: 'the glory of God went up from
Abraham' (Gen. 17. 22, for 'God went up from Abraham'); 'the
mountain upon which the glory was revealed' (Exod. 3. 1, for
'the mountain of God'); 'they saw the glory of the God of Israel'[2]
(Exod. 24. 10, for 'they saw the God of Israel'); 'I saw the glory
of the Lord' (Isa. 6. 1, for 'I saw the Lord').

The last passage quoted is particularly interesting, because it
is alluded to in the New Testament (John 12. 41) in language
which reflects the Targumic paraphrase: 'These things said Isaiah

---

[1] *The Immanence of God in Rabbinic Literature* (1912), pp. 147, 151; quoted by L. Gillet,
Communion in the Messiah (1942), p. 79. For the contrary view, that the 'Word of God'
in the Targums is simply a reverent circumlocution for 'God,' see G. F. Moore, *Judaism*,
Vol. I, pp. 414 ff.

[2] The Septuagint also modifies the original text; see p. 155.

because he saw His glory'. (Note, too, that John takes 'His glory' to refer to Christ, in keeping with what we said about John 1. 14.) There is another passage from the same chapter of Isaiah which is quoted in the New Testament in a form resembling the Targum. This is Isa. 6. 9, 10, as quoted in Mark 4. 12. The closing words of the quotation in Mark ('and it should be forgiven them') appear neither in the Masoretic Hebrew nor in the Greek Septuagint, but they are exactly the words used in the Targum of Jonathan. (As we have said, the Targums of Onqelos and Jonathan contain material much earlier than the dates at which they were written and published.) And this certain point of contact between the quotation and the Targumic text encourages us to interpret in the light of the Targum another part of the quotation (namely, the construction with *hina*, mentioned on p. 67).

In Eph. 4. 8 Paul quotes Psa. 68. 18 with the words 'He . . . gave gifts unto men', whereas the Masoretic and Septuagint texts have 'Thou hast received gifts among men', which means something else. The change from 'Thou' to 'He' is insignificant, because Paul is in any case referring to Christ in the third person in this context; but the change from 'received' to 'gave' is obviously significant, because 'gave' suits Paul's argument as 'received' would not. It is remarkable to find that the Targum on the Psalms gives the passage in a form like Paul's; it runs: 'Thou hast ascended to the firmament [prophet Moses], thou has led captivity captive, [thou hast taught the words of the law,] *thou hast given gifts to men.*' The words within square brackets represent Rabbinical exposition, possibly of a later date; but the actual words of the text, including the important clause at the end, represent an earlier oral Targum. The Syriac (Peshitta) version of the Old Testament,[1] which belongs to the early years of the Christian era, has practically the same reading as the Targum, omitting the phrases which we have bracketed.

Dr. Black points out the similarity between Luke 6. 36, 'Be ye merciful, even as your Father is merciful', and an expansion in the Pseudo-Jonathan Targum of Lev. 22. 28, 'As our Father is merciful in heaven, so be ye merciful on earth'. It is also interesting that the form of this saying in the Matthaean version (Matt. 5. 48: 'Ye therefore shall be perfect, as your heavenly Father is perfect') has a contact with the paraphrase of the preceding verse of Leviticus (22. 27) in this Targum, where 'the virtue of the

---

[1] See p. 193.

perfect man' is mentioned.[1] A thorough study of Old Testament quotations and allusions in the New in the light of the Targums might lead to some interesting results.

A few quotations from the Targums in translation will do more than any general description to indicate their character. First, we give the closing verses of Gen. 3 according to the Onqelos Targum and then according to the expansive Targum of Pseudo-Jonathan.

Genesis 3. 21-24 (Onqelos):

'And the Lord God made unto Adam and his wife garments of glory,[2] on the skin of their flesh, and clothed them. And the Lord God said, Behold, Adam is the only one in the world knowing good and evil; perchance now he might stretch out his hand and take also from the tree of life, and eat, and live for ever. And the Lord God sent him from the garden of Eden, to till the earth whence he was created. And He drove out Adam; and He placed before the garden of Eden the cherubim and the sharp sword, which turns to guard the way to the tree of life.'

Genesis 3. 21-24 (Pseudo-Jonathan):

'And the Lord God made unto Adam and his wife garments of honour, from the skin of the serpent which He had stripped from it, on the skin of their flesh, instead of the beauty which they had cast off; and He clothed them. And the Lord God[3] said to the angels that were ministering before Him, Lo! there is Adam alone on the earth as I am alone in the highest heavens, and there will spring from him those who know to distinguish between good and evil: if he had kept the commandment which I commanded, he would have been living and lasting, like the tree of life, for evermore. Now, since he has not kept what I commanded, we decree against him and expel him from the garden of Eden, before he may stretch out his hand and take from the fruits of the tree of life; for if he ate therefrom he would live and remain for ever. And the Lord God expelled him from the garden of Eden, and he went and settled on Mount Moriah, to till the earth whence he was created. And he drove out Adam from where He had made the glory of His *shekhina* to reside from the beginning,[4] between the two cherubim. Before He created the world[5] He created the Law;

---

[1] M. Black, *An Aramaic Approach to the Gospels and Acts*, pp. 138 f.

[2] The Hebrew text has 'coats of skin'. The Jewish interpreters, by substituting an initial *'aleph* for an initial *'ayin*, read *'ōr* (skin) as *'ōr* (light).

[3] The Palestinian Targum has 'And the word of the Lord God said . . .'

[4] The Palestinian Targum adds, 'at the east of the garden of Eden.'

[5] The Palestinian Targum says 'two thousand years before the world was created.'

He prepared the garden of Eden for the righteous, that they shall eat and delight in the fruits of the tree, because they have acted during their life according to the teaching of the Law in this world, and have kept its commandments: He prepared Gehenna for the wicked, which is likened to a sharp sword that eats from two sides; He prepared within it sparks of light and coals of fire to consume therewith the wicked who rebelled in their lives against the teaching of the Law. Better is this Law to him who acts according to it than the fruits of the tree of life,[1] for the word of the Lord has prepared for him who keeps it, that he shall live and walk in the paths of the way of the life of the age to come.'

The expansions in the later Targums are interesting, not for any real additional information which they give us about the events with which the Scriptures deal, but because of the light they throw on Jewish traditions and methods of exegesis.[2] Here is a further example—the first chapter of Ruth as it appears in the late Targum on the Hagiographa.

Ruth 1. 1-22:

'And it came to pass in the days when the judges judged that there was a mighty famine in the land of Israel. Ten mighty famines have been decreed by heaven to be in the world from the day the world was created until King Messiah comes, to punish the inhabitants of the earth therewith: the first famine in the days of Adam, the second famine in the days of Lamech, the third famine in the days of Abraham, the fourth famine in the days of Isaac, the fifth famine in the days of Jacob, the sixth famine in the days of Boaz (who is called Ibzan the righteous) of Bethlehem-Judah, the seventh famine in the days of David, king of Israel, the eighth famine in the days of the prophet Elijah, the ninth famine in the days of Elisha in Samaria; the tenth famine will not be a famine for eating bread nor yet a thirst for drinking water, but for hearing the word of prophecy from the presence of the Lord.[3]

And when there was that mighty famine in the land of Israel, a certain great man of Bethlehem-Judah departed and went to

---

[1] The Palestinian Targum says, 'Because the tree of life, that is the Law.'

[2] 'Since they were used in worship, their character was necessarily exegetical, and they vary from an almost exact transcript of the Hebrew text into Aramaic to a homiletic discourse in which imagination played a large part. In the greater part of *Judges*, for example, the rendering is fairly close to the Massoretic text, but the Song of Deborah is largely allegorized, and presents a picture which recalls a rabbinic school rather than a battlefield' (T. H. Robinson, in *Ancient and English Versions of the Bible* [ed. H. W. Robinson, 1940], pp. 96 f.).

[3] Cf. Amos. 8. 11.

sojourn in the country of Moab, he, and his wife, and his two sons. And the name of the man was Elimelech, and the name of his wife Naomi, and the name of his two sons Mahlon and Chilion, chief Ephrathites of Bethlehem-Judah. And they came into the country of Moab and were governors there. And Elimelech, Naomi's husband, died, and she was left a widow, and her two sons orphans. And they transgressed the commandment of the word of the Lord and took them foreign wives of the daughters of Moab; the name of the one was Orpah, and the name of the other Ruth, the daughter of Eglon, king of Moab: and they dwelt there about ten years. And because they transgressed the commandment of the word of the Lord and made affinity with foreign peoples, their days were shortened, and Mahlon and Chilion died also, both of them in the polluted land, and the woman was left bereaved of her two sons and widowed of her husband.

Then she arose, she and her daughters-in-law, and returned from the land of Moab, because she was told in the land of Moab by the mouth of the messenger that the Lord had remembered His people, the house of Israel, to give them bread, because of the justice of Ibzan the judge and the prayer which he prayed before the Lord: the same is Boaz the righteous. And she departed from the place where she had been, and her two daughters-in-law with her.

And Naomi said to her two daughters-in-law: Go, return each to her mother's house: may the Lord deal kindly with you as you have dealt with your dead husbands (in that you have refused to take husbands after their deaths) and with me (in that you have nourished and sustained me). The Lord give you a full reward for the kindness which you have shown to me, and through this reward may you find rest, each one for herself in her husband's house. And she kissed them, and they lifted up their voices and wept. And they said to her: We will not return to our people and to our gods,[1] but rather will we return with you to your people to be sojourners.[2] And Naomi said: Turn back, my daughters; why will you go with me? Have I even yet sons in my womb, that they may be husbands for you? Turn back, my daughters, from following me; go to your people, for I am too old to be married to a husband. If I said (as if I were yet a young woman), I have still hope; if I were married to-night to a

---

[1] Literally 'fear(s)'.

[2] In the period when the Targums were composed this would mean not merely 'sojourners' but 'proselytes.

husband and were yet to bear sons; would you perhaps wait for them until they grew up like the woman who waits for a little brother-in-law to marry him:[1] for their sakes would you sit pining so as not to be married to a husband? I pray you, my daughters, do not grieve my soul; for it is much more grievous for me than for you, because a stroke from the presence of the Lord has gone forth against me. And they lifted up their voices and wept again, and Orpah kissed her mother-in-law, but Ruth stuck to her.

And she said: See, your sister-in-law has returned to her people and to her god; go back after your sister-in-law to your people and to your god. And Ruth said: Do not urge me to leave you, to turn back from following you, for I wish to become a sojourner.[2] Naomi said: We are commanded to keep the sabbaths and the holy days, so as not to walk more than 2000 cubits.[3] Ruth said: Wherever you go, I will go. Naomi said: We are commanded not to lodge together with the Gentiles. Ruth said: Wherever you lodge, I will lodge. Naomi said: We are commanded to keep the 613 precepts.[4] Ruth said: Whatever your people observe, I myself will observe, as if this had been my nation formerly. Naomi said: We are commanded not to engage in strange worship. Ruth said: Your God shall be my God. Naomi said: We have four kinds of capital punishment for sinners: pelting with stones, burning with fire, slaying with the sword, and hanging on the gallows. Ruth said: Wherever you die, I will die. Naomi said: We have a sepulchre. Ruth said: And there will I be buried. Then she finished by saying: So may the Lord do to me and so may He add to me if aught but death part you and me. So Naomi saw that she was bent on going with her, and she stopped speaking to her.

So they two went on till they came to Bethlehem; and so it was, when they came to Bethlehem, that all the inhabitants of the city went tumultuously to meet them, and said: Is this Naomi? And she said to them: Do not call me Naomi; call me Bitter of Soul, because Shadday has dealt very bitterly with me. I went out full with my husband and my sons, and the Lord has brought me back empty of them; why, then, do you call me Naomi, when

[1] A reference to the levirate marriage; compare Tamar's waiting for Shelah in Gen. 38. 11.

[2] Here the following conversation makes it clear that 'sojourner' means 'proselyte.'

[3] A Sabbath day's journey: the distance was computed by interpreting Exod. 16. 29 in the light of Num. 35. 5.

[4] The Rabbis calculated that the Law consisted of 613 precepts—365 being negative (one for every day in the year), and 248 being positive (one for every part of the body).

testimony has been borne against me from the presence of the
Lord for my trespass, and Shadday has afflicted me?

So Naomi returned, and Ruth the Moabitess, her daughter-in-
law, with her, who returned from the land of Moab, and they came
to Bethlehem at the commencement of the day of Passover; and
on that day the children of Israel began to cut the sheaf of elevation,
which was of barley.'

The Targum, it will be seen, dotted the i's and crossed the t's
of the Biblical narrative, making sure in particular that it would be
understood in accordance with the tradition of the elders. Apart
from the religious interest, notice how the characters in the story
become more important personages; Elimelech and his family
were *chief* Ephrathites of Bethlehem and became *governors* in Moab;
Boaz is identified with Ibzan, one of the minor judges, because he,
too, was a Bethlehemite (Judges 12. 8), while Ruth turns out to
have been the daughter of Eglon king of Moab (Judges 3. 12 ff.)!

Our last selection will be from the Targum of Jonathan on the
Prophets, and the passage is one of special interest, as it is the
Targum of the great prophecy of the Suffering Servant (Isa. 52. 13-
53. 12).

Isaiah 52. 13-53. 12:
(52. 13) 'Behold my servant Messiah[1] will prosper: he will
be high and will flourish and be very powerful. (14) As the house
of Israel hoped for him many days when their appearance was
diminished among the nations and their countenance more than
the sons of men, (15) so will he scatter many nations: kings will
keep silence over him and place their hands upon their mouths,
because what was not told them they have seen, and they have
perceived what they had not heard.

(53. 1) Who has believed these tidings of ours, and upon
whom has the strength of the Lord's mighty arm now been
revealed? (2) And see: the righteous one will grow up before
Him like blossoming shoots, and like a tree which sends forth its
roots by streams of water, so will the holy generation flourish in
the land which was in need of him. His appearance is not that of
any common man, nor is his awe the awe inspired by an ordinary
person; and a countenance of holiness is his countenance, which
all who see him will look earnestly upon. (3) Then the glory of

[1] The Servant of the Lord is called Messiah in this Targum also in Isaiah 42. 1 and
43. 10.

the kingdoms will be an object of contempt, and will be cut off; see, they will be weak and sad, like a man suffering pain and appointed to afflictions; contemned and disregarded, as though the face of the *shekhina* had departed from us.

(4) Then for our trespasses he will make entreaty and for his sake our iniquities will be forgiven; though we were considered as crushed, stricken from the presence of the Lord and humbled. (5) And he will build the sanctuary which was profaned by our trespasses and betrayed by our iniquities, and by his instruction peace will flourish upon us, and when we follow his words our trespasses will be forgiven us. (6) All we like sheep had been scattered, each one according to his way had we gone astray, and there was good pleasure from the presence of the Lord[1] to forgive the trespasses of us all for his sake.

(7) He prayed and was answered; and before he opened his mouth he was accepted; the strong nations he will deliver up like a lamb for the slaughter, and like a ewe which before her shearers is dumb, so before him none opens his mouth or utters a word. (8) From prison and from punishment he will bring our exiles home, and the wonders which will be done for us in his days who will be able to relate? Because he will remove the dominion of the nations out of the land of Israel, the trespasses wherein my people trespassed he will transfer to them.   (9) And he will deliver up the wicked to Gehenna, and the oppressors, rich in possessions, to the death of destruction, so that those who commit sin may not be established nor speak deceitful things with their mouths.

(10) And there was good pleasure from the presence of the Lord[1] to purify and cleanse the remnant of His people in order to purge their souls from trespasses: they will see the kingdom of their Messiah, they will multiply sons and daughters, they will prolong their days, and those who do the law of the Lord will prosper in His good pleasure. (11) From the servitude of the nations he will deliver their soul; they will see the punishment of their enemies; they will be satisfied with the booty of their kings. By his wisdom he will justify the righteous, in order to bring many into subjection to the Law, and for their trespasses he will make entreaty.   (12) Therefore I will apportion to him the booty of many nations, and the wealth of strong cities will he apportion

[1] This circumlocutory Aramaism for 'the Lord was pleased,' or 'it was the Lord's will,' underlies the Greek of Matt. 18. 14, which runs literally: 'there is not will in the presence of your Father in heaven that one of these little ones should perish.'

as plunder, because he delivered up his soul to death,[1] and the
rebels he brought into subjection to the law, and he will make
entreaty for many trespasses, and the rebels will be forgiven for
his sake.'[2]

The most interesting feature of this Targumic passage is that
while the Servant is clearly identified with the Messiah, all the
ascriptions of suffering to Him are transferred either to the Jewish
people suffering at the hand of their Gentile oppressors or to the
Gentiles receiving retribution at the hand of Messiah. There is
little or no evidence that anyone attributed the sufferings to the
Messiah before the coming of Christ.[3] But the words addressed
to Him at His baptism combined the Messianic idea ('Thou art
My Son', Psa. 2. 7) with that of the obedient Servant ('My beloved
in whom I am well pleased', Isa. 42. 1). Jesus understood, accepted
and fulfilled the role of Messiah as one involving sufferings first
and glory thereafter. The tradition preserved in the Targum,
while it identifies the Servant with Messiah, interprets His rôle
as that of a champion of Israel against the Gentiles. If this was
the view current in the first century, we can understand how the
proclamation of a suffering and crucified Messiah was a stumbling-
block to the Jews. The Targums thus provide us with valuable
background material for the reading of the New Testament.[4]

[1] R. A. Aytoun thinks this is the one clause in the Targum which ascribes suffering to
the Messiah (*Journal of Theological Studies*, 23 [1922], p. 177). C. R. North, however,
thinks the view of Dalman and Seidelin is more probable, that the clause is idiomatic
Aramaic for 'he exposed himself to the risk of death', e.g. in battle (*The Suffering Servant in
Deutero-Isaiah* [1948], pp. 11 f.).

[2] A convenient edition (text and translation) of *The Targum of Isaiah* has been produced
by J. F. Stenning (Oxford, 1949).

[3] The words of John the Baptist: 'Behold the Lamb of God which taketh away the
sin of the world' (John 1. 29), are probably based on Isa. 53, and on an interpretation of it
which attributed the sufferings to the Messiah. But they were not spoken, of course, before
the coming of Christ. They cannot be explained in terms of John's supposed contacts with
the Qumran community, for in that community, while the Servant of the Lord was identified
with the Son of Man of Dan. 7. 13, neither the Servant nor the Son of Man was interpreted
of the Messiah, but rather corporately of the community itself.

[4] The sort of interpretation which the Targums provide, over and above the bare
translation, is what the Jews call *midrāsh*. It may be either logical and legal in character
(*hǎlākhāh*) or anecdotal and popularly homiletic (*haggādāh*). The term *midrāsh* is also
applied to a number of systematic commentaries on various parts of Scripture.

CHAPTER XII

THE OLD TESTAMENT IN GREEK

THE writer remembers being present once at a conference of theologians, where one of the subjects debated was the nature of true theology. One eminent speaker declared on the first day of the conference: 'A man can be a good theologian even if he knows nothing but the Authorized Version of the Bible'. Another speaker, who arrived later and so did not hear this dictum, read a paper on the second day in the course of which he said: 'I would not call a man a theologian unless he could translate from the Septuagint back into Hebrew'. As the late Dr. Joad might have said had he been present: 'It all depends what you mean by a theologian'. This is not what we are going to consider now, but perhaps the present chapter will suggest to the reader some of the reasons which led the second speaker to attach such high value to the Septuagint.

What, then, is the Septuagint? The term itself comes from the Latin word for 'seventy', *septuaginta*, and it is frequently indicated by the Roman numeral sign LXX. The origin of the name is to be found in an ancient document known as the Letter of Aristeas. This document was written not long before 100 B.C., but it purports to have been written over a century and a half earlier by Aristeas, an official at the court of King Ptolemy Philadelphus of Egypt (285-246 B.C.), to his brother Philocrates. Ptolemy was renowned as a patron of literature and it was under him that the great library at Alexandria, one of the world's cultural wonders for 900 years, was inaugurated. The letter describes how Demetrius of Phalerum, said to have been Ptolemy's librarian, aroused the king's interest in the Jewish Law and advised him to send a delegation to the high priest, Eleazar, at Jerusalem. The high priest chose as translators six elders from each of the twelve tribes of Israel and sent them to Alexandria, along with a specially accurate and beautiful parchment of the Torah. The elders were royally dined and wined, and proved their wisdom in debate; then they took up their residence in a house on the island of Pharos (the island otherwise famed for its lighthouse), where in seventy-two days they completed their task of translating the Pentateuch into Greek, presenting an agreed version as the result of conference and comparison.[1]

This story explains the name 'Septuagint' applied to this version,[2] but it was not related to explain a name but to glorify the monotheistic worship and wisdom of the Jews over against pagan idolatry, and incidentally to place the stamp of authority upon a translation. To understand why this latter task was necessary we must look farther back in history.

We read in the book of Jeremiah (chapters 41 to 44) of a large number of the inhabitants of Judah who went down to Egypt to settle there three or four months after the destruction of Jerusalem and the Temple by the armies of Nebuchadrezzar (587 B.C.). From that time to the present day Egypt has never been without a Jewish colony. About the same time as the migration in which Jeremiah was forced to take part, a king of Egypt settled a garrison of Jews on the southern frontier of his kingdom, at Elephantine, at the first cataract of the Nile. They were not members of the group that went down with Jeremiah, but they were their fellow-countrymen. This military colony flourished at Elephantine, and built a temple there some time before 525 B.C.[3]

But the heyday of Jewish colonization in Egypt dawned when Alexander the Great founded Alexandria in 332 B.C. Practically from the first, Jews formed a very important element in the population of this great commercial and cultural capital. Most of the members of the Ptolemy dynasty, which fell heir to Alexander's Empire in Egypt and the neighbouring territories and had its seat of government at Alexandria, favoured the Jews and assigned them a special quarter of Alexandria. By the early years of the Christian era we are told that there were almost a million Jews in Egypt, that two out of the five wards of Alexandria were known as Jewish districts, and that others were scattered throughout the remaining three wards.

Alexandria was from the start a Greek-speaking city, and its Jewish population soon forgot their Palestinian vernacular and came to speak exclusively in Greek. If these people were to make any use of the Hebrew Bible, it must be in a translation. A Greek Targum was as necessary in Alexandria as an Aramaic Targum was

---

[1] Later writers improved on this account by telling how the 72 translators did their work in separate cells, and how after 72 days all their versions were found to coincide exactly—sufficient proof of the divine inspiration of the work!

[2] Note that primarily the term 'Septuagint' applies to the Pentateuch only; it was at the time of Origen (early 3rd cent. A.D.) that it came to denote, as it does now, the whole Old Testament in Greek.

[3] See pp. 53 ff. Compare the Jews of Pathros (i.e. Upper Egypt) in Jer. 44. 1, 15.

in Palestine and Babylonia. And the internal evidence of the Septuagint suggests that this Greek version of the Old Testament was made in the first instance to meet the requirements of the Jewish population of Alexandria, and not to grace the royal library. That a copy ultimately found its way into the royal library is quite likely, but that is another matter.

The exact circumstances under which the Septuagint translation began to be made are unknown. The various ancient reports agree in saying that it was made in Alexandria, and that it was begun in the third century B.C., and this is borne out by the character of the work.

When we are dealing with an ancient work in the language in which it was written, we endeavour by the methods of textual criticism to arrive as nearly as possible at the text of the original document. But in dealing with translations we may have to adopt a quite different procedure. If the translation was an official one from the start, then we can make it our business to determine the original text of the official translation. But the fact is that the official translation very often lies at the end and not at the beginning of the history of the translation of a document from another language. We shall see in Chapter XVI, for instance, that Jerome's Latin version of the Bible, which became the 'Authorized Version' of Western Christendom, was preceded by a large number of individual and unofficial attempts at translation. The evidence suggests that this was so with the Greek translation of the Old Testament. Some of the extant manuscripts of the Septuagint exhibit texts of a few portions of the Old Testament varying from one another to such an extent that they cannot have been derived from a single archetype by the ordinary chances of scribal corruption and so forth. They represent either separate translations from Hebrew into Greek, or successive revisions or editions of the first translation. A similar state of affairs in the first century A.D. has been inferred from the evidence of quotations from the Greek Bible in authors like Josephus, Philo of Alexandria, and some New Testament writers.

Of all the Old Testament, the most important section in the eyes of Jews after the return from the Babylonian exile was the Pentateuch. The Pentateuch, as distinct from the rest of the Old Testament, was read straight through in the synagogue sabbath by sabbath, according to a triennial lectionary cycle, whereas only selections from other parts of the Old Testament were read in public. It must have seemed highly desirable to the leaders of

Alexandrian Jewry that there should be one standard Greek version of the Pentateuch, instead of a number of unofficial versions differing from each other.

Dr. Kahle has argued for many years[1] that it was to invest a new standard version with the necessary authority in the eyes of the people that the Letter of Aristeas was written. He infers from the wording of that Letter that the Greek version of the Pentateuch which it celebrates was intended to supersede previously existing versions which were regarded as inadequate. It represents Demetrius of Phalerum as writing to King Ptolemy:

'Since Your Majesty has given orders for the collection of those books which are lacking to complete the library. . . . I report to you as follows: The books of the law of the Jews are lacking, together with a few others. For they are composed in Hebrew letters and language, *and have been interpreted rather carelessly and not in accordance with the actual sense*, as is reported by those who know; for they have not received royal attention'.

And later in the letter we read that some earlier Greek writers had quoted from the Jewish law, but had come to grief because they used 'the earlier translations which were rather precarious'.

Dr. Kahle's conclusion is that the standard version of the Greek Pentateuch, intended to supersede these earlier translations which were deficient in accuracy, was made about 100 B.C., that the Letter of Aristeas was written to give it the requisite prestige and that the enterprise proved successful in the long run, although some variant translations continued to be used for a considerable time afterwards. Like our English Authorized Version, it was a revision of earlier translations, incorporating their good features, correcting their defects, and ultimately superseding them because of its inherent worth.

Dr. Kahle has overstated his case, to the point where he denies the possibility of using the methods of textual criticism to reconstruct a 'proto-Septuagint' text from which most of our surviving copies are descended.[2] A standard Greek text of the Pentateuch at least was established in the second century B.C., and it is a legitimate exercise of textual criticism to endeavour to reconstruct it.[3] The

---

[1] Cf. *The Cairo Geniza*, pp. 209 ff.

[2] The opposite extreme, namely that the Greek Old Testament began absolutely with one fixed text, is maintained by the American scholar, Professor H. M. Orlinsky; cf. his brief introduction *The Septuagint: The Oldest Translation of the Bible* (Cincinnati, 1949).

[3] One scholar who has given attention to this task in recent years is Dr. P. Katz (W. P. M. Walters) of Cambridge; cf. his *Philo's Bible* (Cambridge, 1950), and 'Septuagintal Studies in the Mid-Century' in *The Background of the New Testament and its Eschatology*, ed. W. D. Davies and D. Daube (Cambridge, 1956), pp. 176 ff. A distinguished pupil of Dr. Katz is Dr. D. W. Gooding; cf. his *Recensions of the Septuagint Pentateuch* (the Tyndale Old Testament Lecture for 1954), and *The Account of the Tabernacle: Translation and Textual Problems of the Greek Exodus* (Cambridge, 1959).

Rylands Library, Manchester, possesses a fragmentary papyrus of Deut. 25-28 in Greek, which dates from the middle of that century at the latest, and yet exhibits a recognizably 'Septuagintal' text.[1] In the rest of the Greek Old Testament the situation may be more fluid, but even so, for most of the books one archetypal Greek text can properly be envisaged behind our extant witnesses. But those features which the Septuagint shares with other Bible translations, on which Dr. Kahle lays such stress, should not be overlooked by textual critics.

The Pentateuch seems to have been the only part of the Greek Old Testament of which a standard text was established by Jewish authorities. The Jews might have gone on at a later time to authorize a standard text of the rest of the Septuagint, but for reasons which will be mentioned below, they lost interest in the Septuagint altogether. With but few exceptions, every manuscript of the Septuagint which has come down to our day was copied and preserved in Christian, not Jewish, circles.[2] The latest exceptions to this general rule have been fragments of the Septuagint from the Dead Sea caves. The fourth cave at Qumran has yielded pieces of two manuscripts of Leviticus and one of Numbers, while the seventh cave has yielded pieces of the Septuagint text of Exodus and of the Epistle of Jeremiah.[3] In an unidentified location west of the Dead Sea (probably on Israel's side of the frontier), occupied by a garrison of Bar-kokhba's in the revolt of A.D. 132-135, there was found an incomplete Greek version of the Minor Prophets, which has been hailed as a missing link in the history of the Septuagint. It is said to resemble closely the Septuagint text used by Justin Martyr (died A.D. 165), and has been tentatively identified with Origen's 'Fifth' Greek version.[4]

There were two main reasons why the Jews lost interest in the Septuagint. One was that from the first century A.D. onwards the Christians adopted it as their version of the Old Testament, and used it freely in their propagation and defence of the Christian faith. It is little wonder that Christians came to attach some degree of divine inspiration to the Septuagint, for some of its translations might almost appear to have been providentially intended to support Christian arguments. The use which Christians made of

---

[1] See C. H. Roberts, *Two Biblical Papyri in the John Rylands Library, Manchester* (1936); Kahle, *The Cairo Geniza*, pp. 220 ff. This manuscript (*p* Ryl. 458) is of comparable date to the Cairo papyrus of the Greek Deuteronomy mentioned on p. 120, n. 1. Cf. W. G. Waddell, *Journal of Theological Studies* 45 (1944), pp. 158 ff.

[2] This is not the only Jewish work which has been preserved by Christians. The same applies to the writings of Philo and Josephus.

[3] See p. 170.   [4] See p. 155.

it can be traced in several New Testament passages. One example is the quotation from Amos 9. 11, 12 in James's speech in Acts 15. 16-18, where the Septuagint version differs considerably from the Masoretic Hebrew text of Amos (represented in our English Old Testament), and where the Septuagint gives more explicit support to James's argument than the Masoretic text does.[1] But it is when we go on to the second century that we realize what an armoury of textual ammunition for disputes against the Jews Christian apologists found in the Septuagint. If we read Justin Martyr's *Dialogue with Trypho the Jew* (the setting of which is at Ephesus shortly after A.D. 135), we find there a good example of this. Trypho on occasion demurs to Justin's quotations from the Septuagint, on the ground that it does not properly represent the Hebrew text; Justin replies that the Rabbis have obviously altered the Hebrew in order to obscure the correspondence between the prophecy and its fulfilment. For example, Justin quotes Psalm 96. 10 in the form, 'Say among the nations that the Lord reigned from the tree', and charges the Jews with having cut out the words 'from the tree' so as to remove a reference to the crucifixion. Trypho answers: 'Whether the rulers of the people have erased any portion of the Scriptures, as you affirm, God knows; but it seems incredible'.[2] Trypho was right, in fact; the phrase, 'from the tree', was not omitted by Jews, but added by Christians.

Another reason for the Jews' loss of interest in the Septuagint lies in the fact that about A.D. 100 a revised standard text was established for the Hebrew Bible by Jewish scholars, in the first instance for the Pentateuch and later for the other Old Testament books. This was the beginning of the process of revision and editing which lasted for several centuries and resulted in the production of the Masoretic text. The standard text fixed about A.D. 100 was the consonantal text which formed the basis of the Masoretes' labours. Variant forms of the Hebrew text which had existed before A.D. 100 were allowed to disappear, with the excep-

---

[1] The LXX version, quoted by James, presupposes Heb. *yidrĕshu* ('will seek') for Masoretic *yîrĕshu* ('will possess'), and *'ādām* ('man') for *'Edōm*; and it neglects the particle *'eth*, the mark of the accusative case, which precedes *shĕ'ērîth* ('remnant'). But the LXX version must represent a variant Hebrew text which has disappeared; and even the Masoretic text would have served James's purpose (if not with the same explicitness), since it predicts that the house of David will regain its sovereignty over the Gentile nations formerly ruled by it —a prediction fulfilled and surpassed by the Gentiles' yielding their allegiance to Christ as Lord.

[2] *Dialogue*, chap. 73; cf. Justin's *First Apology*, chap. 41. The phrase is not present in any copy of the LXX which has come down to us. Cf. the 'Epistle of Barnabas', 8. 5: 'The kingdom of Christ (or the reign of Christ) is on the tree.'

tion of the Samaritan Pentateuch which was preserved outside Jewish circles. But when this authorized text was fixed, any version in another language which was to be fit for Jewish use must conform to it, and this the existing forms of the Greek version plainly did not. So here was a further reason for repudiating the Septuagint, and the version which had once been officially authorized by Alexandrian Jewry and protected from alteration by the most solemn sanctions, the version which Philo regarded as written by inspiration, was now represented as the work of Satan; 'the accursed day on which the seventy elders wrote the Law in Greek for the king' was compared to the day on which Israel had made the golden calf.

A new translation of the Bible into Greek was required for Greek-speaking Jews, and this translation was provided by a man named Aquila. We are told by the fourth-century writer, Epiphanius, that Aquila was a relative of the Emperor Hadrian, a native of Sinope, on the Black Sea, who came to Jerusalem as a civil servant. There he became a Christian, but his inadequate emancipation from some of his pre-Christian ideas and ways brought upon him a public rebuke from the elders of the Church. Aquila thereupon took offence, left the Church, and became a Jewish proselyte. Most of this story is probably fictitious, but that he was a Jewish proselyte from the Black Sea coast is confirmed by earlier and more trustworthy writers, and the evidence suggests that he flourished in the first half of the second century A.D. His translation not only followed the newly established Hebrew text but did so with such slavish literalness that it could hardly be called Greek: the individual words were Greek, but they were put together according to the rules of Hebrew composition. One interesting feature of his translation is that in Isaiah 7. 14 he translated Heb. 'almāh[1] by Gk. neanis, 'young woman', and not by parthenos, 'maiden', 'virgin'. The Septuagint translation was parthenos, which suited the Christian interpretation of this passage as a prophecy of the virginal conception of Christ (as in Matt. 1. 23). The replacement of parthenos by neanis in the later Greek versions blunted the point of this application. Another interesting feature is Aquila's retention of the Hebrew letters יהוה for the ineffable name of God (cf. p. 120). Jerome tells us that people who did not know Hebrew treated these as the Greek letters ΠΙΠΙ, and even pronounced the word as Pipi!

---

[1] While 'almāh is strictly 'young woman', and bĕthūlāh is strictly 'virgin', in Hebrew, yet in the Old Testament 'almāh, which occurs seven times, does not seem to be used in a markedly different way from bĕthūlāh, which occurs fifty times.

Towards the end of the second century A.D. another Jewish proselyte, Theodotion, a native of Ephesus, produced another Greek version of the Old Testament. This was not an original work; what Theodotion seems to have done is to have taken an older Greek translation belonging to the pre-Christian era—one, indeed, which appears to lie behind some of the Old Testament quotations in the New Testament, particularly in Revelation—and revised it in accordance with the standard Hebrew text. It is interesting to note that it was Theodotion's version of Daniel that the Church adopted for purposes of its standard version of the Greek Bible, and not the older version commonly called the Septuagint version of that book. The reason for this was probably the simple fact that in the book of Daniel Theodotion's translation is much the more satisfactory of the two. The 'Septuagint' translation of Daniel is extant only in two manuscripts—the cursive 87, in the Chigi library in Rome (9th or 11th cent. A.D.) and one of the papyrus codices in the Chester Beatty Collection (3rd cent. A.D.). It is also possible that the relation between 1 Esdras in the Septuagint (= 1 Esdras in the English Apocrypha) and 2 Esdras in the Septuagint (= Ezra-Nehemiah of the Masoretic text and the English Bible) is that the former is an older Septuagint version and the latter is Theodotion's version.

Some time after Theodotion another Greek version of the Old Testament was made by Symmachus, who belonged to the Jewish-Christian sect of the Ebionites. His aim seems to have been an idiomatic Greek version, and his method of operation was thus as far removed as possible from Aquila's.

The grandson and translator of Jesus ben Sira, in his prologue to his grandfather's book (Ecclesiasticus), implies that about 132 B.C. a great part of the Old Testament (possibly all of it) was available in Greek. 'Things originally spoken in Hebrew', he says, 'have not the same force in them, when they are translated into another tongue: and not only these, but the law itself, and the prophecies, and the rest of the books, have no small difference, when they are spoken in their original language'.

When the Gospel began to spread among Greek-speaking Jews and Gentiles, the Septuagint was the form of the Old Testament chiefly used by Christians in worship, teaching and evangelization. When we examine the Old Testament quotations which appear in the New Testament, we find that most are taken from the Septuagint as we know it.

The New Testament writers who quote most closely from the

Septuagint as we know it are Luke and the author of Hebrews. The quotation in Heb. 1. 6, 'And let all the angels of God worship Him', is referred in the A.V. margin to 'Deut. 32. 43, LXX'. No such words will be found in Deut. 32. 43 in the A.V., R.V., or R.S.V., which represent the Masoretic text. But the Septuagint text of that verse is longer than the Masoretic; it runs:

> Rejoice, ye heavens, along with Him,
>   And let the sons of God worship Him;
> Rejoice, ye nations, with His people,
>   And let all the angels of God be strong in Him:
> For He takes vengeance for the blood of His children,
>   And will avenge it, and recompense justice upon their foes;
> And to those that hate Him will He render recompense,
>   And the Lord will purify the land of His people.

This longer reading was based on a Hebrew original, as is now made clear by the discovery of a copy of this chapter of Deuteronomy in the fourth cave at Qumran, exhibiting a Hebrew text corresponding closely to the Septuagint. Heb. 1. 6 may echo either the second or fourth lines of this octet, or rather a conflation of the two, neither of which appears in the Masoretic text.[1]

Some Old Testament quotations in the New are evidently translated directly for the occasion from the Hebrew original, others appear to have been derived from non-Septuagintal versions of the Greek Old Testament. The quotations from or allusions to Daniel in the book of Revelation were probably made with reference to the Greek version of Daniel that lies behind Theodotion's revision of that book. Dr. Kahle makes a detailed study of the quotation of Isa. 42. 1-4 in Matt. 12. 18-21 and concludes: 'There can be no doubt that Matthew quoted a translation of Isaiah which differed from the translation found in the Christian "Septuagint".' He continues: 'We can assume that still other forms of text existed in the MSS. of the Greek Bible which were in the hands of the early Christians'.[2] (A further influence on the form of some Old Testament quotations in the New Testament has been mentioned above in our discussion of the Targums.[3])

The Septuagint shows a tendency to avoid anthropomorphisms, but to a much smaller extent than the Targums. For example, 'Enoch walked with God' (Gen. 5. 22, 24) appears in the Septuagint

---

[1] The reference margin of the R.V. at Heb. 1. 6 gives a further reference to Ps. 97. 7 (Worship Him, all ye gods), where the Septuagint has: 'Worship Him, all ye His angels'.

[2] *The Cairo Geniza*, p. 251.   [3] See pp. 137 ff.

as 'Enoch pleased God'; this is the source of the wording of Heb.
11. 5f. Again, where the Hebrew text of Ex. 24. 10 says of the
elders of Israel, 'they saw the God of Israel', the Septuagint says:
'they saw the place where the God of Israel stood.'[1]

Just as the Jews of Alexandria realized the need for a standard
text of the Greek Pentateuch, however, so Greek-speaking Christians
came to feel the need of a standard text of the whole Greek Old
Testament. When this standard text was fixed, in the early
centuries A.D., variant forms of the Greek Old Testament fell into
disuse, and only fragments of them have survived. When we
speak or read of the Septuagint, then, what we understand in
practice is that particular form of the Greek Old Testament,
handed down from pre-Christian Alexandria, which the Church
adopted in preference to variant forms as her standard Greek text
of the Old Testament. The main exception to this definition is,
as we have said, the book of Daniel, for which the Church adopted
the Theodotionic version instead of the old Alexandrian version.

The most important name in the history of the Christian text
of the Septuagint is that of the great Alexandrian scholar, Origen
(A.D. 185-254). In later life, when he had taken up residence at
Caesarea in Palestine, Origen produced a masterpiece of Biblical
learning which is called the Hexapla (Greek for 'sixfold') because
it was an edition of the Old Testament in six parallel columns.
The first column contained the Hebrew text in Hebrew script,
the second contained the same text transliterated into Greek script,
the third and fourth contained the Greek versions of Aquila and
Symmachus respectively, the fifth contained Origen's own edition
of the Septuagint text, the sixth contained Theodotion's version.
In some parts of the Old Testament, especially the Psalms, further
columns were added, containing other Greek versions in addition
to the four just mentioned: these others are known as the 'Fifth',[2]
'Sixth' and 'Seventh' Greek versions. They were probably variant
forms of Greek text which had survived to Origen's day; he found
the 'Sixth', it is interesting to note, in a jar near Jericho (along with
some other Hebrew and Greek books), but not necessarily (as
some have hastily concluded) in one of the Qumran caves.

If Origen's Hexapla had survived entire, it would be a treasure
beyond price. Column 1 would have given most welcome
information on the Hebrew text current in the first half of the
third century; Column 2 would have thrown a flood of light on

[1] See p. 137 for the Targumic treatment of this anthropomorphism.
[2] See p. 150.

the disputed question of the pronunciation of Hebrew (especially the Hebrew vowels); the other columns would have given us equally valuable information about the Greek versions in Origen's time. The fragments of the Hexapla that have been preserved whet our unsatisfied appetite for the vast bulk of the work that has not been preserved. The standard edition of the surviving fragments of the Hexapla is F. Field's *Origenis Hexapla quae supersunt*, published at Oxford in two volumes in 1875; twenty years later about 150 verses of the Psalms in Columns 2 to 6 inclusive were found by Cardinal Giovanni Mercati in the Ambrosian Library at Milan; some other Hexapla fragments and portions of Aquila's translation of the books of Kings were among the discoveries from the Cairo *genizah*.

Origen's Hexapla was preserved at Caesarea until the Saracen conquest of the seventh century, and there it was accessible to later scholars such as Pamphilus, Eusebius, and Jerome.

In editing the Septuagint for the fifth column of the Hexapla, Origen aimed at bringing it into greater conformity with the Hebrew text of the first column. By an elaborate system of critical signs he indicated passages where the Septuagint omitted something which was present in the Hebrew, or added something which was not in the Hebrew. Unfortunately, Origen's successors and copyists did not all preserve these signs accurately when they transcribed his Septuagint text, and this led to the dissemination of a corrupted text. Two other scholars who undertook later recensions of the Septuagint were martyrs in the last great persecution of Christians under the Roman Empire—Hesychius of Alexandria, and Lucian of Antioch. Lucian's recension was based on a conflation of divergent readings and comparison with Hebrew texts,[1] and circulated in the area between Antioch and Constantinople, especially in parts of Asia Minor.[2]

What is the value of the Septuagint for us? Firstly, it represents an underlying Hebrew text over a thousand years older than our Masoretic manuscripts. Hence the importance which the speaker whom we mentioned at the outset of this chapter attached to the ability to translate from the Septuagint back into Hebrew. But the

---

[1] See pp. 186 f.

[2] The two most convenient editions of the Septuagint are that by H. B. Swete in three volumes (Cambridge, 1909), and that by A. Rahlfs in two volumes (Stuttgart, 1935). Publication of the large critical Cambridge edition by the late A. E. Brooke, N. MacLean and H. St. J. Thackeray began in 1906 and is now more than half complete. A comparable edition is being produced at Göttingen, Germany; its publication has begun with books in the second half of the Old Testament.

antiquity of the Septuagint as compared with our surviving manuscripts of the Hebrew Bible must not lead us to exaggerate its textual value. As a translation it is very unequal; the Pentateuch has been done much more carefully than the rest of the Old Testament. The translation of some parts of the Old Testament shows very indifferent workmanship indeed. The Septuagint is a useful adjunct to our Hebrew manuscripts in the textual criticism of the Old Testament; it can never take their place. There are several places where the Septuagint has preserved the true text which has become obscured in the Hebrew transmission, but these are very few in comparison with the places where the Septuagint has mistranslated the Hebrew.

Here are three places where the Septuagint has preserved part of the original text which our Hebrew manuscripts have lost.

(a) Gen. 4. 8. Here the Masoretic text says, 'And Cain said unto Abel his brother', but does not tell us what he said. The Authorized and Revised Versions try to help out the awkwardness thus caused by translating respectively 'And Cain talked with Abel his brother' and 'And Cain told Abel his brother'. Neither of these is an exact translation, but the Revised margin indicates the original text when it says, 'Many ancient authorities have, *said unto Abel his brother, Let us go into the field*'. The ancient authorities are the Septuagint and Samaritan texts. And Cain's suggestion to Abel, 'Let us go into the field', prepares us for the next sentence: 'And it came to pass, *when they were in the field*, that Cain rose up against Abel his brother, and slew him'.

(b) 1 Sam. 14. 41. The Authorized Version makes Saul say to God, 'Give a perfect *lot*' (margin: Shew the innocent); the Revised Version has 'Shew the right' (margin: Give a perfect lot). The Hebrew words in question should really be translated 'Give Thummim', but the difficulty in the reading is due to the accidental omission of some words from the Masoretic text. The Septuagint has preserved these words, and indicates that the verse originally ran as follows:

'And Saul said, O Jehovah, God of Israel, why hast thou not answered thy servant this day? If the iniquity be in me or in Jonathan my son, Jehovah, God of Israel, give Urim; but if thou shouldest say that the iniquity is in thy people Israel, give Thummim. And Saul and Jonathan were taken by lot, and the people escaped'.

The whole narrative becomes lucid, and incidentally welcome light is thrown upon the operation of the priestly oracle, the Urim and

Thummim, which apparently could only indicate one of two alternatives in response to each inquiry.[1]

(c) 1 Kings 8. 12 f. The Masoretic text, represented by our English versions, makes Solomon say: 'Jehovah said that he would dwell in the thick darkness. I have surely built thee an house of habitation, a place for thee to dwell in for ever'. But the Septuagint reading of this passage, which it places not between verses 11 and 14 but after verse 53, runs thus:

> 'Then spake Solomon concerning the house when he had finished building it:
>
>> Jehovah set the sun in the heavens,
>> But he hath determined to dwell in darkness.
>> I have built an house of habitation for thee,[2]
>> A place to dwell in eternally.
>
> (Behold, is it not written in the book of the song?)'

The Septuagint has thus preserved in translation a quatrain of Hebrew poetry. The parenthetic note which follows it may mean that this quatrain was included in a collection of songs or poems, but the similarity in Hebrew script between 'book of the song' (*sēpher ha-shīr*) and 'book of Jashar' (*sēpher ha-yāshār*) suggests that what the Septuagint has preserved is a further item from that treasury of Hebrew poetry from which the poems in Joshua 10. 12-13 and 2 Samuel 1. 19-27 are quoted.

These are but three interesting examples of the way in which the evidence of the Septuagint can be used to throw light on the original text of the Old Testament. The Revised Standard Version of 1952 avails itself of the testimony of the Septuagint for the establishment of the text of these passages, and of others too. It is specially interesting to note that in a number of places where it does so, it has been shown by Qumran discoveries published after the appearance of the R.S.V. Old Testament that the readings which it adopts have Hebrew support as well as Greek. Let one example suffice. In the Song of Moses in Deut. 32 it had long been the view of textual critics, on the basis of the Septuagint, that the original wording at the end of verse 8 was not 'according to the number of the children (sons) of Israel' (as the Masoretic text has it), but 'according to the number of the sons of God' (i.e. the angels). This latter rendering was accordingly adopted in the R.S.V.

---

[1] Note also that, as the Revisers' margin points out, the Septuagint text of 1 Sam. 14. 18 makes Saul say to Ahijah, not 'Bring hither the ark of God . . .', but 'Bring hither the ephod. For he wore the ephod at that time before Israel.' The ephod, not the ark, was the sacred object with which the oracular Urim and Thummim were associated.

[2] Or (quoting a divine oracle): 'Build a house of habitation for me.'

But now a copy of this part of Deuteronomy from the fourth Qumran cave (not the same manuscript as that mentioned on p. 154) exhibits the reading 'sons of God' in *Hebrew*.

The Septuagint text of Jeremiah is substantially shorter than the Masoretic text. Hebrew witnesses to both the shorter and the longer recensions have been identified among the Qumran manuscripts. The Septuagint Psalter adds a hundred-and-fifty-first psalm, purporting to be David's song of victory over Goliath. It was reported in February 1962 that an incomplete Psalter scroll from the eleventh cave at Qumran proved, when unrolled, to contain the Hebrew text of this song and of two or three other uncanonical psalms as well as thirty-six known to us from the canonical Psalter.

The importance of the Septuagint is not restricted to the field of textual and literary criticism. It should in any case be evident that the version of the Old Testament which was so largely used by the New Testament writers and the Church of the first centuries cannot wisely be neglected, because for that very reason, if for no other, it made an immeasurable contribution to Christianity.

It is not always realized that the New Testament writers' task of recording the Gospel in Greek was made easier because the Septuagint already existed. They did not have to invent a Greek theological vocabulary; such a vocabulary lay ready to hand in the Septuagint. The general religious vocabulary of the Greek language was pagan in character, but several elements of that pagan vocabulary had been taken by the Alexandrian translators and used as equivalents of the great words of Old Testament revelation. Thus it came about that in Greek-speaking Jewish circles these words did not bear their original pagan significance but the new significance which they acquired from the Hebrew vocabulary which they represented.

One instance is the Greek word translated 'law'—*nomos*. In Greek the fundamental sense of *nomos* is 'custom', 'convention'. To the Greeks, law was codified custom. But the Septuagint translators used this word to translate Hebrew *tōrāh*, which strictly means 'instruction'. To the Hebrews law meant not codified custom, but divine instruction imparted through the spokesmen of God, Moses and his successors. Thus, when the Septuagint translators used *nomos* to translate *tōrāh* they gave *nomos* a new connotation, which it retains in New Testament and Christian Greek.

Much the same took place with regard to a number of other words, including names and titles of divine beings, psychological terms, and words denoting such things as righteousness, mercy and

truth, sin and atonement. It is particularly important to understand the New Testament words for atonement, sacrifice, forgiveness, propitiation and reconciliation, not in their pagan Greek
senses, but in the senses in which they were used in the Septuagint
to render the corresponding Hebrew words. Take, for example,
the verb *hilaskomai* (propitiate) and cognate words. In pagan
Greek usage *hilaskomai* denotes the appeasing of the wrath of a
capricious power by offering him a gift or by enduring his ven-
geance or in some other way. But in the Septuagint it is used as
the equivalent of the great Hebrew term *kipper*,[1] the word used in
the Old Testament for the wiping out of sin by a gracious and
righteous Covenant-God when the penitent worshipper acknowledged his wrongdoing.[2] Other words derived from the same
root in Old Testament Hebrew which belong to the same context
are *kappōreth*, 'mercy-seat',[3] the place where sin is wiped out,
kippūrīm, 'atonement' (as in *yōm kippūrīm*, 'the day of atonement'),
and *kōpher*, 'ransom'. In the Septuagint *kipper* is rendered by
hilaskomai or its intensive form *exilaskomai*, *kappōreth* by *hilastērion*,
kippūrīm by *hilasmos* or the intensive *exilasmos*. These Greek words
thus take on the meanings of their Hebrew equivalents instead of
the meanings which they had in Greek paganism, and convey
'the sense of performing an act whereby guilt or defilement is
removed'.[4] And in this sense the verb *hilaskomai* and its cognates
lay ready to the hand of New Testament writers when they wished
to speak of propitiation, not in the pagan sense of man's appeasing a
vengeful deity, but in the Christian sense of God's graciously
averting in Christ the wrath which the sin of man had incurred.[5]

[1] The form *kipper* is the Pi'el or intensive form of *kāphar*. In the simple (Qal) form
kāphar is used of wiping or daubing Noah's ark with pitch (*kōpher*): this passage (Gen. 6. 14)
is the only Old Testament instance of the Qal. The intensive *kipper* means not merely 'wipe'
but 'wipe away', 'wipe out'. Some have taken the root sense of the verb to be 'cover'.
But comparative Semitic philology supports the other view: cf. Akkadian *kuppuru*, 'blot
out'. This further supports the translation 'mercy-seat' for Heb. *kappōreth*, as against, e.g.,
the rendering 'ark-cover' adopted by the Jewish translation of the Old Testament.

[2] Whether the repentance was ritually expressed by animal sacrifice, or took the form
of the offering to God of 'a broken and a contrite heart' (Psalm 51. 17).

[3] The same concept is expressed by the 'throne of grace' (Gk. *thronos tēs charitos*) in
Heb. 4. 16.

[4] C. H. Dodd, *The Bible and the Greeks* (1935), p. 93. The opening chapters of this
book contain many examples of the modification of Greek terms through their use in the
Septuagint.

[5] In the New Testament, *hilaskomai* appears in Luke 18. 13 and Heb. 2. 17; *hilasmos* in
1 John 2. 2 and 4. 10; *hilastērion* in Rom. 3. 25 and Heb. 9. 5. In Heb. 9. 5 it means the
literal mercy-seat; in Rom. 3. 25 the same idea may be conveyed figuratively of Christ or
the word may be used adjectivally of Him in the sense 'propitiatory'. (See p. 250 for the New
English Bible rendering of this.) The most important point to notice in all these Biblical
uses of these words is that they denote an act in which God takes the initiative. See also
W. E. Vine, *Expository Dictionary of New Testament Words*, *s.v.* Propitiation (Vol. III, p. 223);
L. Morris, *The Apostolic Preaching of the Cross* (London, 1955), pp. 125-185.

E. W. Grinfield, one of the great Septuagint scholars of last century, expressed the opinion that 'whoever studies the Greek New Testament in conjunction with the Septuagint will obtain such a conception of the unity of the Bible, as never could be obtained from the study of two discordant languages';[1] and although there is an element of exaggeration in his words (as though the study of the Septuagint could be more valuable than that of the Hebrew original), they may still be profitably heeded.

Again, the Septuagint was a great missionary work. Although it was primarily a translation undertaken to meet the requirements of Greek-speaking Jews, it did incidentally make the Old Testament revelation accessible to the Gentile world. Indications are not lacking in the pagan Greek literature of the last three centuries B.C. that it was known and appreciated in some Greek circles. The Hebraistic style of its Greek could never have been pleasing to a Greek ear, but its contents had their own appeal.[2] The unknown author of a Greek treatise *On Sublimity in Style* includes among examples of such sublimity one from the Old Testament:

> So, too, the Jewish lawgiver, no ordinary man, having formed a worthy conception of the divine power, gave expression to it at the very threshold of his Laws, where he says: "God said"—what? "'Let there be light,' and there was light. 'Let there be earth', and there was earth" (9. 8).

He gives the sense rather than exact quotation of Genesis 1. 3, 9; but the source of his information was pretty certainly the Septuagint.

By thus helping to disseminate the knowledge of the living and true God outside Israel the Septuagint paved the way for Christian missionary enterprise among the Gentiles. For the Septuagint was the Bible which the earliest heralds of the Gospel took in their hands as they went on their missionary journeys throughout the Roman Empire, in the earliest decades when as yet there was no New Testament. And when the New Testament was complete, they did not jettison the Old, but added the New Testament in the Greek original to the Old Testament in the Greek translation, thus making up the Greek Bible. The great

---

[1] *An Apology for the Septuagint* (1850), p. 99.

[2] More than one writer, for example, has suggested that the pastoral idylls of the Greek poet, Theocritus (325-267), betray some acquaintance with the LXX version of the Song of Songs. Sir J. Mahaffy, in his *History of Classical Greek Literature*, i (1880), p. 417, n. 1, speaks of the eighteenth idyll of Theocritus 'as perhaps containing the only direct allusion to Hebrew literature which is to be found in classical Greek poetry,' and draws several parallels between it and passages in the Song of Songs. Cf. also D. S. Margoliouth in *Lines of Defence of the Biblical Revelation* (1903), pp. 2 ff.; *New Commentary on Holy Scripture*, S.P.C.K. (1928), p. 413.

Greek Biblical manuscripts—the Sinaitic, Vatican and Alexandrian codices, the Chester Beatty collection, and others—are manuscripts of the whole Greek Bible, and are thus witnesses to the text both of the Greek New Testament and of the Septuagint. The Septuagint had thus, in the providence of God, a great and honourable part to play in preparing the world for the Gospel. 'Greek Judaism with the Septuagint had ploughed the furrows for the gospel seed in the Western world'.[1]

---

[1] A. Deissmann, *New Light on the New Testament* (1907), p. 95.

CHAPTER XIII

THE APOCRYPHAL BOOKS

JOHN BUNYAN relates in his autobiography, *Grace Abounding*, how once, during a time of deep depression, he found great comfort from a verse which came to his mind: 'Look at the generations of old and see; did ever any trust in the Lord and was confounded?' He could not remember where it came from, and being curious to track it down, searched his Bible, but could not find it. Nor could other Christians, whom he asked, help him in his quest. Then, after the lapse of a year, he writes, 'casting my eye upon the Apocrypha books, I found it in Ecclesiasticus, chap. 2. 10. This at first did somewhat daunt me, because it was not in those texts that we call holy and canonical; yet as this sentence was the sum and substance of many of the promises, it was my duty to take the comfort of it. And I bless God for that word, for it was of good to me. That word doth still oft-times shine before my face'.

It is now time to consider these 'Apocrypha books', as Bunyan called them, from which he derived such timely comfort, although they did not belong to 'those texts that we call holy and canonical.'

The sixth Anglican Article of Religion, after listing the thirty-nine canonical books of the Old Testament, goes on: 'And the other Books (as *Hierome*[1] saith) the Church doth read for example of life and instruction of manners; but yet doth it not apply them to establish any doctrine; such are these following:

> *The Third Book of Esdras,*
> *The Fourth Book of Esdras,*
> *The Book of Tobias,*
> *The Book of Judith,*
> *The rest of the Book of Esther,*
> *The Book of Wisdom,*
> *Jesus the Son of Sirach,*
> *Baruch the Prophet,*

[1] Jerome (Latin *Hieronymus*): in his prologue (the so-called *Prologus Galeatus*) to 1 and 2 Samuel (which he calls 1 and 2 Kings) he affirmed that any books not included in the 24 of the Hebrew Bible must be accounted apocryphal (i.e., non-canonical). On the other hand, he sometimes refers to the book of Jesus the son of Sirach (Ecclesiasticus) as 'Scripture', but this is probably an accommodation to popular usage. It is sometimes inferred from certain passages in Ecclesiasticus that it claims the status of Holy Scripture, but this is uncertain, and there is no evidence that it ever succeeded in gaining such status from Jewish authorities. (Sirach is a variant form of Sira.)

The Song of the Three Children
The Story of Susanna,
Of Bel and the Dragon,
The Prayer of Manasses,
The First Book of Maccabees,
The Second Book of Maccabees'.

This is really a very varied assortment of Jewish literature of the period 300 B.C.—A.D. 100; what gives the collection its special interest is the fact that, while none of these books is included in the Hebrew Old Testament, they do (with one exception) form part of the Greek Old Testament. It is very often said that they formed part of the canon recognized by the Alexandrian Jews, but not by the Palestinian Jews; but this is an inaccurate way of stating the difference. There is no evidence that these books were ever regarded as canonical by the Jews, whether inside or outside Palestine, whether they read the Bible in Hebrew or in Greek. The books of the Apocrypha were first given canonical status by Greek-speaking Christians, quite possibly through a mistaken belief that they already formed part of an Alexandrian Canon. The Alexandrian Jews may have *added* these books to their versions of the Scriptures, but that was a different matter from *canonizing* them. As a matter of fact, the inclusion of the apocryphal books in the Septuagint may partly be due to ancient bibliographical conditions. When each book was a papyrus or parchment roll, and a number of such rolls were kept together in a box, it was quite likely that uncanonical documents might be kept in a box along with canonical documents, without acquiring canonical status. Obviously the connection between various rolls in a box is much looser than that between various documents which are bound together in a volume.

The names of the apocryphal books given in the quotation above from Article VI are those which they bear in the Latin Vulgate translation; some of them are known by slightly different names in the English Bible; thus 3 and 4 Esdras in the above list are more commonly known to us as 1 and 2 Esdras,[1] Tobias is known as Tobit, and 'Jesus the son of Sirach' is the book more generally referred to as Ecclesiasticus. In surveying these books, it is convenient to divide them according to their literary character.

[1] The nomenclature of the Esdras books is extremely confusing. These two books (1 and 2 Esdras in the English Apocrypha) are called 3 and 4 Esdras in Article VI because they are so called in the Latin Vulgate. In the Latin Vulgate 1 and 2 Esdras are the names given to our Ezra and Nehemiah respectively. In the Septuagint 1 Esdras is our apocryphal 1 Esdras, and 2 Esdras is our Ezra and Nehemiah. Our apocryphal 2 Esdras is not included in the Septuagint.

1. *Historical*: 1 Esdras, 1 and 2 Maccabees.
2. *'Haggadah', or Religious Fiction*: Tobit, Judith, the Additions to Esther and the Additions to Daniel.
3. *'Wisdom' and Ethical Literature*: Ecclesiasticus, Wisdom, Baruch, Prayer of Manasseh.
4. *Apocalyptic*: 2 Esdras.

In the Septuagint these books (with the exception of 2 Esdras, which never belonged to the Septuagint) are generally arranged alongside canonical books of the same class. Thus 1 Esdras precedes Ezra and Nehemiah (but the books of Maccabees come after the Prophets), Judith and Tobit follow Esther, the Additions to Esther and Daniel appear as parts of the canonical books to which they are attached, Wisdom and Ecclesiasticus accompany the canonical Wisdom books (Job, etc.), Baruch is placed for obvious reasons after Jeremiah, and the Prayer of Manasseh is included in a collection of psalms and hymns which form an appendix to the Septuagint. More or less the same arrangement is followed in the Vulgate and in those versions which are translated from the Vulgate (such as the Douai and Knox versions), but in other English versions from Coverdale's Bible (1535) onward the apocryphal books (if they have been included at all) have been placed together separately after the canonical books of the Old Testament.

Let us now take a brief glance at these books and say something about their character and contents.

1. *Historical*

1 Esdras contains most of the material found in the canonical Ezra, but takes up the tale at an earlier date, for it starts with the Passover celebration of the 18th year of King Josiah, and goes on to tell the story of the closing years of the kingdom of Judah, closely following 2 Chron. 35. 1-36. 21. It ends with an account of the reading of the law by Ezra which is recorded in Neh. 8, but omits all mention of Nehemiah's name from this account. 1 Esdras is, in fact, a variant Greek version of part of the Chronicler's work (for, as we have seen, Chronicles-Ezra-Nehemiah are really one continuous historical work). Some scholars[1] have thought that 1 Esdras was the original 'Septuagint' translation of that part of the Chronicler's work which it contains. It is often called nowadays the 'Greek Ezra' as distinct from the 'Hebrew Ezra' (which is represented by the canonical Ezra). (The name Esdras is, of course, simply a Greek form of Ezra.) The greater part of its contents appears also in the canonical literature, but there is one section (1 Esdras 3. 1-5. 6) which tells of an intellectual competition

[1] In particular A. H. Sayce, H. St. John Thackeray and C. C. Torrey.

between three young men belonging to the bodyguard of Darius I of Persia. The prize is awarded to one of the three named Zerubbabel, who has spoken in praise of Truth: it is from this story that we get the proverbial saying, 'Great is truth and mighty above all things'. Darius bids him choose what he will as his prize, and he asks the king to remember his vow to build Jerusalem. This story is also told by Josephus (*Antiquities* xi. 3).

1 Maccabees is our principal source for the attempt by Antiochus Epiphanes to suppress the Jewish religion and the consequent rising of the Hasmonaean family and establishment of their dynasty; it carries the story down to the reign of John Hyrcanus (134-104 B.C.), and is written with a pronounced pro-Hasmonaean bias. It was written either towards the end of the second century B.C. or in the earlier part of the first century, and although it is no longer extant in any earlier form than the Greek version, it was certainly written originally in Hebrew. The Greek text bears several marks of translation from a Hebrew original, and we have a statement by Jerome that he found this book in Hebrew.

2 Maccabees is not an original work; it is an abridgment of a longer history written in Greek some time about the middle of the first century B.C. by a Jew of Cyrene named Jason. The book relates certain incidents from the persecution under Antiochus and the Hasmonaean revolt from a Pharisaic point of view, with marked emphasis on such things as the sanctity of the Temple, the observance of the Sabbath and the certainty of a blessed resurrection for the martyrs. Its moralizing tendency is indulged at the expense of historical reality; as a source-book for the history of the period it is of much inferior value to 1 Maccabees.

Some copies of the Septuagint have preserved two other 'books of Maccabees'. Of these, 3 Maccabees has nothing to do with the Maccabees; it is chiefly concerned with an attempt by Ptolemy IV of Egypt (221-203 B.C.) to massacre the Jews of Alexandria and with their miraculous deliverance. 4 Maccabees uses the account of certain martyrdoms described in 2 Maccabees to illustrate the power of mind over matter. Both these books were written about the beginning of the Christian era; although extant in the Septuagint they are not part of the Vulgate, and so have not come to be reckoned among the apocryphal books known to Western Christendom.

2. 'Haggadah' or Religious Fiction

The Book of Tobit was written about 200 B.C., and its original language was either Hebrew or Aramaic. Fragments of the book in both Hebrew and Aramaic were found in the fourth cave at Qumran. It purports to tell the story of a pious Israelite named Tobit who was carried away by the Assyrians with many of his fellow-countrymen after the Fall of Samaria. The main purpose of the book is to illustrate the importance of observing the law, with particular emphasis on deeds of charity. It contains features belonging to widespread folk-tales, and shows quite plainly the influence of Persian beliefs and practices. Good and bad angels play an important part in the story; when young Tobias, the son of Tobit, goes to a town of Media to collect from a kinsman some money belonging to his father, he is accompanied by the angel, Raphael, who, under the guise of a travelling companion, serves him very effectively as a guardian angel. When he arrives at Ecbatana, he is able with Raphael's help to drive away an evil spirit named Asmodaeus—who is a well-known character in Persian demonology, where his name appears in its original form, Aeshma-daeva, 'wrathful demon'. The story has left its mark in common life in several interesting ways: the dog Toby traces his descent from the dog of Tobias, who accompanied his young master to Media; and the female name, Edna, first appears in literature as the name of Tobias's mother-in-law.

Judith forms a fierce contrast to the domestic charm of Tobit; it takes its name from a young Jewish widow who, by subjecting the heathen general, Holofernes, to her charm, finds an opportunity to take off his head and thus delivers her city and people from destruction. The book contains the most atrocious historical blunders; Holofernes, for example, is the general of 'Nebuchadnezzar, who reigned over the Assyrians in Nineveh.' If any historical situation at all is reflected in the book, it is an expedition to Syria and Asia Minor by the Persian king, Artaxerxes III (359-338 B.C.); the name Holofernes (Orophernes) was borne by a general of this king. But Judith is not history, but fiction, and it was probably written at some time during the campaigns of Judas Maccabaeus in order to stimulate the ardour of the Jewish patriots. If it has no historical value, however, it has some geographical value, as the author was evidently well acquainted with the region where the action takes place (in Central Palestine), although he disguised the place-names by the use of cryptograms. It was originally written in Hebrew, but no fragment of the Hebrew original has been preserved.

The additions to Esther were mainly intended to compensate

for the absence of the name of God or of any note of true religion from the canonical book. They are popular expansions of the story of Esther, which may have been handed down orally before they were written down in Greek and added to the Greek version of the Hebrew and canonical book.

The additions to Daniel are three in number: the story of Susanna, the story of Bel and the Dragon, and the Song of the Three Children. The story of Susanna gave rise to the proverb 'a Daniel come to judgment', made famous by Shakespeare in *The Merchant of Venice*. It tells how Daniel, as a young man, defended the good name of Susanna, a virtuous and beautiful Jewish lady, against the false accusations of two wicked old men, by examining her accusers separately and exposing the detailed inconsistency of their testimony. The story of Bel and the Dragon is an attack on idolatry. Daniel exposes the fraudulent conduct of the priests who tended the image of the god Bel, and compasses the death of a great dragon which is also worshipped by the Babylonians. The people in wrath demand his death, and he is cast into a lions' den, where he is fed by the prophet, Habakkuk, who is transported by an angel from Palestine to Babylon for this purpose. On the seventh day the king finds Daniel still alive in the den, and has him taken out.

The other addition to Daniel was inserted between verses 23 and 24 of chapter 3. It begins: 'And they walked in the midst of the fire praising God and blessing the Lord'. Then comes a prayer for deliverance, put into the mouth of Azariah (Abednego), after which we read:

> 'And the king's servants that put them in ceased not to make the furnace hot with naphtha, pitch, tow and small wood; so that the flame streamed forth above the furnace forty and nine cubits. And it spread and burned those Chaldeans whom it found about the furnace. But the angel of the Lord came down into the furnace together with Azariah and his fellows, and he smote the flame of the fire out of the furnace; and made the midst of the furnace as it had been a moist whistling wind, so that the fire touched them not at all, neither hurt nor troubled them.'

This is followed by an ascription of praise to God by the three Hebrews, which leads on to the Song proper, beginning 'O all ye works of the Lord, bless ye the Lord; praise Him and magnify Him for ever', which has won a secure place in Christian worship as the canticle *Benedicite omnia opera*.

The Song proper and the Prayer of Azariah seem originally to have been independent compositions and to have been adapted later to the narrative of the three faithful Hebrews in Daniel 3. The language of the Prayer reflects the conditions of the persecution under Antiochus Epiphanes. The stories of Susanna and of Bel and the Dragon may be dated very roughly round 100 B.C. All the additions to Daniel were probably composed at first in Hebrew or Aramaic. The cycle of stories about Daniel and his companions evidently continued to grow after the completion of the canonical Daniel, and there are several stories not included in these apocryphal additions. Josephus, for example, tells us about Daniel's building a tower at Ecbatana in Media,[1] and further additions to the cycle have been identified among the Qumran manuscripts.

3. 'Wisdom' and Ethical Literature

The Apocrypha include two important contributions to Jewish 'Wisdom' literature—the Wisdom of Jesus the son of Sira (commonly called Ecclesiasticus) and the so-called Wisdom of Solomon. The former was written in Palestine about 180 B.C. in Hebrew; the latter was written in Alexandria, and has been variously dated during the two centuries preceding A.D. 40. For many centuries the Hebrew original of Ecclesiasticus was lost (apart from some quotations in the Talmud), but through the discovery of a number of fragments of the Hebrew in the Cairo *genizah* since 1896, and more recently of other fragments at Qumran, we now possess well over half of the original text. The Greek version in the Septuagint was made by a grandson of the author, who left Jerusalem for Egypt in 132 B.C. Ecclesiasticus reflects the outlook of the period preceding the persecution under Antiochus; the only immortality its author cares about is posterity's remembrance of a man's virtues. The best known section of the book deals with this kind of immortality; it is the section in praise of the elders beginning, 'Let us now praise famous men and our fathers that begat us' (44. 1), so frequently read at commemoration services. The Book of Wisdom contains an attack on idolatry remarkably akin to what Paul has to say on the subject in Rom. 1. 18-32.[2] Those who date it about A.D. 40 argue that the subject was keenly relevant just then, for the Emperor Gaius had lately ordered that his image should be erected in the Jerusalem temple to receive divine honours, and this mad policy had serious repercussions

---

[1] Josephus, *Antiquities*, x. 11. 7.

[2] R. A. Knox makes the intriguing revelation that (one wonders how seriously) he has 'toyed with the idea of writing a thesis to prove that it [Wisdom] was written by St. Paul, still unconverted' (*On Englishing the Bible*, p. 89).

among the Alexandrian Jews as well as among those of Palestine.

Baruch purports to be the work of Jeremiah's friend of that name, but actually belongs to a much later date, shortly before or shortly after the beginning of the Christian era. It contains a confession of national sin, a homily on wisdom, which is identified with the law, and a promise of deliverance and restoration. An independent composition appended to Baruch is the 'Epistle of Jeremiah', which contains a warning against idolatry.

The Prayer of Manasseh is a confession of sin and petition for forgiveness, judged appropriate for utterance by King Manasseh when the Assyrians had carried him captive to Babylon, as is related in 2 Chron. 33. 11-13. The Chronicler concludes his account of Manasseh by saying: 'His prayer also, and how God was intreated of him . . . behold, they are written in the history of Hozai (or 'the seers')' (2 Chron. 33. 19). Perhaps some reader in later days, not being able to find this document, decided to make good the deficiency by composing a prayer of repentance in terms which Manasseh would probably have used. It may have been composed in the course of the second century B.C., but its first appearance in literature is in a Christian work of the third century A.D., the *Didascalia Apostolorum*. It is contained in *Codex Alexandrinus* (see p. 183). It was first translated into English for Matthew's Bible of 1537.

4. *Apocalyptic*

Between the Maccabaean wars and the rebellion of Bar-kokhba in A.D. 132, the number of apocalyptic works that appeared in Jewish circles is legion, but only one of them forms part of the Apocrypha proper, the work which we call 2 Esdras. As it stands this is a composite work. The first two chapters are Jewish-Christian in origin and put into the mouth of Ezra a prophecy of the rejection of the Jews in favour of the Christian Church; the last two chapters (15 and 16) contain denunciations of all men in general and certain nations in particular because of their wickedness, and were probably composed in the third century A.D. The kernel of the book (chapters 3-14) is sometimes called the 'Ezra Apocalypse' and consists of seven visions in which revelations of the future were made to Ezra in Babylon; the actual date of composition is *c.* A.D. 100. The Hebrew original of the book is lost, and so is the Greek version; it is, however, extant in other versions based on the

Greek—Latin, Syriac, Ethiopic, Arabic, Armenian and fragments in one or two other languages.[1]

Another important apocalypse, which exercised a deep influence at one time, is the composite work known as the First (or Ethiopic) Book of Enoch, the various parts of which belong to the last two centuries B.C. It throws welcome light on the background of popular thought in Palestine in New Testament times. While it is sometimes quoted as authoritative by early Christian writers, the only Church to accord it canonical status was the Ethiopic Church.[2] It therefore forms to the present day an integral part of the Ethiopic Bible, and that is why Ethiopic is the only language in which it has been preserved complete. Its Aramaic original was lost for long but fragments of it have been found at Qumran; a considerable part of the Greek version is extant.

Having surveyed the apocryphal literature, we have to consider the question, so frequently asked, why these books are not accorded the same authority as the canonical books. The answer is not that they were not written in Hebrew for, as we have seen, many of them were, and were extant in Hebrew well into the Christian era. The answer is rather that they were not regarded as canonical by the Jews, either of Palestine or of Alexandria; and that our Lord and His apostles accepted the Jewish canon and confirmed its authority by the use they made of it, whereas there is no evidence to show that they regarded the apocryphal literature (or as much of it as had appeared in their time) as similarly authoritative.

The early Greek-speaking Church took over the Septuagint from the Hellenist Jews and in general accepted it in its entirety as Scripture without making any distinction between the various classes of books which it contained. Some of the Greek Fathers recognized a distinction in theory: Origen, Athanasius,[3] and others when enumerating the canonical books of the Old Testament restrict the list more or less to the books found in the Hebrew Bible, but in practice they quote the apocryphal books under the same

[1] In the R.V. and R.S.V. there are seventy verses after 2 Esdras 7. 35 which are absent from the A.V.; these were probably deliberately jettisoned from the Latin version at some stage because of their insistence that praying for the dead is useless; they were preserved in Syriac, Ethiopic, Arabic and Armenian versions, from which they were incorporated into German Bibles published in the eighteenth century in Europe and America. Their Latin text was discovered in 1874 in a ninth-century manuscript at Amiens. See B. M. Metzger, *Introduction to the Apocrypha* (Oxford, 1957), pp. 23 f.

[2] The words quoted from Enoch, in Jude 14, 15 appear in 1 Enoch 1. 9. The book is called 1 Enoch to distinguish it from two other specimens of Enochic literature: 2 Enoch (the 'Book of the Secrets of Enoch,' extant in a Slavonic version) and 3 Enoch (a Hebrew mystical treatise). On the Ethiopic canon see also p. 215.

[3] For Athanasius see p. 101.

formulae as they use in quoting from the canonical books. The Latin Fathers for the most part make no distinction; Augustine, for example, reckons the books of the Old Testament as 44 in number, including Tobit, Judith, 1 and 2 Maccabees, Ecclesiasticus and Wisdom[1]. Jerome, however, the greatest Biblical scholar of the Western Church, made a clear distinction between the canonical and apocryphal books; it is to him, in fact, that we owe the term 'apocryphal' as applied to them. The word means etymologically 'hidden', and may primarily have referred to a story in 2 Esdras 14, where Ezra by divine inspiration dictates 94 books, 24 of which are to be published (the books of the Hebrew Canon), while the remaining 70 are to be kept secret (a reference probably to apocalyptic books). Jerome's use of the word, however, has nothing to do with its etymological sense, nor yet does it mean 'unauthentic' or 'untrue'; he simply meant by the term what others meant when they called them 'ecclesiastical books' (books suitable for reading in church) as contrasted with 'canonical books' (books which may be used for the establishment of doctrine).

At the time of the Reformation and Counter-Reformation the Roman Catholics and Protestants diverged markedly in their attitude to these books; the former at the Council of Trent maintained the full canonical status of Tobit, Judith, the additions to Esther and Daniel, Baruch, Ecclesiasticus, Wisdom, and 1 and 2 Maccabees, and they reaffirmed this position at the Vatican Council of 1870.[2] As for the Protestants, there was a divergence within their ranks; the Lutherans and Anglicans, while they did not accord the apocryphal books authority in matters of faith, gave them a sort of deutero-canonical status and continued to use them in church for their ethical value;[3] whereas the Reformed Churches which took their pattern from Geneva accorded them no status different from that of ordinary religious writings. Thus, over against the reference to them in Article VI of the Church of England, we have the *Westminster Confession of Faith* (1647) declaring that:

[1] This is also the reckoning of the Synod of Hippo in A.D. 393 and the Third Synod of Carthage in A.D. 397 (cf. p. 113).

[2] The Roman Catholic Church does not accept the Prayer of Manasseh or the two apocryphal Esdras books as canonical. The books called 1 and 2 Esdras in the Douai Bible are the canonical Ezra and Nehemiah respectively (which appear as 1 and 2 Esdras in the Latin Vulgate). As for the apocryphal books which do appear in the Douai Bible, there is a tendency nowadays among Roman Catholic scholars to class them as 'deutero-canonical'; though it is not clear that this practice is consistent with the decrees of the Trent and Vatican Councils.

[3] The Anglican *Homilies*, which quote the Apocrypha frequently, even refer to them as the 'word of God'.

'The Books commonly called Apocrypha, not being of divine inspiration, are not part of the canon of the Scripture; and therefore are of no authority in the Church of God, nor to be any otherwise approved, or made use of, than other human writings'.

It is not always easy nowadays to buy a copy of the Bible—A.V., R.V., or R.S.V.—that includes the Apocrypha. Few are produced—probably because few are demanded. But in the early days of English Bible-printing the Apocrypha was included as a matter of course. It is interesting to trace some of the stages by which the tendency to omit the Apocrypha from English Bibles steadily increased.

Coverdale's Bible of 1535, following a Zürich Bible of 1524-1529, first separated the apocryphal books from the canonical books of the Old Testament and placed them after Malachi, with a special introduction indicating their less authoritative character. There was one exception: Baruch was still placed after Jeremiah. But in a 1537 edition of Coverdale, Baruch was removed from there and placed after Tobit. Matthew's Bible of 1537 followed Coverdale's, but added the Prayer of Manasseh, which was now for the first time turned into English—from the French of Olivetan. Taverner's Bible of 1539, a revision of Matthew's, omitted the special introduction to the Apocrypha found in Coverdale and Matthew. The Great Bible, also of 1539, another revision of Matthew's, retains the introduction in question, but calls the books Hagiographa instead of Apocrypha. The fifth edition of the Great Bible (1541) omits the introduction, and supplies a second title-page, where the list of apocryphal books is prefaced by the words: 'The fourth part of the Bible, containing these books'. The substitution of these words for Coverdale's introduction obviously reduced the difference between the canonical and apocryphal books.

Becke's Bible, a revision of Taverner's, in 1549-51, has a complete retranslation of 1 Esdras, Tobit and Judith, and adds to the other apocryphal books 3 Maccabees, which now appeared for the first time in English dress. A new introduction to these books justified their separation from the canonical writings, but commended them 'for example of life'.

The Geneva Bible of 1560 prefaced the Apocrypha with an introductory note in more radical terms than those of previous translations. (It printed the Prayer of Manasseh as an appendix to 2 Chronicles, adding a note on its apocryphal character.) On the other hand, the Bishops' Bible of 1568 tacitly treated the

Apocrypha as an integral part of the Bible; it provided these books with a special title-page but no apologetic introduction.   The Puritan party in the Church of England, however, agreed with the followers of the Genevan tradition in their attitude to this as to many other questions.

The first English Bibles to omit the Apocrypha altogether were some copies of the Geneva version published at Geneva in 1599. There is a gap in the page-numbering between the Testaments, indicating that the omission of the Apocrypha was the binder's doing.

In 1611 the translators of the A.V. translated the Apocrypha as part of their work, and in 1615 Archbishop Abbot forbade any stationer to issue the Bible without the Apocrypha, on pain of one year's imprisonment.   But an edition of the Geneva Bible published at Amsterdam in 1640 omitted the Apocrypha deliberately: it was not simply the binder's doing this time.   A defence of the omission was inserted between the Testaments.   This omission was in line with the prevailing tendency in England at this time, where, in 1644, Parliament ordered that the canonical books only should be publicly read in church.   This tendency was reversed after the Restoration, but the exclusion of the Apocrypha became increasingly popular among the Nonconformists.   It is noteworthy that the first English Bible printed in America (1782-3)[1] lacked the Apocrypha.

The fashion of printing Bibles without the Apocrypha received an impetus in the nineteenth century from the example of the British and Foreign Bible Society, which, in 1826, decided to print no more Bibles with the Apocrypha.   It is recorded that this society offered to provide the official copy of the Bible for presentation to King Edward VII at his coronation in 1902, but the offer was declined by Archbishop Frederick Temple on the ground that a 'mutilated Bible' could not be accepted for the purpose.

The translation of the Apocrypha as part of the R.V. was completed in 1894 by the British revisers, but was not undertaken by the American revisers.   In America the Apocrypha was translated by Professor E. J. Goodspeed in 1938 as part of *The Bible: An American Translation*.   The Revised Standard Version of the Apocrypha was published in 1957.   In this country the Apocrypha was naturally included by the late R. A. Knox in his English

---

[1] This was not the first Bible published in America; the first was John Eliot's Algonquin version (N.T., 1661; O.T. 1663).   The first Bible to be published in a European language in America was a German edition of 1743 which did contain the Apocrypha (including the lost seventy verses of 2 Esdras 7; see p. 171).

translation of the Vulgate Old Testament (1949), and it is to be included in the New English Bible.

The best English edition of the apocryphal books, together with other uncanonical literature of a comparable character, is *The Apocrypha and Pseudepigrapha of the Old Testament*, a work containing introductions and commentaries as well as texts, produced by a team of scholars under the editorship of Dr. R. H. Charles, and published in two quarto volumes by the Oxford Press in 1913.

CHAPTER XIV

THE TEXT OF THE NEW TESTAMENT

THE New Testament books were written in Greek within the first century after the death and resurrection of Christ. The original documents were probably written on papyrus in ink. (These two writing materials are explicitly mentioned in 2 John 12.) The shorter writings (like the Epistle to Philemon, the second and third Epistles of John and that of Jude) would require a papyrus sheet of convenient size; the longer works would be written on papyrus rolls. The longest of all—the two parts of Luke's history and the Gospels of Matthew and John—represent about as much writing as could conveniently go on to a papyrus roll of normal length. The letters and the book of Revelation, when written, were sent to the individuals or churches for whom they were intended; Luke's two volumes were presumably sent to Theophilus; the other Gospels were probably deposited with the churches of Rome, Antioch, and Ephesus.

All these autographs have been lost long since. It could not be otherwise, if they were written on papyrus, since (as we have seen) it is only in exceptional conditions that papyrus survives for any length of time. But, providentially, they were copied before they became illegible; otherwise we should have no New Testament. How the first copies of the autographs were made we do not know for certain, but we saw in our chapter on the Canon of Scripture that, about the end of the first century A.D., or the beginning of the second, collections were made of the four canonical Gospels and of the letters of Paul, and the circulation of these collections must have involved a considerable amount of copying and recopying. Other churches than that in Ephesus wanted to have a copy of John's Gospel; other churches than those addressed in the first instance wanted to have copies of Paul's letters. When Clement, a leader in the Roman church about A.D. 95, writes a letter to the Corinthian church, he knows not only the letter which Paul wrote to the Romans, but one at least of those which he wrote to the Corinthians as well. 'Take up the epistle of the blessed Paul the apostle', he writes. 'What did he write first to you in the beginning of the Gospel? Of a truth he charged you in the Spirit concerning himself and Cephas and Apollos, because even then you had formed parties'.[1]

It is plain, then, that by A.D. 95 there was a copy of 1 Corinthians in the archives of the Roman church (and copies of other New Testament writings as well). From the end of the first century to our own day this process of copying and recopying has gone on. Since the fifteenth century the copying and recopying has been done by means of the printing press; before that it was done by hand. It is difficult to copy any documents without making slips; this is so even with modern printing methods, where repeated revisions in proof by a variety of readers reduce the chance of error to a minimum. Yet very curious misprints have crept into some editions of the Bible. One edition of the English Bible displayed the significant misprint in Psa. 119. 161, '*Printers* have persecuted me without a cause'; while another was known as the 'Wicked Bible' because of its inadvertent omission of the word 'not' from the Seventh Commandment.[2]

If misprints can creep into the published text in spite of all the opportunities for previous correction, it was much easier for errors to occur when long texts were copied out laboriously by hand. There are certain types of error which are particularly liable to occur in manuscripts, and these have been classified and named, so that in the majority of instances they are easily detected. Some errors arise more particularly when the scribe is copying by dictation, others arise when he is copying from an exemplar lying in front of him. In the former case he will mistake a word for another that *sounds* like it; in the latter case he will mistake a word for another that *looks* like it. Or, if he is unintelligent, he may divide words wrongly, especially if his exemplar makes no division between words. It may even be that two different divisions make some sort of sense; the question then is, which sense did the author intend? (There is an old moral tale of an infidel father who had the inscription '*God is Nowhere*' hung in his house and invited his little daughter to read it; she spelt it out, '*God is Now Here*'. That was a simple example of 'wrong division'!) The scribe may let his eye wander from a word (say) in line 4 to the same word in (say) line 7 and omit the intervening lines; he may, on the other hand, let his eye wander from the word in line 7 back to the same word in line 4 and write the intervening lines twice. The general name for this kind of mistake is *homoeoteleuton* (Greek for 'similarly

[1] 1 Clem. 47. 1-3.
[2] For this scandalous misprint the King's Printers were fined £300 by Archbishop Land.

ending'). Another form of omission is the writing once only of a word or phrase that should be written twice. This is called *haplography*, and the opposite error is the writing twice of something that should be written only once—*dittography*. The transposition of letters, words, or phrases, is another simple scribal error.

All these errors are the sort that are perpetrated by honest copyists. A man who makes a mistake in transcribing what he thinks he sees in his exemplar is a far more desirable character—from the textual critic's viewpoint, at any rate—than the clever scribe who writes down something which he sees is not in his exemplar, but which he thinks ought to be there. The errors of the former type of scribe are much more easily detected and corrected than those of the latter. But both types of scribes have played their parts in the copying and transmission of the New Testament.

The special character of the New Testament has given rise to special types of errors over and above those which are common in all manuscript copying. Because it is a collection of divinely authoritative writings, an orthodox scribe will not willingly copy out what seems to him to be a discrepancy or contradiction between two authors; hence comes the phenomenon of scribal harmonization. Another form of harmonization is more purely verbal; a scribe who knew one Gospel better than the others (and in early days this was usually Matthew's), would almost automatically copy out parallel passages in the other Gospels in a form approximating that with which he was most familiar. Or, if some Biblical statements seemed hardly orthodox when judged by the standard of later formulations of doctrine, some scribes could hardly resist the temptation to remove what they imagined to be unorthodox wording. Marcion's edition is the most outstanding example of tampering with the text on theological grounds. The wonder really is that there has been so comparatively little of this sort of thing.

In view of the inevitable accumulation of such errors over so many centuries, it may be thought that the original texts of the New Testament documents have been corrupted beyond restoration. Some writers, indeed, insist on the likelihood of this to such a degree that one sometimes suspects they would be glad if it were so. But they are mistaken. There is no body of ancient literature in the world which enjoys such a wealth of good textual attestation as the New Testament. The evidence for the original text of the New Testament is provided mainly by (1) early manuscripts of the New Testament in its original language (Greek), (2) early translations or 'versions' of the New Testament in other languages, from the readings of which we can often infer the underlying Greek, (3) quotations from the New Testament in the works of ancient authors (principally Greek, Latin, and Syriac, but also Coptic and Armenian), (4) lectionaries, both in Greek and in the other languages mentioned, in which passages of Scripture were arranged for systematic reading in church services.

The study of these witnesses to the original text and the restoration by their means of the original text as nearly as it can be determined belong to the science of Textual Criticism. This is not, of course, a science which has to do specially with the New Testament or the Bible as a whole; it makes its contribution to all kinds of literature. In English literature it is a very necessary science in the study of the works of Shakespeare and the determining of his original text by the comparative study of the early editions.

There are four principal stages in the work of the textual critic. First, he makes a study of such individual manuscripts as are available to him, correcting obvious slips and taking cognizance of what appear to be scribal alterations, whether accidental or deliberate. Next, he arranges these manuscripts in groups. Those which share some peculiar feature of spelling or wording, or some common error, are probably related to one another and have a common archetype. There are different ways of grouping manuscripts, according as their evident relation to one another is more or less close. Those whose mutual relation can be fairly precisely established are said to constitute a family. But a number of separate families, while they are diverse from one another in many respects, may have a sufficient number of significant features in common to suggest that they all represent one rather early textual type. In the third place, when the arranging of manuscripts in groups leads to the establishment of an archetype for each of the groups which have been distinguished, these archetypes themselves are subjected to comparative study in the hope that it may be possible to reconstruct a provisional archetype from which the archetypes themselves are descended; if this is achieved, then we have arrived as closely as we can to the autographic text.

Sometimes, after all these processes have been completed, even the ultimate archetype provisionally reconstructed is seen to contain here and there a reading which is manifestly corrupt. No objective textual evidence is available to correct it; the textual critic must perforce employ the art of conjectural emendation— an art which demands the severest self-discipline. The emendation must commend itself as obviously right, and it must account for the way in which the corruption crept in. In other words, it must be both 'intrinsically probable' and 'transcriptionally probable'. It is doubtful whether there is any reading in the New Testament which requires to be conjecturally emended. The wealth of attestation is such that the true reading is almost invariably bound to be preserved by at least one of the thousands of witnesses. Sometimes what was at first put forward as a conjectural emendation has in the course of time turned up in one of our witnesses. For example, it was for long suspected by a number of scholars that in John 19. 29 it was not 'hyssop' (Gk. *hyssōpos*) that was used to convey the sponge filled with vinegar to our Lord's mouth on the cross, but a soldier's javelin (Gk. *hyssos*). But more recently the reading 'javelin', which was previously a mere conjectural emendation, has been recognized in the first hand of a rather late manuscript, and it is adopted in the text of the New English Bible; but even so it is an extremely doubtful reading.

We have seen in Chapter IX how the text of the Hebrew Old Testament, even when no manuscript evidence was extant earlier than the ninth century A.D., was much more securely attested than might have been thought. The New Testament, however, is in a very much better case. I may be permitted to quote here words that I have written elsewhere:

'Perhaps we can appreciate how wealthy the New Testament is in manuscript attestation if we compare the textual material for other ancient historical works. For Cæsar's *Gallic War* (composed between 58 and 50 B.C.) there are several extant MSS, but only nine or ten are good, and the oldest is some 900 years later than Cæsar's day. Of the 142 books of the Roman history of Livy (59 B.C.-A.D. 17), only 35 survive; these are known to us from not more than twenty MSS of any consequence, only one of which, and that containing fragments of Books III-VI, is as old as the fourth century. Of the fourteen books of the *Histories* of Tacitus (*c*. A.D. 100) only four and a half survive; of the sixteen books of his *Annals*, ten survive in full and two in part. The text of these extant portions of his two great historical works depends entirely on two MSS, one of the ninth century and one of the eleventh. The extant MSS of his minor works (*Dialogus de Oratoribus, Agricola, Germania*) all descend from a codex of the tenth century. The History of Thucydides (*c*. 460-400 B.C.) is known to us from eight MSS, the earliest belonging to *c*. A.D. 900, and a few papyrus scraps, belonging to about the beginning of the Christian era. The same is true of the History of Herodotus (*c*. 488-428 B.C.). Yet no classical scholar would listen to an argument that the authenticity of Herodotus or Thucydides is in doubt because the earliest MSS of their works which are of any use to us are over 1,300 years later than the originals'.[1]

[1] *The New Testament Documents: Are They Reliable?* (5th edn., 1960), pp. 16 f. Of course the third kind of textual attestation mentioned above—quotations of their works by other writers—is available for some of these authors too, but to nothing like the same extent as for the Old and New Testaments.

So, when we are considering the textual evidence for the
Biblical writings, we should ask what kind and amount of evidence
we might reasonably expect, having regard to other ancient
writings of comparable date. If we approach the question this
way, we find that even the Old Testament text is astonishingly
well attested as compared with Herodotus and Thucydides, and
that it does not suffer even by comparison with Homer, who has
been more fortunate in this respect than they have. But the
textual evidence for the New Testament is abundant beyond all
comparison with these other works. The number of extant
manuscripts of all or part of the Greek New Testament runs to
about 5000. If the very number of manuscripts increases the total
of scribal corruptions, it supplies at the same time the means of
checking them. Many of these manuscripts are relatively late and
of minor importance (although it does not automatically follow
that a later manuscript must be less important than an earlier one;
sometimes a group of quite late manuscripts will have preserved
here and there an important ancient reading). Our most important
manuscripts, however, come from the fourth, fifth and sixth
centuries, and there are others still older. The oldest of all is the
fragment of a papyrus codex of the first half of the second century,
containing some verses of John 18, and now in the John Rylands
Library, Manchester. Dr. H. Guppy, the late Rylands Librarian,
described it, with pardonable exaggeration, as written 'when the
ink of the original autograph can hardly have been dry. This,'
he added, 'must be regarded as the earliest fragment by at least
fifty years of the New Testament'.[1] Of course such a tiny fragment
cannot make much of a contribution to textual criticism; its real
importance is the testimony it bears to the traditional date of John's
Gospel (c. A.D. 100).[2]

Date is not the only standard by which New Testament
manuscripts may be classified. They are sometimes classified
according to the material on which they are written. The two
main divisions of this classification are papyrus manuscripts and
parchment (vellum) manuscripts. Manuscripts in both divisions

---

[1] *Transmission of the Bible* (1935), p. 4. It is registered as *p* 52.

[2] Another papyrus discovery of comparable date (at any rate not later than A.D. 150)
was published in *Fragments of an Unknown Gospel and Other Early Christian Papyri*, edited by
H. I. Bell and T. C. Skeat (British Museum, 1935). This consists of some papyrus fragments of what has sometimes been thought to be a fifth Gospel having strong affinities
with the canonical four. Actually, however, the fragments represent paraphrases of the
Gospel stories and sayings designed for popular instruction; their chief importance is that
they were obviously written by someone who had the four canonical Gospels before him
and was well acquainted with them.

are denoted by serial numbers, papyrus manuscripts being distinguished by the letter *p*, or the abbreviation *pap.* preceding the number. The number of parchment manuscripts, of course, is far greater than that of papyrus manuscripts. All the papyrus manuscripts are fragmentary. The most important of these are the Chester Beatty Biblical papyri, the discovery of which was announced by Sir Frederic Kenyon in *The Times* of Nov. 17, 1931. These are a collection of papyrus codices, eleven in number, and three of them contain portions of the New Testament in Greek.[1] Of the three New Testament codices, one contained the four Gospels and Acts, another Paul's nine letters to churches and one to Philemon, and the Epistle to the Hebrews, and the third the book of Revelation. They are numbered *p* 45, *p* 46, and *p* 47 in the list of New Testament papyri. The former two belong to the first half of the third century, the third to the second half of the same century. The Pauline-Hebrews codex is most complete of the three; 86 folios have survived out of an original 104.

About 1956 the Bodmer Library, Geneva, acquired a papyrus codex of the Fourth Gospel (numbered *p* 66). The first fourteen chapters are almost complete; the remainder is in a fragmentary condition. This codex was written about A.D. 200, and presents some interesting textual features. Further papyri from the Bodmer collection published still more recently include a codex of *c.* A.D. 200 containing parts of Luke and John (*p* 75), another of comparable date containing the Epistles of Peter and Jude (*p* 72), and one of the sixth or seventh century containing Acts and the Catholic Epistles (*p* 74).

Again, New Testament manuscripts have been classified according to the kind of letters employed. Here again there are two chief divisions—uncial and minuscule manuscripts. Uncial letters were an adaptation of the lapidary capitals used for inscriptions in stone and the like; minuscule letters, as the name implies, were smaller and more akin to ordinary cursive hands. In the enumeration of New Testament manuscripts, those written in uncials are distinguished in that their serial numbers begin with the digit 0 (01, 02, 03, and so on), whereas minuscule manuscripts are numbered ordinarily (1, 2, 3, and so on into the thousands).

[1] The collection represents what was probably the Bible of some Greek-speaking church in Egypt. The other eight papyri in the collection included two manuscripts of Genesis, one of Numbers and Deuteronomy, one of Isaiah, one of Ezekiel, Daniel and Esther, one of Jeremiah (of which only one leaf remains), one of Ecclesiasticus (of which a leaf and a half remain), and one containing some chapters of 1 Enoch and an unidentified Christian homily. All were written in Greek; the Old Testament papyri, therefore, are valuable for the textual criticism of the Septuagint.

For the more important uncial manuscripts, however, an older method of denoting them by capital letters of the Roman, Greek, and even Hebrew alphabets has persisted.

Perhaps the most famous New Testament manuscript is the *Codex Sinaiticus*, denoted by the Hebrew letter א (*'aleph*). It is a parchment copy of the whole Greek Bible (although a good part of the Old Testament has been lost), written in the fourth century A.D., discovered by Dr. Tischendorf in the Mount Sinai Monastery in 1844, presented by the monastery to the Russian Tsar in 1859, and bought by the British Government and people from the Soviet Union for £100,000 on Christmas Day, 1933. It now forms the chief Biblical treasure of the British Museum. The British Museum also houses the *Codex Alexandrinus* (Codex A), another copy of the Greek Bible, written in the fifth century and presented to our King Charles I, in 1627, by Cyril Lucar, Patriarch of Alexandria, and afterwards of Constantinople. Yet another early copy of the Greek Bible is the *Codex Vaticanus* (Codex B), the chief Biblical treasure of the Vatican Library, which was written about the same time as Codex א and exhibits a similar type of text. These three manuscripts are uncials.

Another early uncial forms the chief Biblical treasure of the *Bibliothèque Nationale* in Paris. This is *Codex Ephraemi* (Codex C). It is an incomplete copy of the Greek Bible (64 Old Testament leaves surviving, and 145 New Testament leaves out of an original 238), and dates from the fifth century. It receives its name *Codex Ephraemi* because some time after it was written the Biblical text was rubbed off the parchment in order to use the material for copying out some writings of a fourth-century Syriac Father named Ephrem. The original writing has been revived to a considerable extent by the use of chemical reagents, and can now be read with some difficulty under the darker second writing. Parchment was not too plentiful, and it seemed worth while in those days to rub out earlier writing in order to accommodate something else. A manuscript to which this has happened is called a palimpsest (Greek for 'rubbed out again'). Another important palimpsest among Biblical manuscripts is the Sinaitic Syriac copy of the Gospels mentioned on pp. 198 f.

Another uncial is *Codex Bezae* (Codex D), which bears the name of the Genevan Reformer, Theodor Beza, who presented it to the University of Cambridge in 1581; it is the chief Biblical treasure of Cambridge University Library. It was written in the fifth or sixth century, and contains the Gospels and Acts in both

Greek and Latin.[1] Two important uncial manuscripts of the Gospels may also be mentioned: the *Washington Codex* (Codex W),[2] belonging to the fourth or fifth century, and acquired for the United States in 1906 by C. L. Freer; and the *Koridethi Codex* (Codex Θ), now at Tiflis, a manuscript of the ninth century with a text of the same general type as that of Codex W.

It should be obvious that for textual study the classification of manuscripts by writing material or style of writing is not of high relevance. Even classification by date is of limited value. Other things being equal, an earlier manuscript is likely to have suffered less from successive copyists' slips than a later manuscript; but if a thirteenth-century manuscript has been copied direct from a fifth-century manuscript which has since been lost, it must receive almost the same consideration as its exemplar would have received had it survived. Some scholars have gone too far in judging the value of manuscripts exclusively by their age. Such a scholar was Carl Lachmann, whose writings on the subject of New Testament criticism, published between 1842 and 1850, were epoch-making. Faced with an unmanageable body of manuscript evidence, Lachmann simplified it by disregarding the bulk of later manuscripts. More recently, however, it has become clear that even some quite late manuscripts have preserved some early readings. Even so, Lachmann's procedure marked an important and necessary advance in the study of the New Testament text, which had been impeded by the excessive attachment felt for the traditional text represented by the bulk of later manuscripts. Lachmann's principles were adopted and further applied by S. P. Tregelles and C. von Tischendorf, whose editions of the Greek New Testament supplied the main textual evidence in a most convenient and accessible form. It was in their time, too, that Codex B became accessible to scholarly study and Codex ℵ was discovered.

The text of the Greek Testament established by B. F. Westcott and F. J. A. Hort and published with an explanatory introduction

[1] It once contained the Catholic (or General) Epistles between the Gospels and Acts, but of these only a few verses of 3 John in Latin have been preserved. See p. 225.

[2] This codex inserts after Mark 16. 14 the words: 'And they excused themselves, saying, "This age of lawlessness and unbelief is under Satan, who by his unclean spirits does not allow the true power of God to be comprehended. Therefore now reveal thy righteousness." So they spoke to Christ, and Christ addressed them thus: "The limit of the years of Satan's authority has been fulfilled, but other terrible things are drawing near, even to those sinners on whose behalf I was handed over to death, that they may turn to the truth and sin no more. In order that they may inherit the spiritual and incorruptible glory of righteousness in heaven, go ye into all the world and preach the Gospel to the whole creation . . ."'—and so on to the end of verse 20. Jerome knew this passage as far down as the words 'Therefore now reveal thy righteousness' as occurring in certain copies and especially in Greek codices. (Cf. p. 204, with n. 1.)

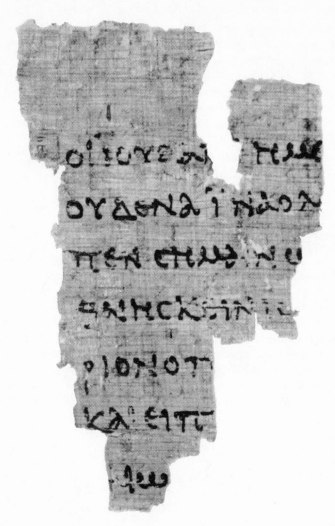

RECTO OF THE PAPYRUS FRAGMENT OF THE FOURTH GOSPEL, OF THE FIRST
HALF OF THE SECOND CENTURY. (ST. JOHN XVIII. 31-33)

and appendices in 1881 introduced a fresh and more scientific method of classification—classification according to textual types or families. This classification has the further advantage that it includes not only Greek manuscripts but also the early versions in other languages and New Testament quotations in ancient authors. Westcott and Hort were pioneers in this matter, and their classification has been corrected and expanded, but classification by types of text has been established as the most rational and fruitful classification of the evidence.

The great centres of Christianity in the early centuries tended, in the course of copying and recopying, to have distinct types of text associated with them. Textual students have been able to distinguish among our sources of evidence for the New Testament text groups of manuscripts, versions and citations associated in particular with Alexandria, Caesarea, Antioch and the West (and the West means primarily Rome). The Alexandrian type is represented in particular by Codices ℵ, B and C, and a few other uncials and minuscules;[1] also by the Coptic (Bohairic) version and by Biblical citations in the Alexandrian writers, Origen, Athanasius, and Cyril. The works of Origen, however, reveal the use of two types of Biblical text. When this was first pointed out (as it was in 1924 by B. H. Streeter in *The Four Gospels*), it was thought that the year 231, in which Origen left Alexandria for Caesarea, marked the time when he exchanged the use of the Alexandrian type of text for the other, which was accordingly called Caesarean. It was later pointed out, however, that Origen may have used this second type of text even before he left Alexandria; and that he certainly used the Alexandrian type of text for a time after he went to Caesarea. Then, when the Chester Beatty papyri were discovered and studied, it appeared that they, too, constituted a witness for the New Testament text which Streeter had called Caesarean, so that this text was current in Egypt in the first half of the third century—that is to say, in the time of Origen. But wherever it originated, this text was certainly used at Caesarea, and radiated from there, and it may continue to be called the Caesarean text. It is the text which was used (in the Gospels at any rate) by Cyril, bishop of Jerusalem, in the middle of the fourth century. Its chief representatives, in addition to the Chester Beatty papyri and the New Testament citations in some

[1] The Bodmer papyrus of John's Gospel (see p. 182) has been assigned by some scholars to the Alexandrian text-type, but care must be exercised in applying to such an early manuscript a method of classification based on the comparative study of later manuscripts. See J.N. Birdsall, *The Bodmer Papyrus of the Gospel of John* (London, 1960).

works of Origen, are Codices W and Θ, some 20 minuscules,[1] and the Palestinian Syriac, Old Armenian and Old Georgian versions.

The Antiochian (or rather the Old Antiochian[2]) text-type has not been isolated among Greek manuscripts, but it is the one to which the Old Syriac version belongs, and it is therefore a reasonable inference that the Greek text from which that version was made was of this type. It had close affinities with the Western text.

The Western text was widely diffused in the early Christian centuries, and is represented not only in several manuscripts (the chief of which is Codex D) and versions (in particular the Old Latin) but also in citations in a large variety of writers (as the African Fathers Tertullian, Cyprian and Augustine, the Latin translation of Irenaeus, and—remarkably enough—Clement of Alexandria). The chief characteristic feature of the Western text is its tendency to expansion. To this text, for example, belongs the famous insertion in the debate about Sabbath-keeping in Luke 6, where between verses 4 and 5 Codex D adds:

> 'The same day, beholding a certain man working on the Sabbath, He said to him: "Man, if indeed thou knowest what thou art doing, blessed art thou. But if thou knowest not, accursed art thou and a transgressor of the law".'

When days of peace came to the Church in the fourth century, and a strong tendency to centralization set in, the new imperial capital of Constantinople (the former Byzantium) exercised great influence on the whole of Greek-speaking Christendom. One feature of this tendency was the dissemination of one particular type of text of the Greek Bible in place of the diverse local types hitherto in vogue. The text of the Greek New Testament which thus became the standard text for Greek Christendom may have been based on a recension made by the same Lucian of Antioch whose recension of the Greek Old Testament was mentioned in Chapter XII. This text has sometimes been called the Antiochian text from its supposed place of origin, but this is liable to lead to confusion with the Old Antiochian text already mentioned, and so the new text had better be called the Byzantine text, since it was certainly adopted by the church of the eastern capital and radiated from that centre. (In Westcott and Hort's nomenclature it is called the 'Syrian' text.)

---

[1] To wit: Codex 1 and allied minuscules (118, 131, 209, 1582), Codex 13 and allied minuscules (69, 124, 230, 346, 543, 788, 826, 828, 983, 1689, 1709), and Codices 28, 565, and 700.

[2] Old Antiochian to distinguish it from the later Antiochian text, thought to have been established by Lucian (died 312). See p. 156.

Whether it was based on the recension of Lucian or not, this Byzantine text was marked by the same feature which we mentioned in connection with its Old Testament counterpart—the conflation of divergent readings from the earlier text-forms. If a textual variant is shown to have arisen from the conflation or mixture of two other variants, it is plainly later than these other two; and this conflate type of variant is very characteristic of the Byzantine text. This in itself suggests that the Byzantine text is later than those other types we have enumerated, and there is the further consideration that the Byzantine text is not represented in the translations or citations of the first three centuries A.D., whereas the other types of text are. Chrysostom is the first Greek Father whose Biblical citations show a Byzantine character (A.D. 347-407).

The Byzantine text is that represented by the bulk of later Greek manuscripts, and it is the text underlying the earliest printed editions of the Greek New Testament[1]—the so-called *Textus Receptus* or 'Received Text',[2] of which our Authorized Version of the New Testament is in the main a translation. It was not without a struggle that the claims of the 'Received Text' to represent the original text of the New Testament were given up; these claims were defended in particular in the closing decades of last century by two great English scholars—moderately by F. H. A. Scrivener and immoderately by J. W. Burgon.[3] But there are now extremely few scholars who hold the primacy of the Byzantine text.

What about the other and earlier forms of text? Westcott and Hort believed that the text which we have called the Alexandrian represented as nearly as could be attained the original autographic text. In their eyes, this text was marked by none of the deviations which they saw in other texts, and they expressed

---

[1] The earliest printed editions of the Greek Testament were the Complutensian, edited by Cardinal Ximenes, printed in 1514 and published in 1520, and that edited by Erasmus, published at Basel in 1516 and re-edited four times (his last edition—the fifth—appearing in 1535). The edition which became standard in England was the third edition (1550) of the Paris printer Estienne (Stephanus). These were followed by the editions of Beza (1565 and following years) and Elzevir (1624 and 1633). See S. P. Tregelles, *An Account of the Printed Text of the Greek New Testament* (1854).

[2] The phrase comes from the preface to Elzevir's 1633 edition of the Greek Testament: 'Textum ergo habes nunc ab omnibus receptum', the publisher says somewhat optimistically ('Now you have the text received by all').

[3] Two names worthy of perpetual veneration among Biblical textual scholars. Scrivener has left memorials of his great work in this field in his edition of the Greek Testament and his *Plain Introduction to the Criticism of the New Testament*; Burgon, for all his temperamental predisposition to be a defender of lost causes, was much ahead of his contemporaries in seeing the importance of early Christian lectionaries and Biblical citations in early authors for textual criticism, and did valuable pioneer work in these fields.

their high regard for it by naming it the 'Neutral' text.[1] But further discovery and study have led to second thoughts on this matter. A number of scholars have adduced weighty arguments for preferring the claims of the Western text to be regarded as the representative of the first-century text. Certainly the Western text has very ancient attestation; it appears in patristic citations earlier than the Alexandrian text does, and in the Gospels and Acts it exhibits a greater number of Aramaizing constructions than the other texts do. For all that, the Western text bears internal signs of being a revision of the first-century text of the New Testament which deviates from it more than the Alexandrian text does. The Alexandrian and Caesarean (and probably the Old Antiochian) texts may also represent revisions of the text, but revisions which represent the first-century text more faithfully than the Western text does. The position is now that we have evidence carrying our knowledge of the textual history of the New Testament well back into the second century. In particular, while we cannot regard the Alexandrian text with the same exclusive veneration as Westcott and Hort showed for it, and must see in it not a 'neutral' text (as they did) but a revised or edited text, yet we recognize that it is a *well* edited text, established by Christians of the second century on the basis of manuscripts far exceeding in antiquity those which have come down to us. The claims of the Caesarean and Old Antiochian texts are less easy to assess. While many, with Streeter, regard the Caesarean as an independent text, it is still possible to hold, as Professor and Mrs. Lake held in 1933,[2] that it is a correction of the Western text by the Alexandrian, and therefore later than both and secondary to them in importance. As for the Old Antiochian text, postulated as the Greek text from which the Old Syriac version was made, it must be earlier than that version, i.e. not later than the middle of the second century. For a similar reason the Western text must be equally old, because the earliest Old Latin version, which is Western in character, cannot be

---

[1] It is much better to avoid all such question-begging titles, and use such as all scholars will agree to, whatever their views of the character of the various texts may be. The geographical designations used above for the various textual types are less open to objection; even more colourless, however, are designations drawn from letters of the Greek alphabet, such as Sir F. Kenyon prefers. He would call the Byzantine text the α text (from Codex A, which is Byzantine in the Gospels), the Alexandrian text the β text (because its chief representative is Codex B) the Cæsarean text the γ text, the Western text the δ text (because its chief representative is Codex D), and the Old Antiochian text the ε text. Obviously this last kind of nomenclature begs no questions—except, indeed, the general question of the existence of text-types at all.

[2] K. Lake, *The Text of the New Testament* (6th edition, revised by S. New, 1933), p. 84.

much later than A.D. 150. (More will be said about the Syriac and Latin versions in the two following chapters.)

If, then, we have been able to carry our research into the text of the New Testament back to the middle of the second century, we should not despair of being able to press it right back into the first century itself—especially if further discoveries of ancient portions of Scripture are made. If Dr. Warfield could write in 1886 of 'the autographic text of the New Testament' as being 'distinctly within the reach of criticism' in 'immensely the greater part of the volume',[1] we need not be less hopeful to-day.

Something more ought to be said, and said with emphasis. We have been discussing various textual types, and reviewing their comparative claims to be regarded as best representatives of the original New Testament text. But there are not wide divergencies between these types, of a kind that could make any difference to the Church's responsibility to be a witness and guardian of Holy Writ. The Authorized Version of 1611 represents, by and large, the Byzantine text. The Revised Version of 1881 and the American Standard Version of 1901, which were produced under the influence of Westcott and Hort's textual theory and work, represent in the main the Alexandrian text. The Revised Standard Version of 1946 reflects the views of contemporary textual scholars, who have traced the various early lines of textual transmission back to the second century, and represents an eclectic text, each variant reading of the second-century textual types being considered on its merits, without marked preference being given to any single one of these types.[2] But the words of one of the editors of this latest revision are perfectly true:

> 'It will be obvious to the careful reader that still in 1946, as in 1881 and 1901, no doctrine of the Christian faith has been affected by the revision, for the simple reason that, out of the thousands of variant readings in the manuscripts, none has turned up thus far that requires a revision of Christian doctrine'.[3]

If the variant readings are so numerous, it is because the witnesses are so numerous. But all the witnesses, and all the types which they represent, agree on every article of Christian belief and practice. Our century has seen no greater authority in this field of New Testament textual criticism than Sir Frederic Kenyon, who died in

[1] B. B. Warfield, *Introduction to the Textual Criticism of the New Testament* (7th edition, 1907), p. 15, repeated from the 1st edition of 1886.
[2] Compare what is said in this respect about the New English Bible (pp. 241 f.).
[3] F. C. Grant, in *An Introduction to the Revised Standard Version of the New Testament* (1946), p. 42.

August, 1952, and we may take his words to heart with confidence:

> 'It is reassuring at the end to find that the general result of all these dis-
> coveries and all this study is to strengthen the proof of the authenticity of the
> Scriptures, and our conviction that we have in our hands, in substantial in-
> tegrity, the veritable Word of God'.[1]

And again:

> 'The interval then between the dates of original composition and the
> earliest extant evidence becomes so small as to be in fact negligible, and the
> last foundation for any doubt that the Scriptures have come down to us sub-
> stantially as they were written has now been removed. Both the *authenticity*
> and the *general integrity* of the books of the New Testament may be regarded
> as finally established'.[2]

[1] F. G. Kenyon, *The Story of the Bible* (1936), p. 144.
[2] F. G. Kenyon, *The Bible and Archæology* (1940), pp. 228 f.

CHAPTER XV

THE SYRIAC BIBLE

'PARTHIANS and Medes and Elamites, and the dwellers in Mesopotamia' are listed among the crowds which came together in Jerusalem on the first Christian Pentecost to hear the disciples. These were Jews who lived in the territories beyond the Euphrates, outside the Roman Empire. Jews had lived in those parts continuously since the captivity of the ten tribes (commonly miscalled the 'lost' tribes) and their numbers ran into millions by the first century. The dominant power east of the Euphrates was in those days the Parthian Empire, under which the Jewish communities seem to have enjoyed much the same degree of religious autonomy as those west of the Euphrates were accorded by the Romans. All the Jews of those parts spoke Aramaic, in common with a considerable part of the non-Jewish population.

Whether any of those eastern Jews who heard Peter speak in Jerusalem brought the Gospel story back home with them we cannot say. Or whether any of the apostles later evangelized those parts we also cannot say with certainty. Legend is abundant on the subject of the later labours of the twelve apostles, but historical evidence is astonishingly scanty outside the pages of the New Testament. However that may be, we know that the Gospel was carried eastward as well as westward in the early Christian decades, although (to our loss) no writer recorded the eastern mission as Luke recorded that in the west.

Before the end of the first century Christianity had been introduced east of the Tigris, in the district round Arbela, to the east of the ancient Nineveh.[1] This district round Arbela forms the setting of an interesting narrative in Josephus,[2] who records how, about A.D. 40, the royal house of the Kingdom of Adiabene, of which Arbela was the capital, was converted to Judaism. For thirty years at any rate this dynasty continued faithful to the Jewish religion (two members of it fought on the Jewish side against the Romans in the war of A.D. 66-70). During those years Jewish influence had every opportunity of spreading in Adiabene and the

---

[1] The rise and progress of Christianity in these eastern territories is recorded in the Syriac *Chronicle of Arbela*, compiled in the sixth century on the basis of good local tradition. Its value has been acknowledged by Harnack and other historical students.

[2] Josephus, *Antiquities*, xx. 2. 1 ff.

neighbourhood. There was a sufficient reading public in those parts for Josephus to produce the first edition of his *History of the Jewish War* in Aramaic for the benefit of the 'Parthians and Babylonians and remotest Arabians, and those of our own nation beyond the Euphrates, and the people of Adiabene'.[1]

This Jewish forward movement in the middle of the first century may well have paved the way for the propagation of Christianity in these lands. At any rate, before long Christianity was securely established in Upper Mesopotamia. In the course of the second century the city of Edessa, east of the Upper Euphrates, appears as the chief centre of Mesopotamian Christianity. From that area the Gospel was carried eastward into the heart of Asia, as far as China. Indeed, right on into the Middle Ages no missionary activity was carried on equal to that in which the Syriac Church engaged.

'It was a campaign of deliberate conquest, one of the greatest that Christian missionaries have ever planned. . . . In the year 1265 the Nestorians[2] reckoned twenty-five Asiatic provinces and more than seventy dioceses. Amongst the latter were Transoxiana, Turkestan, China, and Tangout. Tangout comprised the part of Western China now known as Shensi and Kansu, and the capital of the province was Hsi'en-fu where a great inscription was discovered.[3] . . . From Marco Polo and other travellers we get information of the existence of Nestorian Churches all along the trade routes from Bagdad to Pekin'.[4]

To India, too, the Syriac mission penetrated, and the Syrian Church of the Malabar coast has not only survived to our day, but has shown an increasing vitality during the present century. That Christianity was planted in India at an early date is suggested by the record in Eusebius that when Pantaenus, head of the catechetical school in Alexandria about A.D. 180, went on a mission to India,[5] 'it is reported that his coming had been preceded by the Gospel according to Matthew among some who knew Christ there. Bartholomew, one of the apostles', Eusebius continues, 'had preached to them and left behind Matthew's writing in the script of the Hebrews. This writing is reported to have been preserved

---

[1] Josephus, *Jewish War*, pref., 1, 2.

[2] The Nestorians were so called after Nestorius, patriarch of Constantinople from 428 to 431. He was condemned by the Council of Ephesus in 431 for maintaining Christological views which were held to be heretical. These views, however, triumphed among most of the Syriac Churches. Nestorianism so emphasized the distinction between the Two Natures of Christ as practically to make them two personalities.

[3] This is a Chinese inscription, with a border of Syriac writing, dated in 781, which describes the course of the Syriac mission in China from 636 onward. See Gibbon, *Decline and Fall of the Roman Empire*, chap. 47 (Chandos Classics edition, Vol. III, p. 356, n. 3).

[4] J. R. Harris, *Side-lights on New Testament Research* (1908), pp. 122 f.

[5] 'India' is used by writers of this period in a fairly general sense, and may include any territory on the Asian coast of the Indian Ocean.

to the time mentioned'.[1] The Indian tradition ascribes the first evangelization of the country to the Apostle Thomas. Much of this traditional material is legendary, but it does attest the antiquity of the Syrian Church of India. The official Bible of this Church is the standard Syriac version, and Syriac is still its ecclesiastical language. It should be explained here that 'Syriac' is the name generally given to Christian Aramaic. It is written in a distinctive variation of the Aramaic alphabet.

The standard Syriac version of the Bible is known as the *Peshitta* or 'simple' version. In examining its history we have to consider the Old and New Testaments separately.

The Syriac Old Testament is evidently a translation from the Hebrew original, although it bears some marks of Septuagint influence. When and by whom the translation was made we have no direct information. About A.D. 400 Theodore of Mopsuestia could write of it: 'It has been translated into the tongue of the Syrians by someone or other, for it has not been learned up to the present day who this was'. So we have to form our conclusions on the internal evidence of the version itself. This evidence suggests that we have to do with a translation made from Hebrew by Jews, in fact with a sort of Targum. There are, in fact, some typical Targumic interpretations in the Syriac Old Testament, one of which (in Psalm 68. 18) we have already noticed.[2] Dr. Kahle says that 'there can be no doubt that the closest contact exists between the Syriac Pentateuch and the old Palestinian Targum'.[3] He also suggests that the Syriac version of the Old Testament was carried through in connection with the Jewish mission among the pagan population of Adiabene at the time when the royal house of that country professed the Jewish faith (A.D. 40-70). When the Jewish mission was followed by the Christian mission there and in the neighbouring territories, the Syriac translation of the Old Testament was very likely taken over by the Christians and subjected to Christian editing. To this Christian editing the Septuagint influence detected in the version may well be due. One obvious instance of Septuagint influence appears in the treatment of the musical sign 'Selah' which occurs here and there throughout the Psalms. The Septuagint renders the word by *diapsalma*, which probably denotes the playing of musical instruments during a pause in the singing. The Syriac Psalter simply

[1] Eusebius, *Hist. Eccl.* v. 10.   [2] See p. 138.
[3] *The Cairo Geniza* (1947), p. 187. Cf. 2nd edn. (1959), p. 273. See p. 135 above.

represents the word by a transliteration in Syriac characters of the Greek word *diapsalma*.

There was another Syriac version of the Old Testament, made by Paul, bishop of Tella in Mesopotamia, about 616. This was not a translation from the Hebrew, but a Syriac version of the Septuagint column in Origen's Hexapla, whence it is known as the Syro-Hexaplar text. It never took root among the Syrian Churches, partly, no doubt, because it was so slavishly literal a translation of the Greek as to violate Syriac idiom, but for that very reason the surviving manuscripts of the Syro-Hexaplar are valuable witnesses to the Hexaplaric text of the Septuagint.[1]

As soon as the Christian mission had been set afoot in Mesopotamia, the need would naturally arise for a version of the New Testament in the language of those parts. As regularly happened in the case of translations of Scripture, we find first a period in which several variant efforts at translation are in circulation, none of them being officially authorized, followed by the establishment and imposition of a standard edition. The standard edition of the Syriac New Testament has generally been identified with the revision undertaken by Rabbula, who was bishop of Edessa from 411 to 435. Rabbula's biographer tells us that he undertook his revision because of the variations in the existing texts (which is what we should expect when there was no one 'authorized' text), and that he carried it out accurately, in accordance with the 'authentic' text. As a matter of fact, the 'authentic' text in accordance with which Rabbula produced his revision was the Byzantine Greek text which by this time had become the standard text of Greek Christendom. Together with the Christian recension of the Syriac Old Testament Rabbula's revision of the New Testament constitutes the *Peshitta*, which from his time to our own has remained the 'authorized version' of the Bible in the Syriac Churches. Naturally, Rabbula's revision did not find immediate and universal acceptance; Old Syriac readings can be traced in quotations by Syriac writers down to the beginning of the sixth century, and Rabbula himself was so familiar with the older versions that even in works which he wrote towards the end of his life a large proportion of his Gospel quotations agree with the Old Syriac or Diatessaron texts rather than with the Peshitta. But the fact that the Peshitta is the 'authorized version' of the two main opposed

[1] Fragments also exist of a Christian Palestinian Syriac version of the Old Testament made from the Septuagint some time before the fifth century, and of the version of Philoxenus of Mabug who had the whole Syriac Bible revised c. A.D. 508. Other Syriac versions from the Septuagint are recorded as having been made from time to time.

branches of Syriac Christianity, the Nestorians and the Jacobites, indicated that it must have been firmly established by the time of their final cleavage, well before the end of the fifth century.

It was believed at one time that the Peshitta New Testament was earlier than Rabbula's time, but in point of fact the only forms of Syriac Scripture whose existence and use are attested before the fifth century are some of those texts whose variations impelled Rabbula to undertake his standard revision. For example, Ephrem, the greatest of the Syriac Fathers (c. 308-373), uses in his writings no version of the Gospels other than that known as the Diatessaron (on which indeed he wrote a commentary). This was a harmony of the Gospels very popular in Mesopotamia. Theodoretus, bishop of Cyrrhus near the Euphrates from c. 423 to 457, records that he collected and removed more than 200 copies from the churches in his diocese, replacing them by 'the Gospels of the Four Evangelists.' This last expression probably denotes Rabbula's revision of the Gospels. Rabbula himself seems to have taken similar steps in his neighbouring diocese of Edessa; one of his directions to his clergy ran: 'The presbyters and deacons shall see to it that in all the churches a copy of the "Gospel of the separated ones" shall be available and read'.[1] (The 'Gospel of the separated ones' refers to an edition of the four separate Gospels as distinct from a harmony which weaves them together into one continuous narrative; the edition which Rabbula prescribed would naturally be his own.) It might well seem that the supersession of the Diatessaron was a prime consideration with Rabbula in undertaking his revision.

What, then, was this Diatessaron? The word is by origin a Greek musical term, meaning a 'harmony of four (parts)' (Gk. dia tessarōn, literally 'through four'). It is the name given to a work compiled by Tatian, an Assyrian Christian, shortly after the middle of the second century. The idea of weaving the four Gospels into one continuous narrative is one that has occurred to many people in the course of the Christian era, but Tatian was (so far as we can tell) the first person to do such a thing. He spent several years at Rome, where he became a disciple of Justin Martyr, and returned to his native Assyria about A.D. 172. Where exactly we are to locate the 'Assyria' to which Tatian belonged is a matter on which there has been some difference of opinion, but it is an interesting coincidence with what has been said already about Adiabene that the great German theologian Zahn should have concluded that Tatian came from that area. Zahn reached this

[1] Th. Zahn, Forschungen zur Geschichte des neutestamentlichen Kanons, i. (1881), p. 105.

conclusion on the evidence of the Greek geographers Strabo and Ptolemy.[1] Others, however, have thought of the district round Edessa. In any case, the harmony of the Gospels which Tatian compiled became very popular among the Syriac-speaking Christians, and it required drastic measures even 250 years later, such as those adopted by Rabbula and Theodoretus, to abolish its use and see to it that the faithful read or heard the 'separate' Gospels. For Tatian was not quite orthodox; he founded an ascetic and vegetarian sect called the 'Encratites' (or 'continent' people). It appears that Tatian introduced some of his Encratite ideas into his text of the Diatessaron; for example, John the Baptist is made a vegetarian and instead of eating locusts and wild honey he is fed on milk and honey.[2] It is when mentioning the Encratites that Eusebius makes his solitary mention of the Diatessaron, in terms which suggest that he had never seen a copy: 'Their first leader Tatian composed in some way or other a combination and assembling of the Gospels and called it the Diatessaron, which is current among some people even to the present day'.[3]

But we do not refer to it so vaguely as Eusebius did: we know more exactly in what way Tatian put the Gospel story together. We know, for example, that the Diatessaron was a harmony of the four canonical Gospels (possibly with an occasional insertion from the 'Gospel according to the Hebrews'[4]) and that it began with the first five verses of John's Gospel, after which, instead of the Johannine summary, 'There came a man, sent from God, whose name was John', Tatian reproduced Luke's narrative of the nativity of John the Baptist.

Certain schools of New Testament criticism which flourished in the nineteenth century denied that the Diatessaron was a harmony of the four canonical Gospels. If they had conceded that it was, they would have had to revise their opinions of the date and origin of these Gospels, which they regarded as late in date and possessed of little historical value. Even Bishop Lightfoot, of Durham, in his critique of the book entitled *Supernatural Religion*,[5] could only argue from probability that the Diatessaron did in fact testify to the existence and acknowledged authority of our four

---

[1] *Op. cit.*, p. 269.

[2] We may compare the version favoured by the Ebionites (a Jewish-Christian sect), who replaced the locusts (Gk. *akrides*) in John's diet by pancakes (Gk. *enkrides*).

[3] Eusebius, *Hist. Eccl.*, iv., 29 (early fourth century).   [4] See p. 263.

[5] The anonymous author of this work (1874), later revealed to be W. W. Cassels, argued for the late second-century dating of the Gospels. Bishop Lightfoot's counter-arguments appeared in the *Contemporary Review*, 1874-77, and were reprinted in the volume *Essays on 'Supernatural Religion'* (1889).

Gospels by A.D. 170. 'Yet all the time', as Sir Frederic Kenyon says, 'the decisive proof was lying, so to speak, under their noses'.[1] We have already noticed that the Syrian Father Ephrem wrote a commentary on the Diatessaron. The original Syriac text of this commentary was long lost,[2] but it was accessible in an Armenian translation, which was printed in 1836 by the Fathers of an Armenian convent in Venice, who also published a Latin translation of it in 1876. Not long after, two manuscript copies of an Arabic version of the Diatessaron turned up and this was published in 1888; other evidence of this Arabic Diatessaron has since come to light. The Diatessaron also survives in Latin and Old Dutch forms.

One matter which has not been decisively cleared up concerns the original language of the Diatessaron. Did Tatian compile it in Syriac or did he compile it first in Greek and then translate it into Syriac? On the one hand we have the clear evidence of its circulation and popularity as a Syriac Gospel-harmony. On the other hand we have its Greek title, and also the fact that a third-century vellum fragment of the Diatessaron in Greek was identified in 1933 among a quantity of manuscripts found among the ruins of a Roman fort at Dura-Europos on the Euphrates. However, one textual scholar, Professor A. Baumstark, thinks that this fragment represents a re-translation from the Syriac Diatessaron into Greek. Perhaps the wisest course is to say with Dr. Kahle that Tatian 'produced a Syriac text arranged in the order of the Diatessaron'; he formulates the statement thus in conformity with a suggestion of Professor G. D. Kilpatrick that the Diatessaron was primarily an arrangement of the Gospel material.[3]

But the Diatessaron was not the only form in which the Gospels were known among the Syriac-speaking Churches before the time of Rabbula. It would be the most natural thing in the world to do something in the way of New Testament translation into Syriac soon after the Christian mission had been inaugurated among the Syriac-speaking population. Eusebius[4] tells us that Hegesippus, a Jewish Christian writer who flourished about the

---

[1] *The Story of the Bible* (1936), p. 94.

[2] In September 1957 a considerable portion of the Syriac original of Ephrem's commentary was identified in a parchment manuscript belonging to Sir Alfred Chester Beatty. The editing and translating of the text has been entrusted to Father L. Leloir, O.S.B. It appears that, while the Armenian translation is generally faithful, it is based on a different textual tradition of the commentary from that represented by the Chester Beatty manuscript. As for Biblical quotations, the Armenian translator tended at times to bring these into conformity with the Old Armenian version of the Gospels. The comparative study of these quotations may therefore throw light on the early history of the Armenian Gospel text as well as on the text of the Syriac Diatessaron.

[3] *The Cairo Geniza*, p. 284.   [4] Eusebius, *Hist. Eccl.*, ii., 22.

middle of the second century, quoted Scripture 'from the Syriac'; and it was only in the last few years of Hegesippus's life that the Diatessaron appeared. We have two very valuable manuscripts of the Old Syriac translation of the Gospels, and there is evidence that these two do not represent *all*[1] the Old Syriac Gospel-versions. It was reported in 1950 that a copy of the Four Gospels in Syriac from St. Catherine's Monastery on Mt. Sinai,[2] which was being studied by Professor A. S. Atiya of Alexandria, exhibited the Peshitta text of Matthew, Luke and John, but an Old Syriac text of Mark—but an Old Syriac text of Caesarean type, not of the type represented by the two manuscripts just mentioned. No Old Syriac translation of Acts has survived, but we know that one existed; Ephrem wrote not only a commentary on the Diatessaron but also one on Acts, which has survived only in an Armenian translation. Even the Armenian translation, however, makes it plain that Ephrem's Syriac text of Acts is strongly 'Western' in character and quite distinct from the Peshitta version of Acts. Whether there were also Old Syriac translations of the rest of the New Testament, and (if so) what their character was, must remain an open question until further light is available.

The two Old Syriac copies of the Gospels do not show exactly the same text as each other. As the analogy of other Biblical translations would have led us to expect, there were several varying versions in circulation before these were superseded by an officially authorized edition (which, in the case of the Syriac Bible, was the Peshitta). One of the two copies is called the 'Curetonian', after William Cureton, who discovered it in 1847 and published it in 1858. It is a fragmentary fifth-century manuscript of the Syriac Gospels which was procured from a monastery in the Nitrian Desert of Egypt. The other is called the 'Lewis' or 'Sinaitic' copy, because it was discovered in 1892 by Mrs. A. S. Lewis of Cambridge in the monastery of St. Catherine on Mt. Sinai. This Syriac manuscript is a palimpsest (like the *Codex Ephraemi*),[3] the older writing on which (the Gospel text) has been rendered reasonably legible by chemical means. The later writing was superimposed on the earlier in A.D. 778 at a convent near Antioch; the earlier writing is three or four centuries earlier, but the place where it was written is not known. Of course, we must make a clear distinction between the dates to which the two manuscripts belong, and the dates of

---

[1] See pp. 212 f.

[2] The monastery where Tischendorf in 1844 came upon the great *Codex Sinaiticus*.

[3] See p. 183.

the translations which they bear. There is little difference in date between the two manuscripts, but a comparison of their Gospel texts makes it clear that they are two variant forms of the Old Syriac version, and that the Curetonian text is later than the Lewis and looks like a revision of it. The Lewis palimpsest has traces of Palestinian dialect in its Syriac, which suggests that the translators of the Gospels into Syriac were Palestinian Christians. According to Professor C. C. Torrey, the Curetonian text is 'a revision of the Sinai (Lewis) text improving its language in the direction of pure Syriac, removing the conspicuously Palestinian elements and conforming the text to a later form of the Greek'.[1] Dr. Kahle thinks that the first translation of the Gospels into Syriac was made in Adiabene, where he suggests the first Christian mission to Syriac-speaking people took place.[2]

The original Old Syriac version of the Gospels was earlier than the introduction of Tatian's Diatessaron. But so popular did the Diatessaron become that the text of the 'separate' Gospels in Syriac was (as might be expected) influenced by the text of the Diatessaron. This explains why the two Old Syriac Gospel-texts that have been preserved contain clear signs of Diatessaron influence; they were copied about the time when the Diatessaron was at the height of its popularity, as we know from the evidence of Ephrem, Rabbula and Theodoretus.

It may be that further copies of the Old Syriac version or versions await discovery; it is to be hoped that it is so, for there are still many interesting questions that such discoveries would help to answer. We have mentioned the reported identification of a Caesarean type of Old Syriac text of Mark, which confirms indirect evidence already available that such a' text of all four Gospels existed.[3] Portions are also extant of a Palestinian Syriac version of the New Testament, of a period earlier than the fifth century.

A number of Biblical texts in Palestinian Syriac were discovered in 1952 at Khirbet Mird, some nine miles south-east of Jerusalem. These include fragments of Joshua, Luke, John, Acts and Colossians; many of these fragments are palimpsests.

The standard (*Peshitta*, literally 'simple') text produced and imposed by Rabbula was a revision of the existing version, brought into conformity (as we have said) with the Byzantine Greek text. The older versions did not fall into disuse immediately. In particular, the Diatessaron continued to be used and valued for some

[1] *Documents of the Primitive Church* (1941), p. 250.
[2] *The Cairo Geniza*, pp. 274 ff.   [3] See pp. 212 f.

centuries, in spite of episcopal disapproval, and if at last it died out in its Syriac form, it did not do so before it had been translated into Arabic and Latin.

The original Peshitta version of the New Testament did not include 2 Peter, 2 and 3 John, Jude and Revelation. It was not until 508 that these five books appeared in a Syriac version. This was the Philoxenian version, which was a revision of the whole Bible. It has not survived, however, except in these five New Testament books which it was the first to include in the Syriac Bible. This Philoxenian version was itself revised in turn in 616 by Thomas of Harkel (who later became bishop of Mabug, of which Philoxenus himself had also been bishop). Thomas was responsible only for the New Testament; the Old Testament part of this particular revision was done by Paul of Tella. Thomas's revision of the New Testament (usually called the Harklean version) is an extremely literal translation of the Byzantine Greek text. But it is of great importance because of its inclusion of a number of variant readings, indicated in the margins and by means of a system of critical signs (asterisks and so forth). These readings were found by Thomas in manuscripts of the library of the Enaton, near Alexandria, where he worked on his revision, and they form a valuable contribution to the material for the textual history of the Greek New Testament. The Harklean marginal readings in Acts, for example, give us highly important evidence for the Western text of that book.

Because the Syriac Bible is written in a variant dialect of the language that Jesus spoke, extreme views are sometimes expressed about the forms in which His sayings appear in the Syriac Gospels, as though His actual words in the language in which they were uttered might be found there. The ordinary reader, for example, may readily infer from the writings of Mr. George Lamsa that the Peshitta Gospels preserve the very words of our Lord better than the Greek Gospels do. This, of course, is quite wrong; the Peshitta New Testament is simply a translation of the Greek. Even the Old Syriac forms—Diatessaron and 'separate' Gospels alike—are translations of the Greek Gospels. The most we can say is that some Palestinian idioms in the Old Syriac Gospels may *possibly* go back to a living tradition of the original Gospel story and in particular of the words of Jesus. If the Syriac-speaking Churches were founded by Jewish Christians from Palestine, this is what we might expect.

CHAPTER XVI

THE LATIN BIBLE

THE Latin translation of the Bible is one of quite special importance to us, because of the dominant part that it played for centuries in Western European Christianity. It was from the Latin version that the first knowledge of the Bible came to the British Isles; it was from the Latin version, too, that the first English Bible was translated.

The form in which the Latin Bible has exercised this wide influence is Jerome's Vulgate ('common' or 'popular') version.[1] Jerome played a part in the West similar to that played by Rabbula in Mesopotamia. His translation became the standard version of Western Europe, and remains to this day the official version of the Bible in the Roman Catholic Church. Jerome carried out his work in the last two decades of the fourth century, but his was by no means the first Latin version of the Bible. The inevitable procedure in Bible translations repeated itself here, and in the case of the Latin Bible we can trace its course in much greater detail.

Jerome undertook the work at the bidding of Damasus, bishop of Rome from 366 to 384, whose secretary he was. Damasus was eager to have one standard edition of the Latin Bible which should supersede the bewildering variety of texts already in circulation throughout Latin-speaking Christendom. The position at this time was such that Jerome himself could describe it thus in a letter to Damasus:

'If we are to rely on the Latin types of text, let them tell us in reply which we are to trust, for there are almost as many types of text as there are manuscripts'.

And no wonder, if these types of the Latin text arose in the manner described by Augustine:

'In the earliest days of the faith, when a Greek manuscript came into anyone's hands and he thought he possessed a little facility in both languages [i.e. Greek and Latin], he ventured to make a translation'.

Here we have explicit testimony to the sort of thing that went on

---

[1] This sense of 'Vulgate', with reference to Jerome's translation, goes back to the Council of Trent. Jerome himself used the word with reference to the Septuagint, which he called the 'vulgate edition'.

in the early stages of all Bible translations, as we saw in the case of the Septuagint, Targums and Syriac Bible. The natural result was, as Augustine puts it, an 'infinite variety of Latin translators'.

Before the Vulgate, then, there was an 'Old Latin' version of the Bible (in widely divergent forms), just as before the Peshitta there was an Old Syriac version. But we have much more abundant evidence, in manuscripts and citations, for the history of the Old Latin Bible than we have for the history of the Old Syriac.

We have now to consider the beginnings of the Old Latin Bible.

As we have already mentioned,[1] the Church in Rome was, to begin with, Greek-speaking. For the first two centuries the need of having a Latin version of the Bible does not seem to have been felt in Rome or Italy. Across the Mediterranean, however, lay the Roman province of Africa, covering the territory now represented by Tunisia, Algeria, and Morocco. This territory, which has been a stronghold of Islam from the seventh century to our own day, contained in the early Christian centuries some of the most flourishing Churches in the world. In the roll of Latin Fathers none can stand higher than Tertullian, Cyprian and (greatest of all) Augustine, all of whom belonged to this province. The disappearance of Christianity in this province which followed the Vandal ravages of the fifth century and the Muslim conquest of the seventh has sometimes been attributed to the absence of any Bible in the vernacular Berber tongues. In places where there was a vernacular Bible, such as Egypt and Syria, the Muslim conquest never succeeded in quite obliterating the Christian faith.

In the province of Africa, Latin, and not Greek, was the leading official and civilized language. The indigenous peoples had their own languages, but Latin was the language of administration and culture, and the language of the upper strata in the population. In particular, Latin was the language of the great city of Carthage, which had been razed to the ground by the Romans in 146 B.C., but refounded a century later as a Roman colony. When the Gospel spread to the province of Africa, then, the need for a Latin version of the Scriptures arose at once.

In A.D. 180 there was an outbreak of persecution in parts of the province of Africa. The record of the trial of some Christians of a town named Scillium has been preserved.[2] It tells how they were asked what they had in their chest and replied: 'Books, and letters of Paul, a just man'. It is pretty certain that the language in which

[1] See p. 63.   [2] *Acts of the Scillitan Martyrs* (ed. J. A. Robinson, Cambridge, 1891).

their archives were written was Latin, and that implies that by this
date the letters of Paul had been translated into Latin. If the letters
of Paul, then a *fortiori* the Gospels. But we have more certain
evidence than this. Tertullian, the great jurist-theologian of
Carthage, who was actively writing in the closing years of the
second century and early years of the third, shows clear traces of a
Latin version of the Scriptures. Cyprian, bishop of Carthage, who
was martyred in 258, quotes copiously and accurately from what
must have been a pretty complete Latin Bible. About the middle
of the third century, too, in the writings of the Roman Christian
Novatian, who wrote in Latin, we find evidence of the use of a
Latin version in Europe. The forms in which the Latin Bible
appears in Europe are not altogether independent of the earlier
African forms, and appear to represent progressive revisions of these.

We are not confined to the evidence provided by Bible
citations in the Latin Fathers, however, for our knowledge of the
Old Latin version. Several manuscript copies of parts of the
version have survived, both Old Testament and New Testament,
in the various African and European types of text. The New
Testament is much better attested than the Old. The Old Testament was translated from the Septuagint, not from the Hebrew,
although there are signs of Jewish influence in the translation of
both Testaments (thus occasionally an Old Testament quotation
in the New Testament is given in a form approximating rather
to the Hebrew text than to the Septuagint text reproduced in the
New Testament quotation). The source of this Jewish influence
is not known; we might be better able to identify it if the origins
of the Christian mission in the province of Africa were clearer
than they are. It may be that Jewish Christians played some part
in the evangelization of the province; the Roman Church in its
early days certainly included Jewish Christians.

For the New Testament in the Old Latin version we have
some twenty-seven manuscripts of the Gospels, seven of Acts, six
of the Pauline epistles, and fragments of the Catholic Epistles and
of the book of Revelation. From the variations in these manuscripts we can see how well founded were the statements of
Augustine and Jerome about the manifold divergences of text.

One of the Gospel manuscripts, exhibiting what is called an
African Latin text, is the *Codex Bobiensis* (known by the symbol
'k') in Turin, which now contains only part of Matthew and Mark.
It is particularly interesting because it closes the Gospel of Mark
with the following words, which it adds after verse 8:

'But they reported to Peter and those who were with him all these things which had been commanded them. And after this Jesus Himself also appeared to them and sent through them from the east even to the west the sacred and incorruptible message of everlasting salvation'.[1]

Fragmentary though this manuscript is, it is one of the most important Old Latin manuscripts of the Gospel we have. Of the Gospel manuscripts which exhibit a 'European' text, the most important is the fourth-century *Codex Vercellensis* (denoted by the letter 'b'), which has a text like that of Novatian's Biblical citations.

Particularly important for their citations are those Latin authors who wrote commentaries on various books of the Bible, and quoted almost in its entirety the actual text of the books on which they were commenting. The study of Biblical citations in Latin authors is a field in which a good deal of work yet remains to be done, in spite of much study that has already been devoted to them.[2]

The time came, however, when the multiplicity of texts became too inconvenient to be tolerated any longer, and Pope Damasus, as we have seen, commissioned his secretary, Jerome, to undertake the work. He could not have chosen a better man. Eusebius Sofronius Hieronymus, to give him his full name, was born in Dalmatia in 347 and educated at Rome under the famous grammarian, Donatus. After his Roman education he travelled extensively, acquiring further learning in various parts of the Empire; in particular he learned Hebrew from a Jewish Christian in Syria. When he returned to Rome in 382 he was obviously the very man for the work that Damasus had in mind. He undertook the task unwillingly, all the same. It was a thankless job, to his way of thinking, calculated to stir up blind opposition from those people 'who identify ignorance with holiness' (their race is not *quite* extinct even to-day!). However, he set about it.

---

[1] The same words are found in some Greek manuscripts, in the margin of the Syriac Harklean, in three Coptic manuscripts (once in the text and twice in the margin) and in seven Ethiopic manuscripts. In these authorities they are inserted between verses 8 and 9. As the R.V. margin says, 'The two oldest Greek manuscripts [א and B], and some other authorities [e.g., the 'most accurate codices' known to Eusebius and the Sinaitic Syriac palimpsest, which was not known to the Revisers], omit from ver. 9 to the end. Some other authorities have a different ending to the Gospel [e.g., the ending quoted above from k]' Cf. also p. 184, n. 2.

[2] A monumental critical edition of the Old Latin Bible, based on all the material available at the time, was produced by P. Sabatier at Rheims in 1743-49. A complete revision of this work, in the light of the much greater wealth of evidence now accessible, is being undertaken by the Benedictine Arch-Abbey of Beuron, Germany. Another edition of the Old Latin Old Testament is being prepared by a committee of Oxford scholars for the British and Foreign Bible Society. An independent critical edition of the Old Latin New Testament has also been commenced in Germany; Vols. I, II and III (the texts of Matthew, Mark and Luke, edited by A. Jülicher) were published at Berlin in 1938, 1940 and 1954 respectively.

Perhaps he thought it politic to please Damasus, as he had some hopes of succeeding him in the Roman see. The work of translation and revision was not easy. He was told to be cautious for the sake of 'weaker brethren' who did not like to see their favourite texts tampered with, even in the interests of greater accuracy. Even so, he went much too far for the taste of many, while he himself knew that he was not going far enough. He revised the Gospel text apparently on the basis of the best existing form of European text,[1] correcting it with the aid of Greek manuscripts, and produced his edition of the four Gospels in 384. This was followed by a revision of the Psalter (the so-called 'Roman Psalter'). Jerome later revised the rest of the New Testament, but with a lighter hand.

In 384 Damasus died, and Jerome was not elected to the vacant see. He retired to the east, where, in 386, he settled in Bethlehem and spent the rest of his life there as a monk, pursuing the cause of Biblical learning. At Bethlehem he produced a second version of the Psalter, based on the Septuagint text of Origen's Hexapla. This is generally known as the 'Gallican Psalter' and is the version of the Psalms printed in modern editions of the Vulgate.[2] He went on to translate other Old Testament books from the Septuagint, but realized increasingly that this was an unsatisfactory procedure. At Bethlehem he took the opportunity of perfecting his knowledge of Hebrew under the instruction of a Jewish Rabbi, and at last decided that the only adequate translation of the Old Testament would be a translation from Hebrew. To this task, then, he set himself, and completed it in 405.[3]

Outside the circle of Jerome's friends and admirers his work did not meet with instant appreciation. The rank and file of religious people are normally conservative and suspicious of innovations. Jerome's dependence on the Hebrew text was thought to be a sign of Judaizing, and it was thought outrageous that he should cast doubts on the divine inspiration of the Septuagint. Jerome showed little patience with his critics; in a letter to one of his friends he describes them as 'two-legged asses'!

[1] The best existing form of European text was probably a revision carried out about the middle of the fourth century, representing the correction of a Western text with the aid of texts of the Alexandrian type.

[2] The Gallican Psalter is that traditionally used in the services of the Roman Catholic Church throughout the world except in the city of Rome itself, where Jerome's earlier 'Roman Psalter' has traditionally been used. For a new alternative Latin Psalter see p. 209.

[3] His low estimate of the authority of the apocryphal books led him either to treat them perfunctorily (as in his free paraphrases of Tobit and Judith from an Aramaic text) or to ignore them; it was thus in an Old Latin version that most of them continued to be used in the Western Church.

It was long before the favourite Old Latin version yielded to the sheer intrinsic superiority of Jerome's work. Even so, the older forms of the Latin Psalter, translated from the Septuagint, were so familiar from their liturgical use that they could not be ousted by the translation from the Hebrew. We may compare the way in which Coverdale's Psalter of 1539 has retained its place in the English Prayer Book in spite of the superiority of the 1611 version. So, as we have said, the 'Gallican Psalter', a version made from the Greek, has remained as the Vulgate edition of the book of Psalms.

Theologians of the calibre of Augustine and Pelagius recognized the value of the new translation at once and used it extensively in their works. But it was not until the ninth century that the supremacy of the Vulgate was assured.

The most reliable surviving manuscript of the Vulgate, the *Codex Amiatinus*, now at Florence, was produced at one or other of the twin Benedictine monasteries of Wearmouth and Jarrow (which were founded towards the end of the seventh century). The execution of this manuscript was carried out under the direction of the Abbot Ceolfrid, probably on the basis of copies which he had brought from Italy, and presented to Pope Gregory II in 716.

The fortunes of the Vulgate text form a study in itself. It was copied and recopied so often in the earlier days of its life by men who were well acquainted with the Old Latin text that it became thoroughly contaminated with the Old Latin. Attempts were made from time to time to purify the text. Editions were prepared in South Italy in the sixth century by Cassiodorus,[1] (whose work is reflected in the *Codex Amiatinus*), by Alcuin of York at the instance of Charlemagne about A.D. 800, by his contemporary, Theodulf of Orleans, about the same time on the basis of Spanish manuscripts, and by scholars of the University of Paris in the thirteenth century.[2] It was the Paris revision that formed the basis of the earliest printed editions of the Vulgate.

The first substantial work ever to come off a printing press was the Latin Bible of 1456, properly called the Gutenberg Bible (from the name of the printer, Johann Gutenberg of Mainz), but frequently called the Mazarin Bible (because a well-known copy of it belonged to the library of the seventeenth-century French statesman Cardinal Jules Mazarin). It had been preceded by an

---

[1] It is in the time of Cassiodorus that we first hear of a complete volume (or pandect) of the Latin Bible; there was a copy in his library.

[2] It was in this edition that the Bible was first divided into chapters.

edition of the Latin Psalter, the first book ever to be printed with the printer's name and the date. The Gutenberg Bible was in two volumes, containing 1300 pages of type. It was modelled on manuscript style, with two columns to a page. The typesetting took six years; there were two impressions of it.

The sixteenth century is important in many ways for the history of the Latin Bible. From 1511 onwards the printed editions represent a serious attempt to restore the true text of Jerome's translation by critical methods. In 1546 the Council of Trent decreed that:

'The same holy synod, considering that no small advantage may accrue to the Church of God, if out of all the Latin versions of the sacred books in circulation it make known which is to be held as authoritative, determines and declares that this same ancient and vulgate version which is approved by the long use of so many centuries in the Church herself, be held as authoritative in public lectures, disputations, sermons and expository discourses, and that no one may make bold or presume to reject it on any pretext'.

The reference in the decree to 'all the Latin versions of the sacred books in circulation' reflects the circumstance that, as part of the great activity of those days in translating the Scriptures, many new and independent Latin versions had been produced, both by Protestants and by Roman Catholics, and others were to follow. Among the Latin translators of Scripture in the sixteenth century, Pagninus, Sebastian Münster, Castalio, Erasmus and Beza are outstanding. No judgment was passed by the Council on the intrinsic merit of these new Latin versions, but it was insisted that the ancient Vulgate version alone should be held authoritative (*authentica* is the Latin term). Some members of the Council, such as the English Cardinal Pole, desired that explicit acknowledgment be made in the decree of the authority of the Greek and Hebrew originals, but this was not done, possibly because it was considered self-evident that if a translation was authoritative, so much the more so must its original be, but possibly (so far as some members were concerned) on other grounds.[1]

[1] 'The majority considered this [explicit approbation of the Hebrew and Greek] to be unnecessary', says Professor E. F. Sutcliffe in a most informative and well documented study of 'The Council of Trent on the *Authentia* of the Vulgate' in the *Journal of Theological Studies*, Vol. 49 (1948), pp. 35 ff. He adds that 'some, especially in Spain, strangely misunderstood the decree and put forward extravagant interpretations'—attaching even greater authority to the Vulgate than to the Hebrew and Greek. Pope Pius XII in his encyclical *Divino Afflante Spiritu*, of Sept. 30, 1943, made the position quite clear: 'This authority of the Vulgate in matters of doctrine by no means forbids—nay, to-day it almost demands—the proving and confirmation of this same doctrine from the original texts as well, and the calling into aid everywhere of the same texts, that by their means the right significance of the sacred writings may throughout be more clearly brought out and explained'.

It was all very well to affirm the authority of the 'ancient and vulgate version', but this was quite insufficient in view of the corrupt state of the text and the multiplicity of variants which had crept in since Jerome's time. The faithful might well inquire which edition of the Vulgate was to be regarded as uniquely authoritative. The Council, therefore, decreed that the Vulgate should be edited and printed as accurately as possible. This work was entrusted to a papal commission, but after the commission had sat for forty years it still found itself unable to overcome the difficulties of the task. Then the reigning Pope, Sixtus V, took the matter into his own hands and produced an edition of his own, which appeared in 1590. Unfortunately, Sixtus showed a confidence in the authority and finality of his work unbefitting a scholar (which he undoubtedly was).

> 'By the fulness of apostolic power, we decree and declare that this edition ... approved by the authority delivered to us by the Lord, is to be received and held as true, lawful, authoritative and unquestioned, in all public and private discussion, reading, preaching, and explanation'.

So he enacted, adding that no variant readings were to be published in copies of the Vulgate, that all readings differing from those of his edition were to have no credit or authority for the future, and that his text should be introduced into all the Church's service-books.

But Pope Sixtus died a few months after the publication of his edition, and his enactments were never enforced. For the work was considered by other scholars to be full of faults. In the reign of his next successor but one, Gregory XIV (1590-91), a start was made with a drastic revision of the Sixtine text, and this was completed in the reign of Clement VIII (1592-1605) and published in 1592. The revised edition is commonly called the Sixto-Clementine Vulgate, and remains the 'Authorized Version' of the Roman communion. The preface, by Cardinal Bellarmine, is couched in a temperate and modest style, while it does its best to save the face of the late Pope Sixtus V, by representing that he himself had intended to revise the work on account of the many *misprints* that had crept into it! But in point of fact the Sixtine edition was remarkably free from misprints—more so, indeed, than the Clementine. The differences between the two consist of real textual variations, some 3,000 all told. The suppression of the Sixtine edition may have been due to the influence of the Jesuits, whom Sixtus V had offended (he had, for example, put a treatise of Bellarmine on the *Index of Prohibited Books*). It was in

1604 that the name of Clement VIII was first associated on the title-page of the 1592 revision with that of Sixtus V, whose sole authority had hitherto been claimed for the edition that superseded his own.

Even the Sixto-Clementine edition left room for improvement, for the study of the Vulgate text has not stood still since the sixteenth century, any more than the study of the Hebrew and Greek originals. Much more information is available nowadays on the original text of Jerome's translation, and this information is used to good purpose in two great editions of the Vulgate which have been or are being produced in our day. One of these is the critical edition of the Vulgate New Testament begun by the late Bishop John Wordsworth and Dean H. J. White, publication of which by the Clarendon Press, Oxford, was commenced in 1889 and completed in 1953. The other is a critical edition of the whole Vulgate Bible begun under Papal authority in 1907 and now being carried through by a community of the Benedictine Order. Publication began with the book of Genesis in 1926, and more than half of the Old Testament has now appeared.

Another very interesting enterprise of recent days is the production of a new Latin Psalter, not a revision of Jerome's work, but a new translation from the Hebrew. This was carried through by a Papal commission and completed in 1945, and authority has been given to substitute it for the older and inadequate Latin versions of the Psalms used in the offices of the Church. A new Latin translation of the canticles used in these offices has been published by the same commission.[1]

The Latin versions have played an interesting part in the textual history of the Bible. For example, the mistranslation 'one fold' which we find in the A.V. of John 10. 16 goes back to Jerome's *unum ouile*, although the Old Latin *unus grex* had rightly rendered the Greek *mia poimnē* (rightly rendered by R.V. 'one flock'). Mgr. R. A. Knox, in his recent English translation of the Vulgate New Testament (1945), gives 'one fold' in the text, but adds a footnote: '"One fold": the Greek here is more accurately rendered "one flock". Our Lord evidently refers to the Gentiles who would believe in Him'.

[1] This new Latin version has been published in a free English translation by R. A. Knox: *The Book of Psalms and the Canticles used in the Divine Office* (London, 1947). He also included his English version of the new Latin Psalter as an appendix to his translation of the Vulgate Old Testament (1949). It is understood that the same Papal commission contemplates a new Latin translation (from the original texts) of the whole Bible, and not of the Psalms and ecclesiastical canticles only.

One further example is even more interesting. In the A.V. we find 1 John 5. 7 reading: 'For there are three that bear record in heaven, the Father, the Word, and the Holy Ghost: and these three are one'. No such words are found in the R.V., where 1 John 5. 7 runs: 'And it is the Spirit that beareth witness, because the Spirit is the truth' (words which in the A.V. are printed as the second half of verse 6). The words omitted by the R.V. (usually known as the 'Three Heavenly Witnesses') were no part of the original Greek text, nor yet of Jerome's Vulgate. They first appear in the Spanish Latin writer, Priscillian, who died in 385, and then in a few Old Latin authorities, from which they were later imported into the Vulgate text. Erasmus rightly omitted the passage from his first two printed editions of the Greek New Testament (1516 and 1519). For this he was attacked by champions of the traditional text. He pointed out that the passage was absent not only from the Greek authorities, but even from some Latin copies. In this connection he had a friend ascertain for him the evidence of *Codex Vaticanus* on the point—the first occasion when the authority of this manuscript was appealed to on a point of criticism. Of course it was found to lack the disputed words. Erasmus, however, agreed that if any Greek manuscript could be produced containing the words, he would include them in his next edition. Unfortunately, a Greek manuscript *was* produced which contained the words (in a form which made it clear that they had simply been translated from Latin), and Erasmus included them in his 1522 edition, not because he was convinced of their genuineness, but in order to redeem his promise. (The manuscript containing the words was a sixteenth-century copy [Minuscule No. 61], now in the library of Trinity College, Dublin. They also appear in one or two other late Greek manuscripts, where they also represent a translation from Latin. Apart from these two or three late manuscripts, no Greek manuscript is known to exhibit the passage.)

The passage is present in the authoritative Sixto-Clementine edition of the Vulgate, and an encyclical of Pope Leo XIII towards the end of last century pronounced favourably on its authenticity. Mgr. Knox includes it in his translation ('Thus we have a threefold warrant in heaven, the Father, the Word, and the Holy Ghost, three who are yet one'); he adds a footnote: 'This verse does not occur in any good Greek manuscript. But the Latin manuscripts may have preserved the true text.' It is a pity that, since he undertook to translate the Vulgate, he could not have translated its true reading here. A number of other Roman Catholic versions published in various countries in recent years have indicated more clearly the true state of affairs with regard to this verse. No doubt, when the Benedictine editors of the Vulgate reach this epistle, they will settle the question once and for all by showing that the disputed passage is no part of the authentic Vulgate text, any more than it is of the original Greek text.

The influence of the Latin Bible on the language and thought of Western Christianity has been immense. The genius of the Latin language is different from that of Greek, and in Western Europe a good deal of the Latin genius has found its way into both Roman and Protestant theology. Greek theology tends to be expressed in philosophical terms, Latin theology in legal terms. When we use such elementary Christian terms as 'justify' and 'sanctify' we should remember that we have derived more than the words themselves through Latin. There is a legal connotation about the Latin words *iustificare* and *sanctificare* (especially the former) which is not so apparent in their Greek equivalents *dikaioō* and *hagioō*. These Greek equivalents in turn, as we have already insisted, are to be understood in the light of the corresponding Hebrew expressions. The Greek theologians have been interested rather in those aspects of Christian doctrine which gave scope for metaphysical speculation; the Latin theologians rather in those which lent themselves to legal formulation. Western thought about God has tended to be cast in forensic categories. This is not a misrepresentation in itself, of course, for God is the Judge of all the earth; it simply means that those to whom Christianity has been mediated through the Latin Bible and Latin Fathers appreciate one aspect of the truth, whereas the Greeks appreciate another. The danger arises when the aspect is exaggerated and identified with the whole truth. For that reason among others the re-awakening of interest in Hebrew and Greek learning in the days of the Renaissance and Reformation was salutary in its influence on Western Christianity.

CHAPTER XVII

OTHER EARLY VERSIONS

Primary and Secondary Translations

A TRANSLATION made directly from the original language is called a primary translation. Thus Jerome's Latin Bible is a primary translation, because it was translated directly from the original Hebrew and Greek languages; so also are our English Versions, both Authorized and Revised. The Old Latin version of the Old Testament is a secondary translation, however; that is to say, it was not translated directly from the original tongue, but from a translation of the original—the Greek Septuagint. So, too, the two official versions of the Bible in use among English Roman Catholics—the Douai-Rheims version and the modern version by Mgr. Knox—are secondary translations, because they are translations of the Latin Vulgate and not of the original texts.

Armenian

The missionary activity of the Syriac Christians in the early centuries of the Christian era was responsible for a number of secondary translations of Scripture—translations made, not from the original Hebrew and Greek, but from a Syriac version. North of the region where the Syriac-speaking churches flourished lived the Armenians, who were among the earliest beneficiaries of their neighbours' missionary enterprise. The standard Armenian version goes back, according to two divergent traditions, to the earlier part of the fifth century, when it was produced on the basis of a Greek Bible procured from Constantinople. This Bible had a Byzantine text. But what actually happened at this time—so far, at any rate, as the New Testament is concerned—was that an earlier or 'Old Armenian' version was revised by reference to the new standard Greek text. Our knowledge of the Old Armenian version (which included the Gospels, Acts, Pauline Epistles, and Revelation) is scanty, but it seems likely that part of it was a translation of an Old Syriac text—not, however, an Old Syriac text of the same type as the Sinaitic and Curetonian manuscripts, but one of the Caesarean type.

Georgian

North of Armenia lies Georgia, in the Caucasus; and the Georgians were next to be evangelized after the Armenians, about the close of the third century. The great majority of manuscripts of the Georgian Bible show a Byzantine text, but a few codices (especially the one known as the Adysh manuscript) bear witness to the earlier (Old Georgian) version of the Gospels. The evidence of this version suggests (1) that it was translated from Armenian, and (2) that its text is Caesarean in character. Two other groups of Georgian manuscripts exhibit a mixed text—one in which the Caesarean text has been corrected by the Byzantine in varying degrees. The Old Georgian version (if the above account is right), so far from being a primary version, is not even a secondary, but a tertiary version, being translated from the Armenian, which was in turn translated from the Syriac, which was itself translated from the Greek. It has, however, been held by one or two scholars that the Old Georgian version was translated directly from a Greek text. In spite of the obscurity still surrounding the genesis of this version, it could be a most important witness for a certain phase of New Testament textual history.

The Armenian alphabet probably, and the Georgian alphabet certainly, were expressly devised in order that the Scriptures might be written in these two languages. These two missionary versions are thus the precursors of many more of later date, which required that the language concerned should be reduced to writing before the Bible could be written in it.

Central Asian

We should dearly love to know about further translation activity undertaken by the Nestorian Christians in Central Asia. 'They translated the Scriptures into several languages. There is a record from the ninth or tenth century of their having translated the New Testament into Sogdianese, an Indo-Iranian language'.[1] Rendel Harris reproduces a fragment from a Christian lectionary written in this language in the Syriac character, which contains the sentence:

'at sôqant qat khvardârat qu-'Abraham mâkh pitri-sâ.

This was readily interpreted to mean 'the oath which he sware to Abraham our father' (Luke 1. 73) and then the lesson in which it occurred was easily identified with Luke 1. 63-80.[2] Rendel Harris

[1] E. H. Broadbent, The Pilgrim Church (1931), p. 78.
[2] J. R. Harris, Side-lights on New Testament Research, p. 121.

was even tempted once to think that he had found trace of a Chinese New Testament translated under Nestorian auspices.[1] At any rate, strange finds have been made in ancient monasteries in Central Asia, and more may yet come to light to increase our knowledge of the literary activities of the Nestorian missionaries.[2]

Coptic

Alexandria in Egypt was evangelized soon after the middle of the first century. Alexandria itself was a Greek city. But the Gospel is not restricted to one race or class or culture, and it spread from the city among the indigenous inhabitants of Egypt. These spoke a later form of the ancient Egyptian language, the form which we call the 'Coptic' language ('Coptic' and 'Egyptian' being basically the same word). Up to the beginning of the Christian era Coptic was written in the ancient scripts or in later adaptations of these. But the difficulty of these scripts led to their being superseded by an alphabetic script, based on the Greek alphabet, with the addition of seven signs taken from the 'demotic' script of the native Egyptians. It is this script that is used for all Christian works in Coptic, including first and foremost the Coptic Bible. Coptic died out as a spoken language about the sixteenth century, but it remains the ecclesiastical language of the Copts, the Egyptian Christian minority.

The earlier attempts at writing in the new Coptic alphabet seem to have been made in Upper Egypt, where the Sahidic dialect of Coptic was spoken, and it was in this dialect that the first Egyptian version of the Scriptures was undertaken, probably in the third or fourth century. The Sahidic version, so far as extant manuscripts show, was mainly Alexandrian in type in the New Testament, with a number of Western readings; it may represent an originally Western text corrected by reference to Alexandrian manuscripts. The New Testament was also translated into the Coptic dialect of the Fayyum. But the version which became the standard for the Coptic Church was the Bohairic version, in the dialect of Lower Egypt. Experts differ about the date of this version; it is at any rate later than the Sahidic. In the New Testament it exhibits a very pure Alexandrian text. The Old Testament in both the Sahidic and the Bohairic versions was translated from the Septuagint.

Ethiopic

The standard Ethiopic text of the Bible represents a translation from Greek, though parts of the Old Testament seem to have been

[1] *Op. cit.*, pp. 133 ff.
[2] *Cf.* John Stewart, *Nestorian Missionary Enterprise: the Story of a Church on Fire* (1928).

revised by reference to Hebrew manuscripts. The translation appears to have been a gradual process, carried out between the late fourth or early fifth and the seventh century. Many of the translators seem to have been Syrian monks who came to Ethiopia to escape the imperial persecution of 'Monophysite' Christians.[1] This explains the Syriac element in Biblical and ecclesiastical Ethiopic. The Ethiopic Church has been continuously influenced by the Coptic Church since early times, and this is reflected in Coptic influence on the later manuscripts of the Ethiopic Bible. There are also signs of a revision of the Ethiopic text by reference to an Arabic version. In the New Testament the text is mainly Byzantine; where a reading is of a non-Byzantine type, it is usually Western.

The Ethiopic Bible contains some books which are not accounted canonical by any other Christian Church. One of these, the (First[2]) Book of Enoch, we have already mentioned; another is the 'Book of Jubilees', a Jewish paraphrase of Genesis dating from the second century B.C. and written mainly with the purpose of insisting that one particular calendar (very different from the one used by the Jewish establishment) was ordained by God and was perpetually binding. It derives its name from the fact that it divides the period between the Creation and the Exodus into 50 Jubilee periods of 49 years each, making up 2,450 years in all. Its original language was Hebrew, and fragments of the Hebrew text have been found at Qumran. The Qumran community seems to have followed the Jubilees calendar.

Arabic

The Scriptures do not seem to have been extant in an Arabic version before the time of Muhammad (570-632), who knew the Gospel story only in an oral form, and mainly from Syriac sources. These Syriac sources were marked by Docetism, which explains the statement in the Qur'an that Jesus was only apparently crucified, but did not really die.[3] Of the oldest Arabic versions of the New Testament, some seem to come through Syriac, some through Coptic, and some direct from Greek. The Old Testament was translated from Hebrew into Arabic in the tenth century by the Jewish scholar Saadya Gaon.

[1] The Monophysite heresy was at the opposite pole from that of the Nestorians (see p. 192, n. 2); the Monophysites held that Christ had but one nature. The Coptic and Ethiopic Churches are Monophysite to the present day.

[2] See p. 171.

[3] Docetism was an early Christian 'deviation' which denied that Christ could become truly incarnate (since the material world, including the human body. was inherently evil), and concluded that since He was man only in appearance, He did not really die.

Gothic

The Roman Empire was subjected to continuous and increasing pressure on its northern frontier (formed by the rivers Rhine and Danube) from Germanic tribes. Chief among these were the Goths, who sacked Rome in 410. Augustine, at that time, reflects the general feeling of thankfulness that the Goths had been Christianized before the sack of Rome. What might have happened had they not been Christianized may be seen in what happened later in the incursions of unevangelized barbarians. The first Goths to be evangelized were the Ostrogoths who lived on the lower Danube. Their evangelization began in the third century, and a Gothic bishop, Theophilus, was present at the Council of Nicaea in 325. His disciple and successor, Ulfilas (whose name means 'little wolf'), the 'Apostle of the Goths' (311-381), led his Christian converts across the Danube into the land now known as Bulgaria, but then as the Roman province of Moesia. There he translated the Bible into their language.[1] The translation was made from the recently-established standard text of the Greek Bible (called 'Lucianic' in the Old Testament and 'Byzantine' in the New), so that it tells us little that we did not already know about the history of the text. This Gothic Bible, however, is very important because it is by far the oldest Bible version—and, indeed, the oldest written literature—in any tongue of the Germanic group, to which English belongs. Here and there as we look through this ancient version we still come upon a phrase which looks remarkably familiar; for example, 'This is a hard saying' (John 6. 60) appears in Gothic as *Hardu ist thata waurd*. The Lord's Prayer in Gothic (from Matt. 6. 9-13) runs as follows:

Atta unsar thu in himinam: weihnai namo thein. Quimai thiudinassus theins. Wairthai wilja theins, swe in himina, jah ana airthai. Hlaif unsarana thana sinteinan gif uns himma daga. Jah aflet uns thatei skulans sijaima, swaswe jah weis afletam thaim skulam unsaraim. Jah ni briggais uns in fraistubnjai, ak lausei uns af thamma ubilin. Unte theina ist thiudangardi jah mahts jah wulthus in aiwins. Amen.

There are several manuscripts, more or less fragmentary, of the Gothic Bible, the most famous of which is the 'Silver Codex' in the University library at Uppsala, Sweden, written on purple vellum in silver and partly in gold letters. Gothic is another language whose script (based mainly on Greek uncials and Germanic runes) was expressly devised for the writing of the Scriptures.

Slavonic

So also is Slavonic. In the ninth century, instead of the variety

[1] See p. 80.

of Slavonic languages which are spoken to-day in Eastern Europe, there was one Slavonic language, of which the various Slavonic languages of the present day were but dialects. About the middle of the ninth century a Moravian Empire was formed in East-Central Europe. This Empire professed Christianity, but its church dignitaries were not Slavs but Franks. The liturgy was conducted in Latin, the sermon was preached in the Germanic tongue of the Franks. But the founder of the empire, Rostislav, in order to check the growth of Frankish influence in his realm, asked, in 863, for Slavonic priests to be sent from Byzantium who should conduct the services and preach in the Slavonic language of the people. The Eastern Roman Emperor at Byzantium, Michael III (842-867), sent in response to Rostislav's request two brothers, Constantine and Methodius, natives of Thessalonica, which, though a Greek city, was then surrounded by a Slav population. Constantine (who is also known as Cyril, a name which he assumed on entering the monastic life), devised a Slavonic alphabet[1] and translated the Scriptures from Greek into Slavonic. The form of Slavonic which he used for the purpose was a literary language, not absolutely identical with any spoken dialect; it is known as Old Church Slavonic, and is still used in the liturgy of the Orthodox Slav Churches. After the death of the two brothers the Slav missionaries were expelled from the Moravian kingdom and fled to Bulgaria, where they continued their work. (From its establishment in Bulgaria, the Old Church Slavonic language of the Bible and the liturgy is sometimes, but inaccurately, called Old Bulgarian. At the close of the ninth century the Bulgarian Empire under Tsar Simeon extended from Albania through Macedonia into what is now Hungary.)

Versions from the Latin

During the Middle Ages a number of Bible versions made their appearance in Western and Central Europe, translated (like the Wycliffite versions of the same period in England) from Latin. Most of these versions were carried out as part of the widespread Waldensian activity, and several of them are of some textual interest because of Old Latin readings which they preserve in translation. There are two Provençal versions (one in French Provençal and the other in Piedmontese) which may represent a common original translation into Provençal carried out in the

---

[1] The Glagolitic alphabet of thirty-six letters. This was superseded before the end of the tenth century by the Cyrillic alphabet, also of thirty-six letters, which is still used for Russian, Ukrainian, Serbo-Croatian and Bulgarian.

thirteenth century. Associated somehow with these is a version in the Catalan language of North-east Spain. Then there is a German translation of the New Testament made from the Provençal (and therefore a tertiary version) some time in the fourteenth century. It was printed in several editions between 1466 and 1518: then it was naturally superseded by Luther's translation, the New Testament part of which first appeared in 1522. This older German version seems to have been made in Bohemia. The New Testament was also translated in the fourteenth century into the native language of Bohemia (Czech). In Italy, too, an Italian version of the New Testament had appeared in the thirteenth century. All these versions represent a particular type of Latin text current in Languedoc in the Middle Ages which (apparently under Spanish influence) included several Old Latin readings of a Western character.

Epochs of Translation

It is evident, therefore, that the work of Bible-translation was carried on continuously from the early Christian centuries to the Reformation. Throughout the Christian era, however, we can distinguish three epochs of special activity in this work. The first covers the three centuries from 150 to 450. The second is the age of the Reformation, which (unlike the mediaeval period) saw the revival of translations from the original texts, like Luther's German Bible (1522-34), the French versions by Lefèvre and Olivetan (1534 and 1535), the Spanish and Czech translations of 1602, and Diodati's Italian translation of 1607, not to mention the English translations by Tyndale and his successors. The Counter-Reformation also produced its translations, though these were made on the basis of the Vulgate. The third great age of Bible translation began with the revival of missionary activity at the beginning of the nineteenth century (the British and Foreign Bible Society, for example, was inaugurated in 1804); we may regard it as still being in progress. The Bible has now been translated, at least in part, into more than 1,150 languages; the title of a book published by the American Bible Society in 1938 aptly described it as *The Book of a Thousand Tongues*.[1] But lest we should think that the translator's task is nearly done, the title of another, more recent, book reminds us that there are still *Two Thousand Tongues To Go*.[2]

[1] By Dr. Eric North.
[2] By E. E. Wallis and M. A. Bennett (London, 1960).

CHAPTER XVIII

THE ENGLISH BIBLE

THE history of the English Bible is a subject which deserves a volume to itself,[1] and in a single chapter we can hope only to point out the most important landmarks. Most of the material already dealt with in this book serves as background material for the understanding of the way in which the Bible has come down to us.

Christianity was planted in Britain by the beginning of the fourth century at the latest. In A.D. 314 we have the record of three British bishops (those of York, London, and Lincoln) attending the Council of Arles. The earliest British writer was one of the outstanding figures in early Christian literature—Pelagius[2] (c. 370-450), who in the first decade of the fifth century produced at Rome commentaries on the thirteen epistles of Paul[3]. About the end of the fourth century Ninian, appointed bishop of the district now known as Galloway and Dumfries, evangelized the southern Picts, and established a monastery at Whithorn (*Ad Candidam Casam*) from which the Gospel was carried farther afield, in particular to Northern Ireland.

But there is no evidence of Bible translation having been carried out at this time in the languages of Britain and Ireland. Pelagius wrote in Latin, as did all the other churchmen of Western Europe. And even if the Bible had been translated into the native languages in those days, such translations would have had no place in the history of the *English* Bible.[4] That history has as its starting-point the arrival in Britain of the Germanic-speaking Angles and Saxons and Jutes in the course of the fifth century and their evangelization in the sixth and seventh centuries.

The English (to use this comprehensive name for the Angles, Saxons and Jutes) were evangelized by the Roman mission led by Augustine of Canterbury (597) and by the Irish mission in Lothian

---

[1] I have attempted to supply such a volume in *The English Bible* (Lutterworth Press, 1961).

[2] Augustine calls Pelagius a Briton: Jerome calls him an Irishman (*Scotus*). Gougaud and Bury are probably right in concluding that he was born in Britain of Irish parentage.

[3] These commentaries have been edited by Professor A. Souter (Cambridge University Press, 3 vols., 1922-31).

[4] During the Roman occupation the languages (other than Latin) spoken in the British Isles were the two Celtic languages (British and Irish) and Pictish.

and Northumbria under Aidan and Cuthbert in the seventh century. But some time passed even then before an attempt was made to give the English the Bible or part of it in their own tongue.

Some Old English poems have been preserved which give parts of the Bible story in metrical form, and it is natural to connect these with the story told by Bede of Caedmon, the unlettered poet of Whitby, who 'sang the creation of the world, the origin of man, and all the history of Genesis, and made many verses on the departure of the children of Israel out of Egypt, and their entering into the promised land, with many other histories from Holy Writ; the Incarnation, Passion, and Resurrection of our Lord, and His ascending into heaven; the coming of the Holy Ghost, and the preaching of the apostles; also the terror of judgment to come, the horror of the pains of hell, and the joys of heaven'.[1] Then we have the famous story of Bede himself, completing the dictation of a version of John's Gospel with his dying breath on Ascension Day, 735. Unfortunately, his version has not been preserved. Alfred the Great (d. 901) also played an honoured part in giving his people parts of the Bible in English; his law-code is introduced by an English version of the Ten Commandments, parts of Exodus 21-23 and Acts 15. 23-29, and he is said to have translated part of the Psalter. Later in the tenth century Abbot Aelfric translated considerable parts of the Old Testament into English. Old English versions have come down to us of the Gospels, the Psalter, the Pentateuch and some of the historical books of the Old Testament.

The Old English period ends quite soon after the Norman Conquest of 1066; when the language reappears it has undergone a considerable change under the influence of the invaders' French, and is known as Middle English. The period of Bible translation into Middle English begins about 1300. We have traces of translations of the Psalms[2] and parts of the New Testament leading up to the famous versions associated with the name of Wycliffe (d. 1384). Wycliffe spoke out forcibly on the use of Scripture. 'He constantly appealed to Holy Scripture as the primary and absolute authority in matters of faith and morals, and maintained the desirability of its being made generally accessible to Christians, in these respects at least approximating closely to the standpoint of the Reformers'.[3] The idea that Wycliffe himself translated the

---

[1] Bede, *Ecclesiastical History of the English Nation*, iv. 24.

[2] The best known of these versions of the Psalter is that by Richard Rolle of Hampole (d. 1349), in a northern dialect of Middle English.

[3] S. Leigh Hunt, *Evangelical Quarterly*, 17 (1945), p. 60 (in an article on 'The Real John Wycliffe').

Bible into English rests on a statement of his great Czech disciple, Jan Hus; it is certain, at any rate, that the Wycliffite versions are rightly so called, whether he actually did much translation himself or not, as the work was carried out under his influence and in accordance with his policy. 'Whatever be the final verdict on the subject, Wycliffe's Biblical scholarship cannot be gainsaid'.[1]

There are two Wycliffite versions of the Bible which must be distinguished from each other. One of these was the work of Nicholas of Hereford, a follower of Wycliffe, so far as the Old Testament translation as far as Baruch 3. 20 is concerned; the rest of the version is the work of another, who *may* have been Wycliffe. This version followed the Latin very literally. A more idiomatic 'Wycliffite' version, a revision of the earlier one, was produced towards the end of the fourteenth century by John Purvey, another associate of Wycliffe (who himself was dead by now). Purvey's prologue to his version is interesting and part of it is worth quoting:[2]

'A simple creature hath translated the Bible out of Latin into English. First, this simple creature had much travail, with divers fellows and helpers, to gather many old Bibles, and other doctors, and common glosses, and to make one Latin Bible some deal true; and then to study it anew, the text with the gloss, and other doctors, as he might get, especially Lira on the Old Testament, that helped full much in this work; the third time to counsel with old grammarians and old divines, of hard words and hard sentences, how they might best be understood and translated; the fourth time to translate as clearly as he could to the sentence, and to have many good fellows and cunning at the correcting of the translation'.

He knows that he has not attained perfection; any amendments to his work will be welcome, but let the critic

'look that he examine truly his Latin Bible, for no doubt he shall find full many Bibles in Latin full false, if he look many, namely new; and the common Latin Bibles have more need to be corrected, as many as I have seen in my life, than hath the English Bible late translated'.[3]

But more than linguistic and literary ability is required in a Bible translator:

'A translator hath great need to study well the sense both before and after, and then also he hath need to live a clean life and be full devout in prayers, and have not his wit occupied about worldly things, that the Holy Spirit, Author of all wisdom and cunning and truth, dress him for his work and suffer him not to err'.

And he concludes:

'God grant to us all grace to know well and to keep well Holy Writ, and to suffer joyfully some pain for it at the last'.

---

[1] *Ibid.*
[2] The English has been 'some deal' modernized.
[3] That is, the earlier Wycliffite version.

From this prologue we learn that Purvey had a good grasp of critical principles; before a satisfactory version could be made, a satisfactory Latin text must be established by the comparison of authorities. Moreover, he knew that the Latin itself was a translation and that it should be corrected by reference to the original tongues; and so he availed himself of the work of Nicolas de Lyra, the great commentator of the fourteenth century, celebrated for his knowledge of Hebrew and Greek.[1]

Purvey's translation held the field until Tyndale's translation appeared. A Scots adaptation of it was produced early in the sixteenth century by Murdoch Nisbet.[2]

Between the Middle English and New English versions three events or movements of the greatest importance for our study took place. One was the revival of learning which made the knowledge of Hebrew and Greek much more readily accessible to Western European scholars; another was the introduction of printing about the middle of the fifteenth century; the third was Luther's nailing of his ninety-five theses to the church-door at Wittenberg in 1517, which precipitated the Reformation. The invention of printing made the circulation of books possible on a scale hitherto undreamed of; the spreading of Hebrew and Greek knowledge greatly illuminated the understanding of the Scriptures by enabling men to read them in the original. The first printed Hebrew Bible appeared at Soncino, near Cremona, in 1488;[3] the Greek Testament was first printed in 1514, although the first Greek Testament to be *published* in print was Erasmus's first edition in 1516. Then the Reformation gave a tremendous impetus to the translating and circulating of the Bible in the vernacular. Luther's New Testament, translated into German from the Greek original, appeared in 1522, to be followed three years later by Tyndale's New Testament, translated into English from the Greek original. The influence of Luther's work on Tyndale is obvious to anyone who compares the two versions, but Tyndale is far from being a mere echo of Luther.

[1] Lyra did much to prepare the way for the Reformation by his study of the original languages of Scripture; as the old jingle put it: *Si Lyra non lyrasset, Lutherus non saltasset* (If Lyra had not played the lyre, Luther would not have danced). See A. S. Wood, 'Nicolas of Lyra', *The Evangelical Quarterly* 33 (1961), pp. 194 ff.

[2] Edited in three volumes for the Scottish Text Society by T. G. Law (1901-1905). Of Nisbet's version Sir William Craigie says: 'Unfortunately this remained the only attempt to produce a Scottish version of any part of the Bible' (in *Ancient and English Versions of the Bible*, p. 144). He has overlooked some later efforts, however, notably Dr. P. Hately Waddell's *The Psalms: frae Hebrew intil Scottis* (1877) and his similar rendering of *Isaiah* (1879). For other portions of the Bible in Scots cf. E. North (ed.), *The Book of a Thousand Tongues* (American Bible Society, 1938), p. 121.

[3] The Pentateuch had been printed in Hebrew at Bologna in 1482.

'Luther is extremely free, sturdy, and popular in his decision; Tyndale, working in the white heat of potential martyrdom, rises, at times, to a poetic glow, transcending the style of the original Greek, which, as Goodspeed points out, is on a rather pedestrian level'.[1]

William Tyndale took his Oxford M.A. in 1515 and later moved to Cambridge, where he eagerly pursued the new learning and conceived the ambition to do for England what Luther did for Germany and to 'make the boy that drives the plough in England know more of Scripture' than many a man of learning. Cuthbert Tonstal, bishop of London, had some fame as a patron of the new learning, but when Tyndale sought his patronage in his work of translation he received a discouraging response. He soon found it necessary to leave England for the Continent and prosecute his work there, and his translation of the New Testament began to be printed as a quarto volume by Peter Quentel, in Cologne in 1525. The printing at Cologne was interrupted, however, and Tyndale moved to Worms, where an octavo edition of his English New Testament appeared in 1526; then to Marburg, and later to Antwerp, where he was arrested. His imprisonment and death we have already recorded.[2] Before his arrest he had translated and published the Pentateuch (1530), Jonah (1531),[3] a revised Genesis and a revised New Testament (1534), and *The New Testament yet once again corrected by Willyam Tindale* (1535). As an appendix to his 1534 New Testament he also published certain Old Testament passages prescribed for reading in church in the Sarum lectionary; these were translated from Hebrew, and make it all the more deplorable that he was not spared to complete the translation of the Old Testament.

Tyndale died a martyr's death, vilified by authorities in church and state in England. Nothing was too bad to say about his translation. Thousands of copies were seized on entering this country and publicly burned. Even a man like Sir Thomas More, who himself incurred the wrath of Henry VIII and suffered death for conscience' sake, condemned it in unwarranted terms: 'To study to find errors in Tyndale's book were like studying to find water in the sea'.[4] But when royal policy changed in England,

---

[1] J. T. Hatfield, *Evangelical Quarterly*, 20 (1948), p. 170 (in an article on 'The Hanseatic League and the King James Bible').   [2] See pp. 9 f.

[3] Luther's German Pentateuch appeared in 1523, the historical books in 1524, and Jonah in 1526.

[4] But, in an age when many thought themselves bound to traduce a theological opponent's life and character, it is pleasant to record More's testimony that Tyndale was 'well known, before he went over the sea, for a man of right good living, studious and well learned in Scripture, and in divers places in England was very well liked, and did great good with preaching.'

as it had begun to do even before Tyndale's arrest, and the translation of the Bible into English was authorized, the version which won the royal favour and was placed in every parish church in England was basically Tyndale's, though this fact was not obtruded.

The years which followed the repudiation of papal authority in England were marked by intense activity in Bible translation. In 1535 appeared the translation of Myles Coverdale, later bishop of Exeter, who depended not directly on the original languages but on the Latin Bible and on Luther and Tyndale's versions (though the Reformers were not mentioned by name in the acknowledgment of Coverdale's debt!).[1] In 1537 the version usually called Matthew's Bible was published (it was really the work of John Rogers, a former associate of Tyndale, who was later burned in Queen Mary's reign). Matthew's Bible was really made up of Tyndale's Pentateuch and New Testament, an unassigned version of the books from Joshua to 2 Chronicles,[2] and Coverdale's version of the books from Ezra to Malachi and of the Apocrypha. Both Coverdale's and Matthew's Bibles received the royal licence in 1537. In 1539 a layman named Richard Taverner produced a version which was really a revision of Matthew's Bible, marked by careful scholarship and literary style. The same year saw the appearance of the 'Great Bible', actually a revision of Matthew's Bible carried out by Coverdale, of which a copy was placed in every church in England in accordance with Henry VIII's injunction: 'In God's name, let it go abroad among our people!' The first edition of the Great Bible appeared under the patronage of Thomas Cromwell, as had also the earlier versions of Coverdale and Matthew. Later editions appeared in 1540 and 1541 under the patronage of Archbishop Cranmer, who contributed a preface to it. Cranmer's editions of the Great Bible were also the first to bear the words on the title-page: 'This is the Bible appointed to the use of the churches'. But the Great Bible was really a several-times-revised edition of Tyndale's version (except for the books which Tyndale had not translated); Tyndale's dying prayer for the opening of the King of England's eyes had been abundantly answered.[3]

The reign of Elizabeth saw the production of two further English versions of the Bible, which represented two divergent

[1] Coverdale's Bible was the first to introduce chapter-summaries before each chapter (as distinct from bare chapter-headings which were used in copies of the Vulgate).

[2] It is highly probable that this version of the historical books was actually Tyndale's, translated but never hitherto printed or published.

[3] It is the Great Bible version of the Psalms which is still printed in the Book of Common Prayer.

schools of Protestant thought. The earlier of the two was the Geneva Bible, so called because it was published in 1560 at Geneva (with a dedication to Elizabeth). As might be expected from a version produced in the city of Calvin and Beza, it was marked by accurate scholarship and fidelity to the original text of Scripture and represented the thorough-going Reformed point of view. This point of view found particular expression in the marginal comments. It was the first edition to print each verse as a paragraph, and to print in italics words not in the original texts. It quickly achieved popularity in England, 'and for sixty years it held its own against all rivals, for a time contesting the ground even with our own Authorized Version'.[1] The fact that it was Shakespeare's Bible gives it a special importance in English literary history. It was published in a Scottish edition in 1579 (the first Bible to be printed in Scotland), with a dedication to James VI. It is sometimes called the 'Breeches Bible', because it says in Gen. 3. 7 that Adam and Eve 'sewed figge tree leaves together, and made themselves breeches'.

As for its scholarship, this may be indicated by pointing out that until the appearance of the Revised New Testament of 1881, no English version of the Bible (apart from critical editions intended for students) paid such attention to matters of textual criticism as the Geneva Bible did. Its margins draw attention to variant readings found in a number of manuscripts, including *Codex Bezae*. The codex was not acquired by Beza until 1562, but many of its readings had been recorded in Estienne's 1550 edition of the Greek Testament. A few Bezan readings, however, are mentioned in the Geneva Bible which were not recorded in Estienne's edition; so the translators must have had some other source of information about the codex.

Its outspoken Calvinistic and anti-prelatic sentiments, however, did not please the ecclesiastical leaders in England. At the same time they could not ignore it, because its superiority in translation showed up the imperfections of the Great Bible, which was, in consequence, displaced in general esteem. A revision of the Great Bible was therefore instituted by the English bishops, at the instance of Archbishop Parker. The bishops' revisers incorporated some

[1] J. Paterson Smyth, *How we got our Bible*, pp. 121 f. (The translators' preface in the A.V. quotes Scripture in the Geneva version.) In a footnote on p. 122, Dr. Smyth cites as an example of its marginal comments the note on Rev. 9. 3, where the 'locusts that came out of the bottomless pit' are explained as meaning 'false teachers, heretics, and worldly subtil prelates, with Monks, Friars, Cardinals, Patriarchs, Archbishops, Bishops, Doctors, Bachelors and Masters of Artes, which forsake Christ to maintain false doctrine.' No wonder it was disliked in episcopal and academic circles!

of the Genevan renderings and also some of its external features, such as the division of the whole Bible into verses. Controversial notes, however, were avoided. The Bishops' Bible appeared in 1568, and a second edition followed in 1572. It represented an advance on the versions which had appeared in the first half of the sixteenth century, though for the most part it did not reach the standard of the Geneva Bible.

It looked now as if English-speaking Protestantism was to have two versions of the Bible, representing the Anglican and Genevan standpoints respectively. The prevention of this unfortunate state of affairs stands to the credit of the version of 1611. But before we go on to this, we must refer to the Roman Catholic translations into English, which appeared in the interval between the Bishops' Bible and the Authorized Version. These were the New Testament version produced in the English college at Rheims in 1582 and the Old Testament produced at Douai (to which the college had returned in the meantime) in 1609-10. Both Old Testament and New Testament are faithfully translated from the Latin Vulgate. When the New Testament appeared, the Sixtine and Clementine editions of the Vulgate had not yet been produced; accordingly, when the whole Bible was revised at a later date (1749) by Bishop Challoner, vicar-apostolic of the London district, and made much more 'English', the New Testament was also brought into conformity with the Sixto-Clementine text.

The Douai-Rheims translation is markedly Latinate in many of its renderings, containing such unfamiliar words and expressions as 'Azymes', 'the parasceve of the pasch', 'the bread of proposition', 'exinanited', 'odible to God', 'longanimitie', 'archisynagogue', 'commersation', 'contristate', 'donanes', 'agnition', 'superedified', 'prefinition of worlds', 'scenopegia'. A fair example of the style of the Rheims New Testament is given by its version of Eph. 3. 8-11:

> 'To me the least of al the sainctes is giuen this grace, among the Gentils to euangelize the vnsearcheable riches of Christ, and to illuminate al men what is the dispensation of the sacrament hidden from worlds in God, who created al things: that the manifold wisedom of God may be notified to the Princes and Potestats in the celestials by the Church, according to the prefinition of worlds, which he made in Christ Jesus our Lord'.

This has been improved as follows in Challoner's 1749 revision:

> 'To me, the least of all the saints, is given this grace, to preach among the gentiles the unsearchable riches of Christ, and to enlighten all men that they may see what is the dispensation of the mystery which hath been hidden

from eternity in God, who created all things: that the manifold wisdom of God may be made known to the principalities and powers in the heavenly *places* through the church, according to the eternal purpose, which he made in Christ Jesus our Lord'.[1]

In fairness to the Rheims translators, however, it must be said that they provided at the end of the book a glossary giving the sense of fifty-eight of these Latinisms.

While the Rheims translators admitted that they were moved to undertake this version by the wide circulation of other English versions of Scripture, they produced a work which really did make the New Testament accessible to English Catholics of the Roman obedience, despite its inferiority to the Protestant versions. In the notes with which the text was provided they spared no pains to interpret the text conformably with Roman doctrine. The Rheims translation was one of those which lay before the translators of the 1611 version; the Douai Old Testament, however, did not appear in time to be similarly used.

The Authorized Version, as we call it, or the King James Version, as it is frequently called in America, was a happy by-product of the Hampton Court Conference, which King James convened in 1604 (the year after his accession to the English throne) for the statement and discussion of the divergent views of rival parties in the Church of England. James, who was something of a scholar himself, took up with eagerness a suggestion by the Puritan leader, Dr. John Reynolds, that there might be a new translation of the Bible, and insisted at the outset that the new translation should be without marginal notes. By this he did not mean notes necessary to elucidate the sense, but notes expressing a sectional point of view, such as those in Tyndale's Bible[2] and the Geneva Bible. Some of the Genevan notes were characterized by James as 'very partiall, untrue, seditious, and savouring too much of dangerous and traytorous conceits'. Two notes which he seems to have particularly disliked were those at Exod. 1. 19 and 2 Chron. 15. 16. The former said, with regard to the midwives' refusal to kill the baby boys as Pharaoh commanded: 'Their disobedience to the king was lawful, though their dissembling was evil'. The very suggestion that it could ever be lawful to disobey a king did not commend itself to James. And he suspected that some readers

---

[1] See Mgr. Knox's chapter on 'Challoner and the Douay Version,' in *On Englishing the Bible* (1949), pp. 41 ff.

[2] An often-quoted marginal comment of Tyndale's is the one he provided to Exod. 32. 35: 'The Pope's bull slayeth more than Aaron's calf.' From the other side we may compare a heading to Acts 8 in the Rheims version, quoted by Mgr. Knox (*op. cit.*, p. 47): 'Simon Magus more religious than the Protestants.'

might think of his mother, the late Mary Queen of Scots, when they read the note anent Asa's deposition of *his* mother for idolatry: 'Herein he showed that he lacked zeal, for she ought to have died'.

But whatever James's motives were in disapproving of these and similar comments, his advice that the new version should be free from them was wholly sound. It meant in the sequel that all the non-Roman English-speaking world received one and the same English Bible as a common heritage. It is not the Bible of high church or low church, state church or free church, Episcopalian, Presbyterian or Independent, Baptist or Paedobaptist, Briton or American; it has remained The Bible *par excellence* wherever the English tongue is spoken for over three hundred years. And its excellencies have not been appreciated by Protestants only. Dr. Alexander Geddes, priest of Enzie in Banffshire, and a great Roman Catholic Biblical scholar of the end of the eighteenth century, gave it as his opinion that 'if accuracy and strictest attention to the letter of the text be supposed to constitute an excellent version this is of all versions the most excellent.' And as regards the Old Testament section of the Authorized Version, its high quality as a worthy representative of the sacred Hebrew has been widely acknowledged by Jewish scholars.

The procedure followed by the translators, who included most of the leading classical and Oriental scholars in the country, need not be detailed here. The reader should by no means ignore the preface which they set in the forefront of their work, entitled 'The Translators to the Reader' (composed by Dr. Miles Smith, later bishop of Gloucester). It is unfortunate that this preface is generally omitted nowadays from editions of the Authorized Version; but it is still printed in some (e.g. in the Two-Version edition of the Oxford Press). (It is not to be confused, of course, with the much shorter dedication 'To the Most High and Mighty Prince James', though even this contains some interesting inform-ation about the translators' policy of avoiding the extremes repre-sented on the one hand by 'Popish Persons at home or abroad', and on the other by 'selfconceited Brethren' of Puritan outlook or Nonconformist temper.)

In this preface the translators justify the general principle of Bible translations in the vernacular, and the particular work of translation on which they were engaged. They acknowledge the worth of the earlier English translations, and assert that their present concern is not 'to make a new translation, nor yet to make of a bad one a good one . . . but to make a good one better, or out of many good ones one principal good one, not justly to be excepted against'. They defend their disagreement with those who 'peradventure would have no variety of senses to be set in the margin, lest the authority of the Scriptures for deciding of controversies by that shew of uncertainty should somewhat be shaken'. As for the use or avoidance of technical terms, they followed a middle course; 'we have on the one side avoided the scrupulosity of the Puritanes, who leave the old Ecclesiastical words, and betake them to other, as when they put *washing* for *baptism*, and *congregation* instead of *Church*: as also on the other side we have shunned the obscurity of the Papists, in their *azymes, tunike, rational, holocausts, prepuce, pasche*, and a number of such like, whereof their late translation is full'. And they state quite clearly their policy of using a variety of synonyms, instead of translating each Hebrew or Greek word as far as possible uniformly by the same English word. This policy, while a stylistic advantage, is not an aid to accurate study, and was reversed by the Revisers of 1881 and 1885.

The Authorized Version was formally a revision of the 1602 edition of the Bishops' Bible. But all the existing English versions lay before the translators, and every available foreign version, Latin translations ancient and recent, the Targums and the Peshitta —all as aids to the elucidation of the Hebrew and Greek originals. But the abiding influence of one man in particular may be traced throughout great portions of their work, and that man was William Tyndale. Of their sixteenth-century predecessors the translators justly say: 'they deserve to be had of us and of posterity in everlasting remembrance. . . . blessed be they, and most honoured be their name, that break the ice, and give the onset upon that which helpeth forward to the saving of souls'. But of all these, the one who actually broke the ice was Tyndale.

Great as its excellencies were, the 1611 version was not immune from criticism. One great scholar, Dr. Hugh Broughton, thought it so ill done that he declared that he 'had rather be rent in pieces with wild horses, than any such translation by my consent should be urged upon poor churches'. (Broughton had not served on the panel of translators, for all his scholarship; he was not much of a team-worker.) And for some decades the popularity of the Geneva Bible endured, but its last edition appeared in 1644. By sheer merit the Authorized Version established itself as The English Bible.

If we compare an early edition of the Authorized Version

with a recent one, we shall notice several changes. The spelling has been considerably modernized, and other alterations have been introduced, all unauthorized, some intentional, some accidental, some good, some bad. One obvious misprint has persisted in most editions since the first one of 1611 in Matt. 23. 24, where 'strain at a gnat' should be 'strain *out* a gnat', which is the rendering of the previous versions from Tyndale's onwards. Indeed, many of the earliest editions of the A.V. were very carelessly printed, the most flagrant instance being the 'Wicked Bible'[1] of 1641; it was left for two Cambridge editions (1629 and 1638) to give a really accurate presentation of the text as decided upon by King James's revisers. In the course of time the rather full chapter summaries have been abbreviated,[2] while the marginal references have been considerably expanded. In 1701 dates were introduced into the margin for the first time; these were mainly, but not entirely,[3] based on the chronological works of Archbishop Ussher.

Some other attempts were made in the seventeenth century to translate the Bible or revise the work already done, and the Long Parliament appointed a committee to supervise the matter, but nothing came of it. A variety of translations and paraphrases appeared in the eighteenth century, including a revision by John Wesley in 1755. The nineteenth century saw the appearance of many more.

The Authorized Version, despite its many excellencies, was not perfect. The English language continued to develop after 1611, and some words gradually changed their meaning. Some inaccuracies and infelicities in the Authorized Version called for amendment. But the most important consideration of all was the progress in textual studies that was made throughout the seventeenth, eighteenth, and nineteenth centuries. The Authorized Version of the New Testament represents, by and large, the 'received text' of the Greek.[4] The textual work of Brian Walton, John Mill, and Richard Bentley did something to reveal the inadequacy of such a basis; and the labours of Lachmann, Tregelles, and Tischendorf in the nineteenth century, together with the fresh

---

[1] See p. 177.

[2] It is a pity to lose a fine old word such as appeared at the end of the chapter summary of Genesis 50: 'He [Joseph] dieth and is chested'. These chapter summaries frequently do impose interpretations on the text, but rarely of a character which divided Protestant readers in the seventeenth century. Editions of the Bible with chapter summaries (or even chapter headings) can hardly, however, be described as editions without note or comment.

[3] E.g., in the dating of the books of Ezra and Nehemiah, Ussher's individual view of the date of Artaxerxes I is not followed.

[4] See p. 187.

evidence which they discovered or drew attention to, made it plain that a revision of the existing version was necessary if the Greek text was to be represented with all desirable accuracy. Before these considerations gave rise to the official revision of the Authorized Version which appeared in 1881 and 1885, they found expression in several private ventures, such as the translations of Dean Alford, Conybeare and Howson, and J. N. Darby.

The Revised Version was initiated by a resolution passed in the Upper House of Convocation of the Province of Canterbury in 1870, that a committee of both houses should be appointed to confer with any committee which the Convocation of the Province of York might appoint, to consider and report on the desirability of revising those passages in the Authorized Version which required amendment. The Province of York declined, whereupon the Canterbury committee met and formulated its report, finding that a revision was desirable and indicating its scope. When the report was adopted, a fresh joint committee of both houses was appointed to take the appropriate steps for implementing it. This new committee decided to form two companies, one to revise the Old Testament and one to revise the New; and each company invited other scholars, both Anglican and Nonconformist, to join it. The New Testament company worked for over ten years, the Old Testament company for some fourteen years.[1] The co-operation of parallel American companies was arranged.

The aims and procedure of the Old and New Testament companies will be found set out in the 'Revisers' Preface to the Old Testament' and 'Revisers' Preface to the New Testament', which are printed in most copies of the Revised Version.

The reception given to the Old Testament revision when it appeared, though not uncritical, was generally favourable. The Old Testament revision was more conservative than that of the New in the matter of departures from the 1611 text, and it represented no revolution in the textual criticism of the original, being based on the Masoretic Hebrew. On the fiftieth anniversary of the publication of the complete Revised Version, a leading article in *The Times*, while severely critical of the New Testament revision, went on to say:

'The Old Testament company were far more successful. In one of his Cambridge lectures Professor Quiller-Couch protested "against the injustice

---

[1] It is good to record (and that with admiration) that the Revisers received no remuneration for their arduous labours—unless the gratitude of those who appreciated their work be counted as remuneration. The revisers of 1611 also worked without remuneration, but their services were not forgotten when royal or episcopal preferment came round.

of treating the two revisions—of the New Testament and of the Old—as a single work, and saddling the whole with the sins of a part". He declared that "the Revisers of the Old Testament performed their work delicately, scrupulously, with great good judgment; they have clarified the sense of the Authorized Version while respecting its consecrated rhythms". His tribute is well deserved. Even as a mere matter of arrangement, it was an immense gain that the Revised Version, unlike its predecessors, printed the poetical books of the Old Testament as poetry instead of as prose. It was an even greater gain when numerous passages in the poetical and prophetical books which had been simply unintelligible in the older version became lucid in the new, and were found to have beauty of thought as well as beauty of sound. To compare, for example, the two renderings of the noble drama of Job is to agree with Dean Bradley of Westminster when he declared that the Revisers "for the first time made this great book intelligible to ordinary English readers"'.[1]

The New Testament revision, on the other hand, had a very mixed reception. It was attacked on two scores—its quality as a translation, and the principles of textual criticism which it embodied. On the former score it must be acknowledged that it was open to criticism. The elegance and beauty of the Authorized Version have often disappeared in the course of the revision. In the words of the article already quoted from *The Times* of May 14, 1935:

'The real trouble with the selected company of Revisers was that, while it included the most eminent authorities of the time on New Testament Greek, it included no men of letters versed in the rhythm, cadence, and euphony of good English. The Revisers began by setting before themselves a pedantic code, and for the sake of conformity with that code they cheerfully ruined many of the loveliest passages in English literature'.

But *did* they ruin 'many of the loveliest passages in English literature'? These passages remain. As a monument of English literature the Authorized Version stands where it ever did and can never be displaced. On the other hand, it must be considered that the stylistic elegance of the New Testament in the Authorized Version is a quality largely absent from the Greek original, just as much as the academic pedantry[2] of the New Testament in the Revised Version is absent from it. Dr. C. J. Cadoux, discussing the question, points out that there are two ideals of translation, roughly corresponding to the characteristic tendencies of Oxford and Cambridge Universities.

'The Oxford method aims at conveying the sense of the original in free idiomatic English without too much regard to the precise wording of the former: the Cambridge method is to pay meticulous attention to verbal

---

[1] *The Times*, May 14, 1935. The article goes on to suggest that the University Presses might publish a composite edition, giving the Old Testament and Apocrypha in the R.V., and the New Testament in the A.V.

[2] These words are used in a purely descriptive and not in any derogatory sense.

accuracy, to translate as literally as is possible without positive violence to
English usage, or positive misrepresentation of the author's meaning, and to
leave it to the reader to discern the sense as well as he can from the context.
For good or ill, the Cambridge genius presided over the English Revision'.[1]

Much depends on what the reader really wants. If he is not concerned with smaller points of accuracy, but wants a literary masterpiece, with old haunting associations and beautiful cadences, he
will prefer the Authorized Version. If he wants an accurate and
severely literal representation of the original, calculated to serve
the requirements of the careful student, he will prefer the Revised.
One obvious advantage of the Revised Version from this point of
view is the Revisers' policy of rendering a single word of the original
by a single English word where the sense permits: a policy in
which they markedly departed from the deliberate practice of their
1611 predecessors, and in which they would have had the cordial
approval of Hugh Broughton (for the deliberate variations of the
A.V. constituted one of its many demerits in his sight).[2]

    On the other score, that of the underlying text, something
has been said already in Chapter XIV.[3] The great access of textual
information since 1611 made it necessary for the Revisers to decide
what form of Greek text was to serve as the basis for their revision.
Among the New Testament revisers the claims of the Byzantine
text were ably maintained by Dr. Scrivener, and those of the
Alexandrian text by Dr. Westcott and Dr. Hort. In general, the
views of Westcott and Hort commanded the assent of their colleagues, and the textual (as distinct from merely translational)
differences between the Authorized and Revised Versions correspond more or less to those between the Byzantine and Alexandrian
types of Greek text. This aspect of the Revisers' work was fiercely
attacked, and especially by Dean Burgon, whose great scholarship
lent weight to the powerful critiques which he contributed to the
Quarterly Review in 1881 and 1882 and republished in The Revision
Revised (1883). In making these criticisms Burgon appealed
confidently to the verdict of succeeding days, but subsequent
textual research, while it has not upheld the supremacy of the
Alexandrian text with Westcott and Hort's confidence, has vindicated their estimate of the late and secondary character of the
Byzantine text. On this score the Revised Version did represent a

----

[1] In *Ancient and English Versions of the Bible*, p. 251. In a footnote Dr. Cadoux refers
to W. Sanday in *The Expositor*, April, 1882, pp. 249-252. In a choice between the Oxford
and Cambridge ideals the present writer feels no hesitation.
[2] The Revised Standard Version of 1946-52 reverts in some degree to the 1611 practice.
[3] See pp. 184 ff.

great step forward as compared with the Authorized, but not, of course, the last step.

The Revised Version of the Apocrypha appeared in 1895. In 1898 an edition of the Revised Bible with newly-prepared marginal cross-references was published; in this edition the textual and translational variants and other notes appearing in the margins of the ordinary editions of the Revised Version are printed as footnotes. It would be difficult to think of a more useful edition of the English Bible for the serious student than this edition of 1898. But even more useful, so far as the New Testament is concerned, is *The New Testament in the Revised Version of* 1881 *with Fuller References,* edited by A. W. Greenup and J. H. Moulton (Oxford, 1910).

The points in which the American Revision companies differed from their British colleagues were listed in appendices to the British edition, until in 1901 the Americans published their own edition of the Revised Version, usually known as the American Standard Version.[1] A new edition of this version, in which the English is slightly modernized, is being prepared by the Lockman Foundation of La Habra, California, under the title: *The New American Standard Bible.* The first sample of this work, *The New American Standard Gospel of John,* appeared in 1960.

New Testament study has not stood still since the Revised Version appeared, and the Revisers' work both in textual criticism and translation is capable of further improvement. The advances in textual criticism have been mentioned in Chapter XIV; they have largely been the result of fresh discoveries, such as the Sinaitic Syriac palimpsest and the Chester Beatty papyri. As regards the Revisers' translation work, it was carried out too much as though the Greek of the New Testament should be treated like the classical Greek of the fifth and fourth centuries B.C. As we have seen in Chapter V, the true character of New Testament Greek began to be appreciated shortly after the date at which the Revisers' work appeared. To say these things, of course, is not to blame the Revisers; their work was accomplished in the light of the best knowledge available to them. But with the access of fresh knowledge their work calls for further revision.

At various times since the end of last century fresh translations of the Bible in part or in whole have appeared. *The Twentieth Century New Testament* (1898-1901; revised edition, 1904) was a

---

[1] One of the most immediately apparent differences between the A.S.V. and the R.V. is the former's use of 'Jehovah' for the Ineffable Name in the Old Testament instead of 'the LORD' or 'GOD'. The R.S.V. (1952) reverts to the earlier usage.

dignified modern translation of Westcott and Hort's Greek text.[1]
Dr. R. F. Weymouth's *New Testament in Modern Speech* (1902 and
later) represents the Greek of the translator's own *Resultant Greek
Testament*, based on the consensus of the best critical editions; it
pays special attention to grammatical accuracy in such matters as
the proper translation of the Greek tenses (as befitted the work of a
headmaster). Professor James Moffatt's version of the New
Testament appeared in 1913 and his Old Testament in 1924; the
English is idiomatic, except where the translator's native Scots
intrudes; the translation, though vigorous, is rather free; the Old
Testament is less accurate than the New; in both Testaments
Moffatt takes excessive liberties with the text.[2] Yet of all modern
translations Moffatt's has proved the most popular. To read
through one of the New Testament epistles in Moffatt's version is
one of the best ways of getting a grasp of the general argument.
Many readers dislike it because its style is so much more colloquial
and less stately than that of the Authorized Version. They feel
like the old lady whose minister visited her and (being a modern
young man) read her a portion of Moffatt's translation. When he
had done, she said: 'Yes, that was very nice, but won't you read a
bit of the Word of God before you go?'[3] But Moffatt's version
was not intended to be a substitute for the Authorized Version,
and cannot be fairly blamed for not being what it never set out to
be. Much of the Authorized Version sounds foreign to those who
have not been brought up to appreciate its wording, and there can
be no doubt that to such people Moffatt has made the Bible message
intelligible, in spite of the imperfections of his version. In the
United States special mention must be made of *The Bible: An
American Translation* (1935), which comprises Dr. E. J. Goodspeed's
version of the New Testament (1923) and Apocrypha (1938), and
the version of the Old Testament edited by Dr. J. M. Powis Smith
(1935), in modern literary American idiom.

Among Roman Catholics, the Rheims-Challoner New Testa-
ment was revised in America by the Episcopal Committee of the
Confraternity of Christian Doctrine and published under the title
The New Testament of our Lord and Saviour Jesus Christ (Paterson,

---

[1] See K. W. Clark, 'The Making of the Twentieth Century New Testament', *Bulletin
of the John Rylands Library* 38 (1955-56), pp. 58 ff.

[2] At the very outset of his Old Testament translation, for example, he transposes Gen.
2. 4a and makes it the first sentence of the Bible. For this he was vigorously criticized by
the late Dr. W. L. Baxter in a pamphlet entitled, *The Bible's First Verse: Moses? or Moffatt?*

[3] Similarly an eminent Roman Catholic scholar remarked of Mgr. Knox's translation
when it first appeared: 'I shouldn't call it the Word of God!'

1941). This work represents a very real improvement. The companion version of the Old Testament, which is now well advanced, is not a revision but a completely new and refreshing translation from the original texts. In England the Rheims-Challoner version has not been revised; instead, a completely new translation of the Vulgate New Testament was produced by Mgr. Ronald A. Knox and published in 1945 with the authorization of the Roman Catholic hierarchy of England and Wales, so that English and Welsh Roman Catholics have now the choice of two official versions. Mgr. Knox subsequently completed (1949) a translation of the Vulgate Old Testament.[1] After some revision, this also received hierarchical authorization, and the approved edition of the complete Knox Bible was published in 1955. But a translation of a translation, no matter how accurately revised by reference to the original, can never be so adequate as a translation of the original text; and this is provided for Roman Catholics in this country by the excellent *Westminster Version of the Sacred Scriptures*, a translation with commentary, edited by the late Father C. Lattey (1913 onwards).

The Jewish Publication Society of America published in 1917 *The Holy Scriptures According to the Masoretic Text*, a translation of the Old Testament by Jewish scholars preserving the order and arrangement of the Hebrew Bible. Its debt to the Authorized and Revised Versions is obvious. It has more recently been revised by an editorial board under the chairmanship of Professor H. M. Orlinsky.

Other revisions of the older versions, such as *The Book of Books* (1938), and the *Letchworth New Testament* (1948), may be passed over with a bare mention. So also may *The Bible in Basic English* (New Testament, 1940; complete Bible, 1949), with the inherent limitations of its medium (although it has a positive value as an independent translation from the original tongues). *The New Testament in Plain English*, by C. K. Williams (1952), makes use of a vocabulary over half as large again as the 'Basic' Bible. *The Expanded Translation of the New Testament*, by Kenneth S. Wuest, in three volumes (1956-59), attempts to bring out philological and theological nuances more fully than an ordinary translation could do. Something similar was attempted by the translators of *The Amplified New Testament* (1958).[2] The *Berkeley Version* of the whole

---

[1] See p. 209, n. 1, for Mgr. Knox's version of the Psalms and canticles.

[2] Produced by the Lockman Foundation (see p. 234), whose Research Secretary, Dr. Frances E. Siewert, took a major part in the work. *The Amplified Old Testament* is now being produced; Volume II (Job-Malachi) appeared early in 1962; Volume I is in preparation.

Bible (1959) is the most outstanding among recent translations of both Testaments sponsored by private groups. The New Testament has been paraphrased in vigorous modern English by J. B. Phillips in *Letters to Young Churches* (1947), *The Gospels* (1952), *The Young Church in Action* (1955) and *The Book of Revelation* (1957), the whole work being issued as *The New Testament in Modern English* (1958). A fine translation of *The Four Gospels*, by a classical scholar, E. V. Rieu, has lately (1952) been added to the 'Penguin Classics,' followed by a fairly fully annotated translation of *The Acts of the Apostles* by his son, C. H. Rieu (1957). Olaf M. Norlie's *Simplified New Testament* (1961) is a version for young people based on the Received Text; it is bound up with *The Psalms for Today*, a scholarly version by R. K. Harrison.

More important is the Revised Standard Version of the Bible (New Testament, 1946; complete Bible, 1952), a revision of the versions of 1611 and 1901, carried through by a committee of American scholars. The Apocrypha followed in 1957. This latest revision makes full use of the most recent textual and linguistic discoveries. Archaisms have been removed, but the language is not the American idiom of the mid-twentieth century but good literary English of a quality that is acknowledged as standard on both sides of the Atlantic. It shows little of the Cambridge ideal of translation which is so marked in the Revised Version, and therefore the Revised Version (or the American Standard Version) may still be preferred by exact students. But for more general purposes the Revised Standard Version makes a strong bid to replace the Authorized Version. Its publication was announced and welcomed with great enthusiasm, although in certain quarters it met with keen criticism. This, of course, is no unprecedented experience for a new version of the Bible. The principles on which the new revisers have worked have been interestingly set out in two hand-books, *An Introduction to the Revised Standard Version of the New Testament* (1946) and *An Introduction to the Revised Standard Version of the Old Testament* (1952).

It may be questioned, however, whether at this time of day successive revisions of older revisions are adequate. It may well be argued that what is required to-day is a completely new translation, based on the most reliable information available on all the subjects involved, linguistic and textual, and carried out under an urgent sense of the constraint of the Word of God. Dr. C. J. Cadoux stated in 1940 that 'all serious Christians are fundamentally at one in needing a version of the Scriptures which is as truthful as human skill, aided by the divine grace, can make it'.[1] It remains for us now to describe the latest attempt to supply this need.

[1] In *Ancient and English Versions of the Bible*, p. 274.

CHAPTER XIX

THE NEW ENGLISH BIBLE

A.D. 1961 has been a notable year in the history of the English Bible, and that for two reasons. It marked the three hundred and fiftieth anniversary of the publication of the Authorized Version, and it witnessed the publication of the first instalment of the New English Bible.

When the copyright of the Revised Version was running out in the 1930's, one of the two University Presses which owned the copyright approached two well-known scholars, Professor G. R. Driver of Oxford and Professor J. M. Creed of Cambridge, and invited them to revise and submit specimen passages of the Old and New Testaments respectively. The idea was to bring the Revised Version abreast of contemporary linguistic and textual knowledge. Specimens were prepared and submitted, but when World War II broke out in 1939 Professor Driver undertook work of national importance, and Professor Creed died in 1940. The plan to revise the R.V. thus came to nothing. After the war a much more ambitious and radical plan was launched, the production of what has come to be called the 'New English Bible'.

The initiative in regard to the New English Bible was taken by the General Assembly of the Church of Scotland in 1946, in response to an overture from the Presbytery of Stirling and Dunblane. The ministers and elders of Stirling and Dunblane may well take some pardonable pride in contemplating the effect of their overture! The Church of Scotland warmly adopted the overture, and approached the Church of England and the principal Free Churches, who also approved of the suggestion. A joint committee was set up in 1947, including representatives of the chief non-Roman Churches of Great Britain and Ireland, the Oxford and Cambridge University Presses, the British and Foreign Bible Society and the National Bible Society of Scotland. Its task was to prepare a new translation of the Bible into modern English.

After hearing reports from advisory and consultative panels, the joint committee appointed three panels of translators—for the Old Testament, New Testament, and Apocrypha respectively. A fourth panel was also set up by the joint committee: this was a panel of literary and stylistic advisors. The joint committee determined that the criticisms of style and language which had been brought against the Revised New Testament of 1881 should not lie against the new translation.

The first Chairman of the joint committee was Dr. J. W. Hunkin, Bishop of Truro; when he died in 1952, he was succeeded by Dr. A. T. P. Williams, Bishop of Winchester, whose name appears beneath the Preface to the New Testament in the New English Bible. The first Secretary was Dr. George S. Hendry, formerly Church of Scotland minister at Bridge of Allan—most fittingly, for it was he who presented the overture of the Presbytery of Stirling and Dunblane to the General Assembly in 1946. When he left the country in 1949 to become Professor of Systematic Theology in Princeton Theological Seminary, U.S.A., he was succeeded by another Church of Scotland theologian, Professor J. K. S. Reid, now of Aberdeen University. The Director of the whole enterprise is Professor C. H. Dodd, formerly of Cambridge, who has also acted as convener of the New Testament translators' panel. The appearance of his name as a Companion of Honour in the Queen's Birthday Honours List of June 1961, so soon after the publication of the new version of the New Testament, was a mark of appreciation of his work in this connexion, over and above his more personal contributions to Biblical scholarship over many years. Professor Dodd is, by general consent, the most distinguished Biblical scholar in the British Isles today, and it is both gratifying and encouraging to know that such an important work as the New English Bible is being carried on under his direction. But he is 'Director', not 'Dictator'; here and there in the New Testament version one comes upon renderings which would probably not be his personal preference, to judge by what he has written elsewhere. While individuals have contributed in many ways to the translation, their contributions have been subject to the judgment of the whole panel, whose members accept corporate responsibility for the work.

The Deputy Director, and convener of the Old Testament translators' panel, is Dr. G. R. Driver, Professor of Semitic Philology at Oxford; the convener of the Apocrypha panel is Professor W. D. McHardy, of the Regius Chair of Hebrew at Oxford.

As for the procedure adopted, each book (or sometimes part of a book) is entrusted to an individual translator, who need not be a member of one of the panels. He produces a first draft, which may bear very little resemblance to the finally approved version.

This draft is then sent to all members of the appropriate panel, who work through it along with the translator in the course of their next meetings.

In the case of the Old Testament, the first draft goes first of all to Professor Driver, who studies it in the light of his expert knowledge of Semitic linguistics, before it is submitted to other members of the panel. When the draft has been thoroughly discussed and revised by the panel, it goes to the literary panel. The members of the literary panel make their suggestions for improvement of the English style, and the appropriate translation panel then adopts such of these suggestions as it thinks fit. The version finally agreed upon by the translation panel is lastly submitted to the joint committee, with whom the final decision rests.

The New Testament translators completed their work on December 18, 1958, ten years to the day from the date of their first meeting. Their names deserve to be put on record. In addition to Professor Dodd, they are Principal G. S. Duncan, formerly of St. Andrews; Professor R. V. G. Tasker, of King's College, London; Professor C. F. D. Moule, of Cambridge; Professor G. D. Kilpatrick, of Oxford; Dr. J. A. T. Robinson (now Bishop of Woolwich); the Rev. G. M. Styler, of Corpus Christi College, Cambridge. Three of the most distinguished members of the panel died before its work was finished; Professor T. W. Manson, of Manchester; Principal W. F. Howard, of Birmingham; and Dr. E. G. Selwyn, Dean of Winchester.

During 1959 the text of the translation was finally prepared for printing. In March 1960 it was adopted by the joint committee, at a meeting held in the historic Jerusalem Chamber of Westminster Abbey; on March 14, 1961, it was published by the Oxford and Cambridge University Presses. There were two editions—a larger Library Edition with full translators' notes and introduction, and a smaller Popular Edition with a minimum of notes and a shorter introduction. Within twelve months from the date of publication some four million copies had been sold. One reviewer has described the New English Bible as 'The Bible for Jones' ('Jones' being our old friend, the man in the street); if that is so, then Jones has certainly taken to it in a big way, and vast numbers of his contemporaries are doing their best to keep up with him.

The translators of the New English Bible, like the revisers of the R.S.V., have made an eclectic text the basis of their work. The Introduction to the New English Bible points out that there is at present no critical text which would command the same general degree of acceptance as the Alexandrian text did in the days when the R.V. appeared. 'Nor has the time come', the Introduction continues, 'in the judgment of competent scholars, to construct such a text, since new material constantly comes to light, and the debate continues. The present translators therefore could do no other than consider variant readings on their merits, and, having weighed the evidence for themselves, select for translation in each passage the reading which to the best of their judgment seemed most likely to represent what the author wrote. Where other readings seemed to deserve serious consideration they have been recorded in footnotes'.

This decision in favour of an eclectic text is inevitable and wise in the present situation; although one might wish that the footnotes sometimes, instead of merely saying that 'some witnesses read' something different from what appears in the text, could have given a little indication of the relative support given to variant readings. But then it was no part of the translators' responsibility to provide an *apparatus criticus* to their text.

The New English Bible is a totally fresh translation, made direct from the original texts. It is not a revision of earlier versions. Therefore, it will make a very different impression from the Revised Standard Version of 1952. With all of its deviations from the text of the A.V. and American Standard Version, the Revised Standard Version is recognizably a revision of these previous versions. This is not the case with the New English Bible. The difference between it and the older versions is therefore much greater than the difference between the R.S.V. and the older versions. In fact, the R.S.V. appears positively conservative, not to say old-fashioned, alongside the New English Bible!

In a memorandum circulated at a fairly early stage in the course of the new translation, Professor Dodd said that the translators aimed at a 'timeless' English, something which would be genuinely English in idiom, avoiding archaisms and transient modernisms; intelligible to any reasonably intelligent person, but not bald or pedestrian; more concerned with conveying a sense of reality than with preserving 'hallowed associations'; accurate without being pedantic. The unit in the translation is not the word but rather the clause or the sentence; sometimes, indeed, it may be more extensive still. It is remarkable how close this principle is to that which guided John Purvey when he edited the second Wycliffite version of 1395—'to translate as clearly as he could to the sentence'.[1] Indeed, we may go farther back in the history of English translation, and listen to Alfred the Great telling us how he 'began, amidst other diverse and manifold cares of the kingdom, to turn into English the book which is called *Cura Pastoralis* in Latin, and in English *The Shepherd's Book*—sometimes word for word, and sometimes meaning for meaning'. In these words he indicates two ways in which translators may go about their task, and the conflict between these two ways can be abundantly illustrated from the history of the English Bible. A word-for-word translation will be criticized for being too slavishly literal; a meaning-for-meaning translation will be criticized for being too free.

But there is, in fact, a place for both kinds of translation. The Bible student who, without possessing an acquaintance with the original languages, yet wishes to be brought as close to them as possible through the medium of his own language, will appreciate an accurate word-for-word translation. The ordinary reader who wishes to have the sense of what the Biblical writers said conveyed as effectively as possible in his own idiom will be best served by a meaning-for-meaning translation.

So far as English versions are concerned, the man who wants an accurate word-for-word translation has in the Revised Version the best of its kind that he is ever likely to have. But those who want a meaning-for-meaning translation will welcome the New English Bible, for this is precisely what its sponsors have set out to provide. They have made the sentence, and not the individual word, the unit of translation; they have made it their business to replace Greek constructions by English ones. Whereas the Revisers of eighty years ago went as far as they could in rendering the same Greek word throughout by one selected English word, the new translators have reverted in large measure to the pattern of the Authorized Version, in which considerable liberty was exercised in the choice of now this synonym and now that. Indeed, the new translators may have gone too far in this respect, partly because each translator was left to exercise his own judgment in the choice of English equivalents while preparing his first draft, and no attempt was made to impose uniformity afterwards. Take, for example, the Greek word *xylon* (literally meaning 'wood'), which is used five times in the New Testament in reference to the cross (which elsewhere is indicated by another Greek word, *stauros*). For those five occurrences the older versions have 'tree'; the New English Bible has 'gibbet' in Acts 5. 30; 10. 39; 13. 29; 'tree' in Gal. 3. 13

[1] See p. 221.

(quoting from Deut. 21. 23); 'gallows' in 1 Pet. 2. 24. (The other word, *stauros*, is regularly rendered 'cross'.)

Again, the variation in the selection of synonyms makes it impossible to follow Paul's use of one and the same word throughout his letters, or to trace the degree of verbal identity existing between parallel passages in the Gospels. All this means that the new version of the New Testament will not be of much use for the more specialized interests of Bible students; if they want an English version maintaining the necessary precision in such matters, they will continue to use the R.V. The New English Bible, in fact, was not primarily intended for students; had it been so, it would in all likelihood not have attracted general readers, any more than the R.V. has done.

Yet the translators have aimed at producing a translation in the proper sense of the term, not a paraphrase. Sometimes they have gone back to even earlier models than the Authorized Version. The translators of the Authorized Version claim to have avoided 'the scrupulosity of the Puritanes, who leave the old ecclesiastical words, and betake them to other, as when they put . . . *congregation* instead of *Church*'. But whether it was Puritan scrupulosity or some other consideration that moved the new translators, they have shown a preference for 'congregation' over 'church' where a local church is in view. In Matthew 16. 18 they make Jesus say, 'on this rock I will build my church'; but in Matthew 18. 17 we find 'report the matter to the congregation, and if he will not listen even to the congregation, you must then treat him as you would a pagan or a tax-gatherer.' So Tyndale comes into his own again.

Some books on the English Bible have quoted for its quaintness the rendering of 1 Corinthians 16. 8 in most of the older English versions from Wycliffe to Geneva: 'I will tarry at Ephesus until Whitsuntide.' Now the New English Bible can be added to the list: 'I shall remain at Ephesus until Whitsuntide.' But it does not follow Tyndale and Coverdale in Rev. 1. 10 and make John say that he was in spirit 'on a Sunday'. 'It was on the Lord's day' is the rendering here. Nor has Passover reverted to Easter in Acts 12. 4. The preceding verse says: 'This happened during the festival of Unleavened Bread.' But the translators' propensity for using now one phrase and now another to represent the same original appears when we compare Acts 20. 6; here 'after the days of Unleavened Bread' is relegated to a footnote as the literal rendering, while the text reads, 'after the Passover season.'

Whether the New English Bible will lend itself to use in public worship is something that experience will show; the private reader can scarcely assess its suitability for this.[1] Some bishops have cautiously confined its use in their dioceses to certain occasions where 'hallowed associations' do not count for so much; but a surprising number of ministers of various denominations have testified decidedly to the welcome impact which it makes on hearers in church services.

There is certainly something fine and sonorous about the opening words of the *Magnificat* (Luke 1. 46-55):

> '*Tell out, my soul, the greatness of the Lord,*
> *rejoice, rejoice, my spirit, in God my Saviour . . .*'

But as the canticle proceeds, we are conscious of something more than the dignity of the diction. It has often been pointed out that the *Magnificat* provides an excellent example of the power of familiar cadences to lull the understanding to sleep; it would be difficult otherwise to account for the complacency with which comfortable congregations voice such revolutionary sentiments as it contains. 'He hath put down the mighty from their seats'—that is the familiar Prayer Book version, but it does not strike home to our condition in the 1960's so tellingly as the New English Bible does: 'he has torn imperial powers from their thrones.' (If that rendering had been thought up by churchmen in some countries, they would have been accused of being crypto-Communists!)

One feature which has had to be recognized from the day of publication onwards is the thoroughly readable character of the new version. The wording and the format, added to the inherent and abiding fascination of the subject-matter, draw the reader on, so that, before realizing it, he has read through ten or twelve chapters. The fact that people whom one would not class as 'Bible-readers' have been seen reading page after page of it in public vehicles is testimony enough to its attractiveness.

It has been suggested that the new version may not lend itself so well to memorizing as the Authorized Version does; if that is so, it may be a good thing in some ways, as it will retain its 'newness' and therefore its special effectiveness longer. It is not as though it was intended to supersede the Authorized Version; if both versions are used side by side, as the sponsors of the New English Bible hope,

---

[1] The records which have just been produced, on which one may hear the Gospel of John and other parts of the New English Bible read aloud from beginning to end, suggest that the sound as well as the sense has received due attention.

then the New English Bible will serve as a kind of commentary on the Authorized Version, showing what the older version *means*. There will inevitably be a tendency to ask from time to time: 'Why have they changed this?'—when in fact they have not *changed* anything, since they were translating from the original text, and not revising the Authorized Version. But to so many people the A.V. is 'The Bible' in a unique sense that any other translation is felt to be a 'change' which must be asked to justify itself if it is to be accepted.

'Surely they could have left the Lord's Prayer alone', one hears it said. But it would have been a complete departure from their principles had the translators, instead of providing a direct rendering from the Greek of Matt. 6. 9-13 or Luke 11. 2-4, simply 'lifted' the rendering of their predecessors. After all, it will be a long time before people spontaneously follow the New English Bible when saying the Lord's Prayer, and when they do, one wonders what meaning they will attach to the petition 'And do not bring us to the test' (Matt. 6. 13; Luke 11. 4).[1]

Of course many people will not *feel* that it is the Bible, because to them the Bible is bound up with the traditional phraseology and binding and so forth. We have heard of the little girl who said 'It's quite good, I suppose, but it's not so *holy* as the old one, is it?'—and one distinguished reviewer has said that he would not feel that an oath sworn on the New English Bible would be so binding as one sworn on the Authorized Version. Well, it will be a long time, no doubt, before anyone is asked to swear an oath on the New English Bible; that was not what the sponsors and translators had in view when they embarked upon their work. Indeed, the New English Bible has something pertinent to say on this very subject: 'You are not to swear at all . . . plain "Yes" or "No" is all you need to say; anything beyond that comes from the devil' (Matt. 5. 34, 37).

There are some rather colloquial expressions which have not hitherto been associated with 'Bible English'. Such are the words of our Lord's disillusioned hearers in John 6. 60: 'This is more than we can stomach! Why listen to such words?' Or the wording of 1 Tim. 5. 15, 'For there have in fact been widows who have taken the wrong turning and gone to the devil'—but it is surprising to find how literal a translation this is when it is compared with the Greek. The warning in 1 Cor. 5. 9 to 'have nothing to do with

---

[1] The translators knew what they meant, but how is the general reader to know? Surely a preferable rendering would have been 'Grant that we may not fail in the test.'

loose livers' is a rare instance of ineptness; one wonders how the literary panel passed it.

The prologue to the Fourth Gospel provides a useful sample of the translators' work.

The older versions present us with a word-for-word rendering of verse 1 of this chapter: 'In the beginning was the Word, and the Word was with God, and the Word was God'. The new version presents us with a 'meaning-for-meaning' rendering; that is to say, the translators have asked themselves, 'What does this sentence *mean*?' and have then set themselves to express that meaning in the best English they could find for the purpose. What is meant by the clause: 'In the beginning was the Word'? 'In the beginning' is probably a deliberate echo on the Evangelist's part of the opening words of the book of Genesis. At that time, he wishes us to understand, when God created heaven and earth, the Word through whom He created them was already in existence. The new translators have conveyed the Evangelist's purpose clearly by their rendering 'When all things began, the Word already was.' Whether the echo of Genesis 1. 1 will be as clear in the N.E.B. as it is in the older versions we cannot say until we see the Old Testament part of the work and examine its rendering of Genesis 1. 1—and that will not be for some years yet.

The second clause of John 1. 1 ('The Word dwelt with God') does not call for comment here, but the third clause makes us stop and think. 'The Word was God' is the old-established translation of this clause, and evangelicals have been at pains to defend this translation against such forms as 'the Word was divine' (which says less than the Evangelist intended) or even 'the Word was a god' (which says something quite different from what the Evangelist intended). Is the Evangelist's meaning better expressed by the N.E.B.? 'What God was, the Word was' could be ambiguous out of its context; but in the context it clearly means that the Word was the perfect expression of all that God was—a thought which is repeated in a variety of forms throughout this Gospel. As Professor C. K. Barrett says—and our translators would certainly agree— 'John intends that the whole of his gospel shall be read in the light of this verse. The deeds and words of Jesus are the deeds and words of God; if this be not true, the book is blasphemous.'[1]

The next thing to be noted in the prologue is that the translators have adopted for their text at the end of verse 3 the punctuation which the R.V., A.S.V., and R.S.V. record in the margin. This

[1] *The Gospel according to St. John* (1960), p. 130.

punctuation, which has strong and early support, puts a full stop after 'was not anything made' and begins the next sentence: 'That which hath been made was life in him' (R.V. mg.). It is rendered in the N.E.B.: 'All that came to be was alive with his life.' Here the crucial question is one of punctuation more than translation, and on the whole the punctuation adopted in the text of A.V., R.V., A.S.V., and R.S.V. seems preferable. The words as thus punctuated are translated in the margin of the N.E.B.: 'No single created thing came into being without him. There was life in him . . .' (It may well be that this is the punctuation personally preferred by Professor Dodd; at least this is what one could infer from a passage on page 318 of his book *The Interpretation of the Fourth Gospel*. But if that is so, it simply indicates that the new translation is a true joint-production, and that, as we have hinted already, even the preference of the Director could be outvoted.)

The remainder of the prologue illustrates the care which the translators have taken to express the full meaning of their text, and the considerable success which they have achieved. The rendering of John's testimony in verse 15 shows up clearly the two senses in which 'before' is used (A.V., 'preferred before me, for he was before me'), and makes the emphasis on our Lord's pre-existence as unmistakable as could be desired: 'This is the man I meant when I said, "He comes after me, but takes rank before me"; for before I was born, he already was.'

Later on in this Gospel it is gratifying to see John 4. 9b properly rendered: 'Jews and Samaritans, it should be noted, do not use vessels in common.'

In Acts 17, Paul's speech at Athens is admirably rendered. For one thing, the new translation makes it plain that the speech was delivered not 'in the midst of Mars' hill' (A.V.) but 'before the Court of the Areopagus' (Acts 17. 22). Did Paul tell his hearers that they were 'too superstitious' (A.V.) or 'very religious' (R.S.V.)? The New English Bible tells us: 'I see that in everything that concerns religion you are uncommonly scrupulous.' The words at the beginning of verse 25 are rendered in a way that makes the sense plainer than it is in most versions. 'Neither is worshipped with men's hands', says the A.V., and the R.V. and R.S.V. are not noticeably better. For God is and should be worshipped by the hands of His people as well as with their other organs and faculties. 'It is not because he lacks anything that he accepts service at men's hands', says the new version, and that is exactly what is required. 'He fixed the epochs of their history and the limits of their territory,' says the new translation in the second half of verse 26, but the variant reading in the footnote is probably to be preferred: 'He fixed the ordered seasons.' It is likely that what Paul refers to here is the seasonal succession of seed-time and harvest (cf. Acts 14. 17) and the provision of the habitable zones of the earth for men to live in, rather than the rise and fall of nations and their territorial frontiers (although these too are matters of divine overruling, as the book of Daniel and Deut. 32. 8 remind us). In verse 28 I should have put quotation-marks round the words 'in him we live and move, in him we exist' as well as round 'We are also his offspring'; the former passage is as much a poetical quotation (from Epimenides) as is the latter (from Aratus).

Paul's brief statement of the gospel in Rom. 1. 16, 17, is rendered: 'It is the saving power of God for everyone who has faith—the Jew first, but the Greek also—because here is revealed God's way of righting wrong, a way that starts from faith and ends in faith; as Scripture says, "he shall gain life who is justified through faith"'. Here we may observe the care taken throughout this translation to distinguish the imperfective aspect of the verb 'to believe' (rendered 'have faith' or the like) from the aorist tense (rendered, e.g. in Rom. 4. 3, 'Abraham put his faith in God'). Moreover, when the word 'faith' appears as part of the phrase used to express the idea of believing, the connection between the verb 'to believe' and the noun 'faith' is more immediately apparent. It may be said that God's righteousness is more than 'a way of righting wrong' in the abstract, that it is a way of righting *sinners*; but this appears clearly enough in the context. 'From faith to faith' (Rom. 1. 17, A.V., etc.) is none too easy a phrase to interpret; one version is suggested in the text of the New English Bible, but a footnote suggests the alternative, 'based on faith and addressed to faith,' which is perhaps to be preferred. The translation of the quotation from Habakkuk certainly conveys Paul's understanding of that scripture.

The heart of the gospel is plainly unfolded in Rom. 3. 21-26, where incidentally we see how effectively the translators can deal with one of Paul's long sentences. In verses 21 f. the twofold aspect of God's 'righteousness' is conveyed by two expressions—'God's justice' and 'God's way of righting wrong.' The significance of the reference to the blood of Christ in verse 25 is indicated by rendering it 'his sacrificial death.' But serious questions have been raised about the rendering of Gk. *hilastērion* in that verse. What are the implications of these questions?

'Retribution' is the word preferred for the Greek term which is rendered 'wrath' in the older versions (although 'wrath' is used in John 3. 36). The reason may be that to our ears 'wrath' conveys an emotional connotation which is absent from the biblical concept (but what are we to say of 'the fury of retribution' in Rom. 2. 8?). Whichever rendering is used, the wrath or retribution is God's; we may say this while acknowledging that in the Bible it is something foreign and uncongenial to Him, His 'strange work', slowly and reluctantly embarked upon, in contrast to His mercy, which He hastens joyfully to lavish upon undeserving penitents. And if 'we see divine retribution revealed from heaven and falling upon all the godless wickedness of men' (Rom. 1. 18, N.E.B.), we see in the gospel how this retribution is removed by the act of God. This is what Paul asserts in Rom. 3. 25 when he says that God has provided Jesus to be our *hilastērion*[1], which the new version translates 'the means of expiating sin' (cf. R.S.V. 'expiation'). This seems inadequate to express Paul's thought. We can understand perfectly the avoidance of 'propitiation' if that is understood as implying that God required to be appeased or persuaded to show mercy. But since God is the subject of the sentence, since the *hilastērion* is something that He has provided, would not 'propitiation' or some equivalent word ('atonement,' perhaps) take its proper meaning from the context as clearly as *hilastērion* and related Greek words did from their earlier context in the Septuagint?[1]

We note a preference for 'splendour' to 'glory' as the rendering of Gk. *doxa*, effective sometimes, as in Rom. 9. 5, where the phrase 'the splendour of the divine presence,' denotes the *shekhina*; less effective at other times, as in Rom. 8. 30, 'to those whom he justified he has also given his splendour,' or in the closing verses of 2 Cor. 3. We may hope, at least, that in such a passage as the last-mentioned close liaison has been maintained between the Old and New Testament panels. The subjunctive reading has been preferred in Rom. 5. 1 ('let us continue at peace with God . . .'), the indicative being relegated to a footnote. (Professor Dodd's commentary on Romans would support the indicative, and rightly so.) At the end of Rom. 9. 5 the words 'May God, supreme over all, be blessed for ever!' appear as an independent doxology; a footnote gives two alternative renderings, one of which puts the words in apposition with 'the Messiah' (A.V. 'Christ'); this last construction, unpopular in recent translations, has lately had some weighty words spoken in its support by Oscar Cullmann.[2]

[1] See p. 160.   [2] *The Christology of the New Testament* (1959), pp. 312 f.

Another great theological paragraph, Heb. 1. 1-4, is superbly rendered. 'All orders of existence' is a particularly happy rendering for Gk. *aiōnes* in verse 2; on the other hand, in Heb. 11. 3 the same term is rendered 'universe.' One may wonder whether the phrase 'purgation of sins' in verse 3 is not a little archaic; it may be no more than a coincidence that the same expression appears in the Wycliffite version of 1382 and the Rheims version of 1582.

But the critic who tried to find a Romeward tendency here would be sadly astray. Some critics, indeed, have detected such a tendency in Matt. 16. 18: 'You are Peter, the Rock; and on this rock I will build my church.' But what the translators have done here is to try as far as possible to convey in English the assonance between the Greek words for 'Peter' (*petros*) and 'rock' (*petra*)—an assonance which would have amounted to identity in the Aramaic lying behind the Greek, for in Aramaic both 'Peter' and 'rock' are *kēphā*.

There is nothing in the way of denominational or sectional bias in the New English Bible; that really goes without saying, in view of the many Churches represented on the panels, not to mention the reputation of the individual translators. The great verities of the historic Christian faith come to clear expression; that, too, is only what was to be expected in a version whose sole aim is to let the Biblical writers convey their own message in mid-twentieth century English.

While the Roman Catholic Church in this country took no part in the production of the New English Bible, some interesting judgments on the work were expressed by Roman Catholic scholars after its publication. Father Thomas Corbishley, a leading English Jesuit, is quoted as saying that, while some features of the translation would have to be modified to make it acceptable to Roman Catholic sentiment, yet 'broadly speaking, it is safe to say that the new translation, based as it is on strict scholarship and not seeking to be "the expression of any denominational or doctrinal leaning", could at least serve as a basis for an agreed text.' Across the Atlantic Father Philip J. King, Professor of Sacred Scripture at St. John's Seminary, Boston, said that the publication of the new version 'affords us an opportunity to salute our Protestant brothers who have made such outstanding contributions to the field of sacred scripture' and spoke of the Bible as 'the natural bond uniting Catholics and non-Catholics'.

These courtesies have made some people jump to the conclusion that the production of a common version of Scripture,

agreed upon by Protestant and Roman Catholic Churches alike,
is just around the corner. It is safe to say that anything of the kind
is a long way off, so far as official action by Churches as such is
concerned. On a private and unofficial level, however, the situation
is different. Right now a team of Protestant, Roman Catholic and
Jewish scholars in America is working together on a new translation
of the Bible. The team is headed by Professor W. F. Albright. It
is planned to publish the version in thirty paperback volumes in
Doubleday's Anchor Book Series.

But our present concern is with the New English Bible. The
New Testament is here, and here to stay. Prolonged private and
public use must precede a mature assessment of its worth. But
one need not wait until then to recognize that, as a faithful rendering
of Holy Writ, it not only has power to make its readers wise and
lead them to salvation through faith in Christ, but also (to quote
its own translation of the following words, 2 Tim. 3. 16 f.) 'has its
use for teaching the truth and refuting error, or for reformation
of manners and discipline in right living, so that the man who
belongs to God may be efficient and equipped for good work of
every kind.' The contribution which the New English Bible as a
whole will have to make to the spiritual life of the English-speaking
world must depend in part on the Old Testament side of the work,
which we cannot expect for six or seven years yet. But this is a
day of spiritual hunger, and it is evident that many thousands of
people have begun to find in the New Testament volume of the
New English Bible true spiritual food. We may well pray that
many more readers will share their experience, and that in due
course the New English Bible in both Testaments may bring the
divine message home with fresh power to the hearts of men. The
reign of the second Elizabeth will then stand alongside the reign of
her illustrious namesake as a time when the Word of God became
the dominant force in the daily lives of English-speaking people.

APPENDICES

LOST BOOKS

HERE and there throughout the Bible reference is made to writings which no longer exist. Numbers 21. 14 f. quotes a fragment of poetry from 'the book of the Wars of the LORD' commemorating the Israelites' advance through Transjordan. The other quotations in that chapter are possibly derived from the same source. So, too, may the song of Deborah in Judges 5, though it could also have been contained in 'the book of Jashar',[1] like the piece of poetry quoted in Joshua 10. 12 f., about the sun and moon standing still. David's lament over Saul and Jonathan, 'the song of the bow', was also included in that collection (2 Sam. 1. 17 ff.), as were Solomon's words in 1 Kings 8. 12 f., recovered from the Septuagint text (see page 158). These two lost books were evidently collections of poetry.

The writers of the books of Kings and Chronicles make mention of court records and prophetic writings dealing with the persons and times they relate. 'The book of the chronicles of the kings of Israel' and 'the book of the chronicles of the kings of Judah' mentioned in 1 and 2 Kings (cf. 1 Kings 14. 19, 29, etc.) were not, of course, the Biblical books of Chronicles (which were written after the books of Kings); they were the court annals of the two kingdoms. The author of 1 and 2 Kings writes with a religious purpose; he is not interested in matters of secular history as such, but when he ends his treatment of a king's reign, he says in effect: if you want to know more about his reign than is necessary for the purpose of this work, you will find it in the ordinary records.

The author of Chronicles makes particularly full mention of the earlier works dealing with his subject-matter. Much of his material, of course, is repeated from the earlier historical books, from Genesis to 1 and 2 Kings, but in addition he refers to 'the chronicles of king David' (1 Chron. 27. 24), and mentions 'the history of Samuel the seer', 'the history of Nathan the prophet', and 'the history of Gad the seer' as authorities for David's reign (1 Chron. 29. 29); and as authorities for Solomon's reign 'the

[1] Several mediæval and modern attempts have been made to 'supply' the missing book of Jashar.

history of Nathan the prophet', 'the prophecy of Ahijah the Shilonite', and 'the visions of Iddo the seer concerning Jeroboam the son of Nebat' (2 Chron. 9. 29). Rehoboam's reign, he says, is recorded 'in the histories of Shemaiah the prophet and of Iddo the seer, after the manner of genealogies' (2 Chron. 12. 15). 'The commentary (*midrash*) of the prophet Iddo' is also quoted for the doings of Abijah. Jehoshaphat's reign, says the Chronicler, is recorded 'in the history of Jehu the son of Hanani, who is mentioned in the book of the kings of Israel' (2 Chron. 20. 34, R.V. *m.*; cf. 1 Kings 16. 1, 7). The particulars of the reign and family of Joash of Judah 'are written in the commentary (*midrash*) of the book of the kings' (2 Chron. 24. 27)—that is, presumably, not our canonical books of Kings but an expansion of it. Our canonical book of Isaiah, which simply mentions King Uzziah's name twice (Isa. 1. 1; 6. 1), cannot be the book in which the same Isaiah wrote 'the rest of the acts of Uzziah, first and last' (2 Chron. 26. 22); although it may be the book intended in 2 Chron. 32. 32 ('Now the rest of the acts of Hezekiah, and his good deeds, behold, they are written in the vision of Isaiah the prophet, the son of Amoz, in the book of the kings of Judah and Israel'), with particular reference to Isa. 36-39, the chapters which recur in 2 Kings 18. 13-20. 19. 'The acts of the kings of Israel' (2 Chron. 33. 18) are not to be identified with any part of the Old Testament, for nowhere outside 2 Chronicles itself do we now read of Manasseh's prayer and the 'words of the seers that spake to him in the name of the LORD'. What relation these 'acts' bore to 'the history of Hozai' (or 'the history of the seers') mentioned in the next verse as relating the same matters, we cannot say. In the light of the Chronicler's copious references to literature extant in his day, it is interesting to find Professor W. F. Albright writing: 'Every pertinent recent find has increased the evidence for the early date of the Book of Chronicles (about 400 B.C. or a little later) and for the care with which the Chronicler excerpted and compiled from older books, documents and oral traditions which were at his disposal' (*The Biblical Archaeologist*, Vol. 5 [1942], p. 53).

In the New Testament we have Luke's reference to the many who had undertaken to draw up accounts of the Gospel events (Luke 1. 1 f.). Before the canonical Gospels appeared, there were likely several written summaries of the story of Jesus and digests of His teaching, compiled for private use, or for use in evangelizing and teaching.[1] The nativity narratives of Luke's first two chapters

[1] Cf. *Some Notes on the Gospels*, by the late Dr. D. M. McIntyre (I.V.F., 1943).

look as if they were derived from one or two Hebrew memoirs, preserved, perhaps, among the disciples of John the Baptist or in the Holy Family.[1] There is also some evidence in the New Testament epistles of the existence of catechetic summaries in the churches in the very early days of the Christian mission: this has been worked out particularly by Archbishop Carrington[2] and Dean Selwyn.[3] And another very early document—perhaps the earliest of all—may have been a collection of 'Testimonies' or Messianic prophecies of the Old Testament fulfilled in Jesus;[4] such a collection would certainly have depended on the teaching which Jesus Himself gave when He expounded the Scriptures to His disciples and showed the necessity of His suffering before entering into His glory (Luke 24. 25 ff., 44 ff.). These are not really 'lost' documents, however; in due course they were incorporated in the New Testament. When the early Christian writer, Papias, bishop of Hierapolis, in Asia Minor, soon after the beginning of the second century, says that 'Matthew compiled the Oracles [that is, the oracles uttered by the Lord[5]] in the Hebrew speech, and everyone translated them as best he could',[6] he is probably referring not to our Gospel of Matthew but to a collection of sayings of Jesus on which both Matthew's and Luke's Gospels drew.

The 'epistle from Laodicea' mentioned by Paul in Col. 4. 16 is unknown, although some have identified it with the Epistle to the Ephesians. This epistle was listed as the Epistle to the Laodiceans in Marcion's canon. (Ephesians appears to have been a circular letter, not meant for any single church; the words 'at Ephesus' in Eph. 1. 1 are omitted by some early copies.) But later readers, finding in Col. 4. 16 what they took to be a reference to a lost epistle, undertook to make good the imagined loss by writing an 'Epistle to the Laodiceans'. This spurious effort is extant in a Latin translation, which is printed in Bishop Lightfoot's commentary on Colossians and Philemon (pp. 285-287).[7]

Whether the names Jannes and Jambres (or Mambres), given to the Egyptian magicians in 2 Tim. 3. 8, were derived from some

---

[1] Cf. W. Sanday, *Outlines of the Life of Christ* (1906), pp. 193 f.; A. S. Geyser, 'The Youth of John the Baptist', *Novum Testamentum* 1 (1956), pp. 70 ff.

[2] P. Carrington, *The Primitive Christian Catechism* (1940).

[3] E. G. Selwyn, *The First Epistle of Peter* (1946).

[4] Cf. J. R. Harris, *Testimonies*, i. (1916), ii. (1920).

[5] Others think Papias refers to the oracles *concerning* the Lord, i.e., Messianic 'Testimonies'. But a compilation of the sayings of Jesus seems more probable.

[6] Quoted by Eusebius, *Hist. Eccl.*, iii. 39.

[7] See translation in M. R. James, *The Apocryphal New Testament*, pp. 478-480.

book it is impossible to say. They are found in the Pseudo-Jonathan Targum to the Pentateuch,[1] but that, of course, was not written until long after the New Testament age, although the names may have been part of the oral Targum much earlier. Origen[2] mentions a 'book of Jannes and Mambres', which is no longer extant, but it may well have been composed on the basis of the reference in 2 Tim. 3. 8.

Origen, along with his fellow-Alexandrians, Clement and Didymus, is likewise our authority for ascribing the story of the contention between Michael and the devil for the body of Moses, mentioned in Jude 9, to a work called the *Assumption of Moses*.[3] A work bearing this title has come down to us,[4] but there is no such reference in it, so either the book known to these Alexandrian writers was a different one, or it was more comprehensive. As for Jude's quotation of Enoch's prophecy (Jude 14 f.) we have already noted that it is also extant in the (First) Book of Enoch.[5]

---

[1] See p. 134. They are also mentioned in the Babylonian Talmud, *Menachoth* 85a, and elsewhere in Rabbinical literature, where they are said to be Balaam's sons. The *Zadokite Work*, a Qumran document of *c.* 100 B.C., speaks of 'Jannes and his brother' as being raised up by Belial when Moses and Aaron were raised up by the 'Prince of Lights'.

[2] *Commentary on Matthew*, 27. 9.

[3] Origen, *De Principiis*, iii. 2. 1; Clement and Didymus in their respective expositions of Jude.

[4] Translated with notes in R. H. Charles's *Apocrypha and Pseudepigrapha*, ii, pp. 407 ff.

[5] See p. 171, n. 2.

THE NEW TESTAMENT APOCRYPHA AND
OTHER EARLY CHRISTIAN BOOKS

THE preface of a book written in 1820 begins with the question: 'After the writings contained in the New Testament were selected from the numerous Gospels and Epistles then in existence, what became of the Books that were rejected by the compilers?'[1]

The very form of the question betrays a misconception, as the reader of our chapter on 'The Canon of Scripture' (pp. 95 ff.) will realize. But it is a misconception that is still quite generally entertained: that at some Church Council or other, membership of which was determined by who knows what principle, a body of men sat down with a pile of writings on the table before them and said, 'Now, let's decide which of these are to be accepted as authoritative and which are to be rejected'. In fact, there never was any such Church Council: the Church and the New Testament grew up together.

But were there not other Christian books in existence, and may not some of these have been worthy of canonical recognition? There were other Christian books; if anyone wishes to decide for himself if they were worthy of canonical recognition or not he has only to read them and see, for many of them have survived and are accessible in translation.

The earliest Christian writers outside the New Testament are known as the Apostolic Fathers: they belong to the century between A.D. 80 and 180. Their works are not to be classed as 'New Testament Apocrypha'; they are simply what they profess to be, the writings of Christian men, designed for the edification of their fellow-Christians. But why are they not regarded as canonical? Because they do not bear the marks of canonicity. They themselves recognize the superior authority of the apostolic writings. Ignatius,

---

[1] William Hone, *The Apocryphal New Testament*, 'a misleading and an unoriginal book' (M. R. James): misleading, for the reason mentioned above and others as well; unoriginal, because it combines Jeremiah Jones's edition of the New Testament Apocrypha (1736) with Archbishop Wake's edition of the Apostolic Fathers (4th edn., 1737). The Apostolic Fathers, of course, are quite improperly included in a work entitled *The Apocryphal New Testament*. Hone's work was reprinted in America in 1926 by the Alpha Publishing Company under the title, *The Lost Books of the Bible*. See E. J. Goodspeed's discussion of 'Modern Apocrypha,' in his *New Chapters in New Testament Study* (1937), pp. 189 ff.

bishop of Antioch, author of seven epistles written while he was on his way to be thrown to the lions in the Roman amphitheatre about A.D. 115, says in his Epistle to the Romans (4. 3): 'I do not enjoin you, as Peter and Paul did. They were Apostles, I am a convict; they were free, but I am a slave to this very hour'. Ignatius was very sure of the rightness of his views, and very anxious that they should be accepted, but he does not enforce them with apostolic authority.[1] The 'Epistle of Barnabas', another work included among the Apostolic Fathers (too late in date to be the work of the New Testament Barnabas), among other improbable fancies tells us that the hyena changes its sex year by year and that the hare acquires an additional orifice for each year of its life (these interesting details come out in its allegorization of the Levitical food-laws which distinguish between clean and unclean animals). Clement of Rome, writing to the Corinthian Church about A.D. 95, adduces the fable of the phoenix in illustration of the resurrection. He is a good man, with a pastoral concern for the welfare of his own and other Churches; but how far short he falls of the New Testament level is indicated by the fact that, in spite of his familiarity with the Epistle to the Hebrews, he 'turns his back on its central argument in order to buttress his own arguments about the Church's Ministry by an appeal to the ceremonial laws of the Old Testament', a procedure which Professor T. W. Manson rightly describes as 'a retrogression of the worst kind'.[2] The *Shepherd*, an allegory written by a member of the Roman Church called Hermas early in the second century, was, as we have seen (p. 110), read publicly in church as a work of edification, but not accorded canonical status. And it was the people who produced and enjoyed writings like these who recognized the superior and divine authority of the New Testament writings, guided by a wisdom which has been acknowledged by the approval of successive Christian generations.[3]

The New Testament Apocrypha properly so called are the various Gospels, Acts, Epistles, and Apocalypses produced during the second century and later under the names of apostles and other associates of our Lord. Most of these belong to the category of

[1] The authority which he exercised in his own Church of Antioch is, of course, another matter.

[2] T. W. Manson, *The Church's Ministry* (1948), pp. 13 f. The failure of most of the Apostolic Fathers to grasp the central Biblical doctrine may be gathered from Dr. T. F. Torrance's study, *The Doctrine of Grace in the Apostolic Fathers* (1948).

[3] The writings of the Apostolic Fathers are accessible, in the original Greek and in translation, in Bishop Lightfoot's one-volume edition (Macmillan, 1891) and in Kirsopp Lake's two-volume edition in the Loeb Library (Heinemann, 1912-13).

religious fiction. Some of our apocryphal Gospels were intended to satisfy the desire for information about the 'hidden years' of our Lord's life before His entry upon public ministry; these include several 'Infancy Gospels', relating the prodigies performed by Jesus as a child. The apocryphal Acts were largely intended to supply information about the later career of those Apostles who disappear from the New Testament record at an early date. Among the apocryphal Epistles are the letters exchanged between Christ and King Abgar of Edessa and the 'Epistle to the Laodiceans' mentioned in the previous Appendix. Of the apocryphal Apocalypses the most interesting is the 'Apocalypse of Peter,' mentioned in the Muratorian Canon (see p. 110). We know from Clement of Alexandria, Eusebius and Sozomen, that it was read in some churches; it has a literary interest in that its lurid descriptions of the torments of the damned coloured much mediaeval and even more recent pictures of hell, including in particular Dante's *Inferno*.

Some of these apocryphal writings were designed to lend support to various heretical beliefs and practices; one example which we have already mentioned (p. 196) is the Ebionite Gospel which gave John the Baptist a vegetarian diet. This Gospel was perhaps not a new invention but simply an adapted edition of one of our canonical Gospels or of a similar one.

The ancient document called 'The Gospel according to Thomas' has received considerable publicity in the religious and secular press over the last three or four years. It was discovered in Upper Egypt in 1945 or 1946, along with 48 other documents written, like it, in Coptic. These 49 works, from the ancient Christian monastery at Chenoboskion, were contained in 13 papyrus codices. The great majority of them proved on examination to be Gnostic in character, that is to say, they represent a more developed form of the sort of heresy which Paul refutes in the Epistle to the Colossians.

The 'Gospel according to Thomas,' however, is not a directly Gnostic work. It is a collection of about 114 sayings attributed to Jesus, introduced by the preface, 'These are the secret words which the living Jesus spoke, and Didymus Judas Thomas wrote them down'; and ending with the title, 'The Gospel according to Thomas'. When scholars began to study it, they realised that portions of it had been known previously. About the end of the nineteenth century and beginning of the twentieth, much excitement was aroused by the discovery in Egypt of papyrus fragments exhibiting utterances ascribed to Jesus, each of them introduced by the words

'Jesus said'. These fragments are commonly called the 'Oxyrhynchus Sayings', from the ancient name of the place where they were found. They were written in Greek, whereas the recently-discovered 'Gospel according to Thomas' is written in Coptic. But it is now clear that the 'Oxyrhynchus Sayings' were fragments of a much larger Greek compilation, which was subsequently translated into Coptic for the benefit of the rank and file of the Egyptians who did not know Greek. And it is this Coptic translation that has now come to light as the 'Gospel of Thomas'. The Greek original of the compilation may be dated about the middle of the second century A.D., the Coptic translation is a century or two later. We may hope that the complete Greek original will yet be found.

The 114 sayings contained in this document are of a varied nature. Many of them are sayings recorded in the canonical Gospels, some of these being almost verbally identical while others have been subjected to greater or less modification. It is not certain, however, that they were directly derived from the canonical Gospels; some at least appear to have been handed down independently by word of mouth until they were recorded in this form. There are other sayings in the compilation which are not paralleled in the New Testament. Some of these could conceivably be genuine; at least they are sufficiently in keeping with our Lord's character and teaching to deserve serious consideration. But the company which they keep makes them suspect, for some of the sayings ascribed to Him in this work are self-evidently spurious, and reflect the Gnostic outlook of the community to whose library this particular copy of the work belonged.

A judicious and reliable account of the whole matter is provided in the recently published Fontana paper-back entitled *The Secret Sayings of Jesus: From the Gospel according to Thomas*.[1] The authors of this little book point out that the Thomas Gospel differs from the New Testament Gospels in that it minimizes the historical basis of Christianity. To call it a 'Fifth Gospel' is wide of the mark; properly speaking, it is not a Gospel at all. No compilation of sayings of Jesus, even if they were all genuine, can properly be called a Gospel. For a Gospel must declare God's good news; it must tell of Christ's

---

[1] By R. M. Grant and D. N. Freedman, with an English translation of the Gospel of Thomas by W. R. Schoedel (1960). I have dealt with this document further in *Faith and Thought* 92 (1961-62), pp. 3 ff. See also R. M. Wilson, *Studies in the Gospel of Thomas* (1960) and B. Gärtner, *The Theology of the Gospel of Thomas* (1961). On the other manuscripts found at Nag Hammadi see W. C. van Unnik, *Newly Discovered Gnostic Writings* (1960). A useful survey of sayings ascribed to Jesus outside the four canonical Gospels (as they were known before the discovery of the 'Gospel of Thomas') is given by J. Jeremias in *Unknown Sayings of Jesus* (1957).

redemptive death. And even those sayings of Christ which refer to His death are significantly absent from the 'Gospel of Thomas'.

Some of the sayings ascribed to Jesus in the 'Gospel of Thomas' are paralleled in other uncanonical Gospels. One of the sayings, for example (one which was preserved in Greek in an Oxyrhynchus papyrus), is quoted by Clement of Alexandria (c. A.D. 180) as coming from the 'Gospel according to the Hebrews'; he quotes it in the form: 'Let not him that seeks [the Kingdom], cease until he find it, and when he finds it he will be astonished. Astonished he shall attain to the Kingdom, and having attained, he shall have rest.'

This 'Gospel according to the Hebrews', now extant only in fragments, seems to have been a sort of Jewish-Christian Targum or expanded paraphrase of our Gospel of Matthew, circulating in Egypt and Transjordan. It contains some other sayings ascribed to Jesus not found in the canonical Gospels, but they are at best of doubtful authenticity. Jerome identified the 'Gospel according to the Hebrews' with a document which he found in Caesarea, called the 'Gospel of the Nazarenes', and which he mistook at first for the Hebrew or Aramaic original of Matthew's Gospel. Probably the 'Gospel of the Nazarenes' was simply an Aramaic translation of Matthew and a different work from the 'Gospel according to the Hebrews'. At any rate, both these 'Gospels' bore some relation to the canonical Matthew, and are therefore to be distinguished from the great mass of apocryphal Gospels, which are not only apocryphal but fictitious even when not heretical.

One of the apocryphal books of 'Acts'—the 'Acts of Paul'— while admittedly a romance written by an orthodox presbyter of Asia about A.D. 160,[1] contains a pen-portrait of Paul which, from its vigorous and unconventional character, was thought by Sir William Ramsay to embody a genuine tradition of the Apostle's personal appearance. He is described as 'a man small in size, with meeting eyebrows, with a rather large nose, bald-headed, bow-legged, strongly built, full of grace, for at times he looked like a man, and at times he had the face of an angel'.[2]

Many of these apocryphal writings, with the 'Gospel according to the Hebrews' and that of the Nazarenes and some unattached sayings of Jesus, are accessible in English in *The Apocryphal New*

---

[1] The poor man's incursion into novel-writing was not appreciated by his brother-clerics, and he was degraded from the presbyterate, despite his plea that he had written the romance 'for love of Paul'—which was no doubt true. We may compare the disapproval with which Bunyan's *Pilgrim's Progress* was greeted by some of his more severe brethren.

[2] Cf. W. M. Ramsay, *The Church in the Roman Empire* (1893), pp. 375 ff.

Testament, translated with most helpful preface and notes by Dr. M. R. James, late Provost of Eton, and published by the Oxford Press in 1924. The reader who wishes to form his own judgment on the relative merits of these apocryphal writings and the canonical books will find his material there.

SUGGESTIONS FOR FURTHER STUDY[1]

GENERAL

FINEGAN, J.	Light from the Ancient Past* (Oxford, 1959).
GRANT, F. C.	Translating the Bible* (Edinburgh & London, 1961).
KENYON, F. G.	The Story of the Bible* (London, 1936).
" "	Our Bible and the Ancient Manuscripts,* revised edition (London, 1958).
" "	The Bible and Archæology* (London, 1940).
MACGREGOR, G.	The Bible in the Making (London, 1961).
ROBINSON, H. W. (ed.)	Ancient and English Versions of the Bible, 2nd edn. (Oxford, 1954).
RYPINS, S.	The Book of Thirty Centuries (New York, 1951).
SCHWARZ, W.	Principles and Problems of Biblical Translation (Cambridge, 1955).
SMYTH, J. PATERSON	How we got our Bible* (London, 1886; revised, 1938).

CHAPTERS I AND II

DIRINGER, D.	The Alphabet (London, 1947).
" "	The Story of the Aleph Beth* (London, 1958).
DRIVER, G. R.	Semitic Writing: from Pictograph to Alphabet (Oxford, 1948).
GELB, I. J.	A Study of Writing (London, 1952).
PINNER, H. L.	The World of Books in Classical Antiquity* (London, 1949).

CHAPTERS III, IV AND V

AUVRAY, P., POULAIN, P. and BLAISE, A.	The Sacred Languages (London, 1960).

HEBREW

DRIVER, G. R.	Problems of the Hebrew Verbal System (Edinburgh, 1936).
DRIVER, S. R.	Hebrew Tenses (Oxford, 1892).
HARRISON, R. K.	Teach Yourself Hebrew* (London, 1955).
ROBINSON, T. H.	The Genius of Hebrew Grammar (Oxford, 1928).
THOMAS, D. W.	The Recovery of the Ancient Hebrew Language (Cambridge, 1939).
WEINGREEN, J.	Practical Grammar for Classical Hebrew (Oxford, 1939).

[1] These works more suitable for beginners are marked with an asterisk.

ARAMAIC

BLACK, M.	*An Aramaic Approach to the Gospels and Acts*, 2nd edn. (Oxford, 1954).
COWLEY, A. E.	*Jewish Documents of the Time of Ezra** (London, 1919).
COWLEY, A. E.	*Aramaic Papyri of the Fifth Century B.C.* (Oxford, 1923).
DALMAN, G. H. ..	*The Words of Jesus** (Edinburgh, 1902).
,, ,, ..	*Jesus-Jeshua** (London, 1929).
KRAELING, E. G. ..	*The Brooklyn Museum Aramaic Papyri* (New Haven and Oxford, 1953).
ROWLEY, H. H.	*The Aramaic of the Old Testament* (Oxford, 1929).
TORREY, C. C.	*Documents of the Primitive Church* (New York, 1941).

GREEK

ARNDT, W. F., and GINGRICH, F. W. ..	*A Greek-English Lexicon of the New Testament and Other Early Christian Literature* (Cambridge, 1957).
ATKINSON, B. F. C. ..	*The Greek Language* (London, 1930).
BLASS, F.	*The Philology of the Gospels* (London, 1898).
BLASS, F., and DEBRUNNER, A. ..	*A Greek Grammar of the New Testament and Other Early Christian Literature* (Cambridge, 1961).
DEISSMANN, G. A. ..	*Bible Studies** (Edinburgh, 1909).
,, ,, ..	*New Light on the New Testament* (Edinburgh, 1907).
,, ,, ..	*Light from the Ancient East* (London, 1927).
,, ,, ..	*The Philology of the Greek Bible* (London, 1908).
,, ,, ..	*The New Testament in the Light of Recent Research* (London, 1929).
HUDSON, D. F. ..	*Teach Yourself New Testament Greek** (London, 1960).
MEECHAM, H. G. ..	*Light from Ancient Letters** (London, 1930).
MOULE, C. F. D. ..	*An Idiom Book of New Testament Greek* (Cambridge, 1953).
MOULTON, J. H., and MILLIGAN, G. ..	*The Vocabulary of the Greek Testament* (Edinburgh, 1930).
NUNN, H. P. V. ..	*Elements of New Testament Greek** (Cambridge, 1948).
,, ,, ..	*A Short Syntax of New Testament Greek* (Cambridge, 1924).
SIMPSON, E. K. ..	*Words Worth Weighing in the Greek New Testament* (London, 1944).
VINE, W. E. ..	*A New Testament Greek Grammar** (London, 1947).
,, ,, ..	*Expository Dictionary of New Testament Words** (4 vols., London, 1939-41).

CHAPTERS VI, VII AND VIII

BENTZEN, A.	*Introduction to the Old Testament* (Copenhagen, 1949).
BLACKMAN, E. C. ..	*Marcion and his Influence** (London, 1948).
DODD, C. H.	*According to the Scriptures** (London, 1952).
FILSON, F. V.	*Which Books Belong in the Bible?** (Philadelphia, 1957).
GREGORY, C. R. ..	*Canon and Text of the New Testament* (Edinburgh, 1907).
HARNACK, A.	*The Origin of the New Testament** (London, 1925).

HEBERT, A. G.   ..   ..   *The Throne of David* (London, 1941).
"   "   ..   ..   *The Authority of the Old Testament* (London, 1947).
HUNTER, A. M. ..   ..   *The Unity of the New Testament** (London, 1943).
PHILLIPS, G. E.   ..   ..   *The Old Testament in the World Church** (London, 1942).
ROWLEY, H. H. ..   ..   *The Re-discovery of the Old Testament** (London, 1945).
"   "   ..   ..   *The Unity of the Bible** (London, 1953).
RYLE, H. E.   ..   ..   *The Canon of the Old Testament* (London, 1904).
SNAITH, N. H. ..   ..   *The Distinctive Ideas of the Old Testament** (London, 1944).
SOUTER, A.   ..   ..   *Text and Canon of the New Testament* (London, 1954).
TASKER, R. V. G.   ..   *The Old Testament in the New Testament** (London, 1954).
WESTCOTT, B. F.   ..   ..   *The Canon of the New Testament* (London, 1870).

CHAPTERS IX, X AND XI

AP-THOMAS, D. R.   ..   *A Primer of Old Testament Text Criticism** (London, 1947).
BOWMAN, J.   ..   ..   *Samaritan Studies* (Manchester, 1958).
BRUCE, F. F.   ..   ..   *Second Thoughts on the Dead Sea Scrolls,** 2nd edn. (London, 1961).
CROSS, F. M.   ..   ..   *The Ancient Library of Qumran and Modern Biblical Studies* (New York and London, 1958).
GEDEN, A. S.   ..   ..   *Introduction to the Hebrew Bible* (Edinburgh, 1909).
GINSBURG, C. D.   ..   *Introduction to the Massoretico-Critical Edition of the Hebrew Bible* (London, 1897).
KAHLE, P. E.   ..   ..   *The Cairo Geniza*, 2nd edn. (London, 1959).
MONTGOMERY, J. A.   ..   *The Samaritans* (Philadelphia, 1907).
ROBERTS, B. J.   ..   ..   *The Old Testament Text and Versions* (Cardiff, 1951).
ROBINSON, H. W.   ..   'The Hebrew Bible'; Chapter I in *Ancient and English Versions of the Bible* (Oxford, 1954).
WÜRTHWEIN, E.   ..   ..   *The Text of the Old Testament* (Oxford, 1957).

CHAPTER XII

GOODING, D. W.   ..   *Recensions of the Septuagint Pentateuch* (London, 1955).
HOWARD, W. F.   ..   ..   'The Greek Bible': Chapter II in *Ancient and English Versions of the Bible* (Oxford, 1954).
KAHLE, P. E.   ..   ..   *The Cairo Geniza* (London, 1959), pp. 209-264.
KENYON, F. G.   ..   ..   *The Text of the Greek Bible* (London, 1937).
MEECHAM, H. G.   ..   *The Oldest Version of the Bible** (London, 1932).
"   "   ..   ..   *The Letter of Aristeas* (Manchester, 1935).
ORLINSKY, H. M.   ..   *The Septuagint: The Oldest Translation of the Bible* (Cincinnati, 1949).
OTTLEY, R. R.   ..   ..   *A Handbook to the Septuagint** (London, 1920).
ROBERTS, B. J.   ..   ..   *The Old Testament Text and Versions* (Cardiff, 1951), pp. 101-187.
SWETE, H. B.   ..   ..   *Introduction to the Old Testament in Greek* (Cambridge, 1914).

CHAPTER XIII

BROCKINGTON, L. H.   ..   *A Critical Introduction to the Apocrypha* (London, 1961).
CHARLES, R. H. (ed.)   ..   *The Apocrypha and Pseudepigrapha of the Old Testament* (2 vols., Oxford, 1913).

METZGER, B. M.	..	An Introduction to the Apocrypha* (Oxford, 1957).
OESTERLEY, W. O. E.	..	Introduction to the Books of the Apocrypha (London, 1935).
PFEIFFER, R. H.	..	History of New Testament Times, with an Introduction to the Apocrypha (New York, 1949).
TORREY, C. C.	..	The Apocryphal Literature (Oxford, 1945).

CHAPTER XIV

FOX, A.	.. ..	Meet the Greek Testament* (London, 1952).
GREGORY, C. R.	..	Canon and Text of the New Testament (Edinburgh, 1907).
HARRIS, J. R.	..	Side-lights on New Testament Research* (London, 1908).
HOWARD, W. F.		'The Greek Bible': Chapter II in Ancient and English Versions of the Bible (Oxford, 1954).
KENYON, F. G.	..	The Text of the Greek Bible (London, 1949).
KILPATRICK, G. D.	..	'The Transmission of the New Testament and its Reliability', Journal of Transactions of the Victoria Institute 89 (1957), pp. 91 ff.*
LAKE, K. and S.	..	The Text of the New Testament (London, 1933).
MILLIGAN, G.	..	The New Testament Documents (London, 1915).
PARVIS, M. M. and WIKGREN, A. P. (ed.)	..	New Testament Manuscript Studies (Chicago, 1950).
ROBERTSON, A. T.	..	An Introduction to the Textual Criticism of the New Testament (New York, 1928).
SCRIVENER, F. H. A.	..	A Plain Introduction to the Criticism of the New Testament (4th edition, revised by E. Miller, London, 1894).
SOUTER, A.	..	Text and Canon of the New Testament (London, 1954).
STREETER, B. H.	..	The Four Gospels (London, 1929), Part I: pp. 25-148.
TAYLOR, V.	.. ..	The Text of the New Testament* (London, 1961).
TWILLEY, L. D.	..	The Origin and Transmission of the New Testament* (Edinburgh & London, 1957).
WEIGLE, L. A. and others	..	An Introduction to the Revised Standard Version of the New Testament* (New York, 1946).
WESTCOTT, B. F., and HORT, F. J. A.		The New Testament in the Original Greek, with Introduction and Appendices (2 vols., London, 1881).
ZUNTZ, G.	.. ..	The Text of the Epistles (London, 1953).

CHAPTER XV

HILL, J. H	.. ..	The Earliest Life of Christ: Being the Diatessaron of Tatian* (Edinburgh, 1894).
HOGG, H. W.	..	The Diatessaron of Tatian* (Edinburgh, 1896).
KAHLE, P. E.	..	The Cairo Geniza (London, 1959), pp. 265-313.
LEWIS, A. S.	..	A Translation of the Four Gospels from the Syriac of the Sinaitic Palimpsest* (London, 1894).
„	.. ..	Light on the Four Gospels from the Sinai Palimpsest* (London, 1913).
ROBERTS, B. J.	..	The Old Testament Text and Versions (Cardiff, 1951), pp. 214-228.

ROBINSON, T. H.	..	'The Syriac Bible': Chapter III in *Ancient and English Versions of the Bible* (Oxford, 1954).
STEWART, J.	.. ..	*Nestorian Missionary Enterprise**★** (London, 1928).
VINE, A. R.	.. ..	*The Nestorian Churches**★** (London, 1937).
VÖÖBUS, A.	.. ..	*Investigations into the Text of the New Testament used by Rabbula of Edessa* (Pinneberg, 1947).
„	.. ..	*Researches on the Circulation of the Peshitta in the Middle of the Fifth Century* (Pinneberg, 1948).

CHAPTER XVI

BURKITT, F. C.	..	*The Old Latin and the Itala* (Cambridge, 1896).
CHAPMAN, J.	..	*Early History of the Vulgate Gospels* (Oxford, 1908).
ROBERTS, B. J.	..	*The Old Testament Text and Versions* (Cardiff, 1951), pp. 237-265.
SOUTER, A.	..	*Text and Canon of the New Testament* (London, 1912), pp. 33-54.
SOUTER, A.	..	*The Earliest Latin Commentaries on the Epistles of St. Paul* (Oxford, 1927).
SPARKS, H. F. D.	..	'The Latin Bible': Chapter IV in *Ancient and English Versions of the Bible* (Oxford, 1954).

CHAPTER XVII

See especially B. J. Roberts, *The Old Testament Text and Versions*, pp. 229 ff., 266 ff., and B. M. Metzger, 'The Evidence of the Versions for the Text of the New Testament', in Parvis and Wikgren, *New Testament Manuscript Studies*, pp. 25 ff.; also the works in the bibliography on Chapter XIV by Gregory, Harris, Kenyon, Lake, Scrivener, and Souter; and the symposium, *Ancient and English Versions of the Bible*, pp. 97 ff., etc. The bibliographical notes in these works will give fuller guidance for those who desire it.

CHAPTERS XVIII AND XIX

BRUCE, F. F.	.. ..	*The English Bible**★** (London, 1961).
BURGON, J. W.	..	*The Revision Revised* (London, 1883).
BUTTERWORTH, C. C.	..	*The Literary Lineage of the King James Bible* (Philadelphia, 1941).
CADOUX, C. J.	..	'The Revised Version and After': Chapter VIII in *Ancient and English Versions of the Bible* (Oxford, 1954).
CRAIGIE, W. A.	..	'The English Versions (to Wyclif)': Chapter V in *Ancient and English Versions of the Bible* (Oxford, 1954).
DAICHES, D.	..	*The King James Version of the English Bible* (Chicago, 1941).
DEANESLY, M.	..	*The Lollard Bible* (Cambridge, 1920).
„	..	*The Significance of the Lollard Bible* (London, 1953).
GOODSPEED, E. J.	..	*The Making of the English New Testament**★** (Chicago, 1925).
GRANT, F. C.	..	*Translating the Bible**★** (Edinburgh, 1961).
HARRISON, F.	..	*The Bible in Britain**★** (London, 1949).

ISAACS, J. .. .. .. 'The Sixteenth-Century English Versions': Chapter VI in *Ancient and English Versions of the Bible* (Oxford, 1954).

" .. .. 'The Authorized Version and After': Chapter VII in *Ancient and English Versions of the Bible*.

KNOX, R. A. .. .. *On Englishing the Bible*★ (London, 1949).

MAY, H. G. .. .. *Our English Bible in the Making* (Philadelphia, 1952).

MOULTON, W. F. .. *The History of the English Bible*★ (London, 1911).

MOZLEY, J. F. .. .. *William Tyndale* (London, 1937).

" .. .. *Coverdale and his Bibles* (London, 1953).

POPE, H. .. .. *English Versions of the Bible* (London, 1952).

POLLARD, A. W. .. *Records of the English Bible* (Oxford, 1911).

PRICE, I. M. .. .. *The Ancestry of our English Bible* (second revised edition, New York, 1949).

WEIGLE, L. A. .. .. *The English New Testament*★ (London, 1949).

WEIGLE, L. A. and others *An Introduction to the Revised Standard Version of the New Testament*★ (New York, 1946).

" " .. .. *An Introduction to the Revised Standard Version of the Old Testament*★ (New York, 1952).

WESTCOTT, B. F. .. *A General View of the History of the English Bible* (revised by W. A. Wright, London, 1905).

APPENDICES I AND II

CARRINGTON, P. .. .. *The Primitive Christian Catechism* (Cambridge, 1940).

FERRAR, W. J. .. .. *The Early Christian Books*★ (London, 1919).

FINDLAY, A. F. .. .. *Byways in Early Christian Literature*★ (Edinburgh, 1923).

GRANT, R. M. .. .. *Second-Century Christianity* (London, 1946).

" .. .. *Gnosticism and Early Christianity* (Oxford, 1959).

" (ed.) .. .. *Gnosticism: An Anthology* (London, 1961).

HARRIS, J. R. .. .. *Testimonies*, i. (Cambridge, 1916).

HARRIS, J. R., and .. *Testimonies*, ii. (Cambridge, 1920).
BURCH, V.

JAMES, M. R. .. .. *The Apocryphal New Testament* (Oxford, 1924).

LAKE, K. .. .. *The Apostolic Fathers* (2 vols., London, 1912-13).

LIGHTFOOT, J. B. .. *The Apostolic Fathers* (London, 1891).

VAN UNNIK, W. C. .. *Newly Discovered Gnostic Writings* (London, 1960).

NOTE.—The articles on Canon, Texts and Versions in the standard Bible Dictionaries and Encyclopedias should also be consulted. The articles on these subjects in *The Twentieth Century Encyclopedia of Religious Knowledge* were reprinted separately under the title *The Text, Canon and Principal Versions of the Bible*, by E. E. Flack, B. M. Metzger and others (Grand Rapids, 1956). Above all, the articles 'Canon of the Old Testament', 'Canon of the New Testament', 'English Versions of the Bible', 'Language of the Apocrypha', 'Language of the Old Testament', 'Language of the New Testament', 'Text and Versions', in *The New Bible Dictionary* (Inter-Varsity Fellowship, London, 1962), contain material of high value.

INDEX OF NAMES AND SUBJECTS

SCRIPTURE REFERENCES—OLD TESTAMENT

SCRIPTURE REFERENCES—NEW TESTAMENT

APOCRYPHA